THE ESSENTIAL
BRAND
BOOK

To my parents, Rob and Jan, for their encouragement
and support throughout all the years.

THE ESSENTIAL
BRAND
BOOK

over 100 techniques to increase brand value

SECOND EDITION

IAIN ELLWOOD

KOGAN
PAGE

First published in 2000
Reprinted 2001
Second edition 2002

Kogan Page Limited
120 Pentonville Road
London N1 9JN
www.kogan-page.co.uk

© Iain P Ellwood, 2000, 2002

British Library Cataloguing in Publication Data

A CIP record for this book is available from the British Library.

ISBN 0 7494 3863 0

Cover design by Richard Crighton
Typeset by Saxon Graphics Ltd, Derby
Printed and bound in Great Britain by Biddles Ltd, Guildford and King's Lynn
www.biddles.co.uk

CONTENTS

Brand equity

Brand strategy

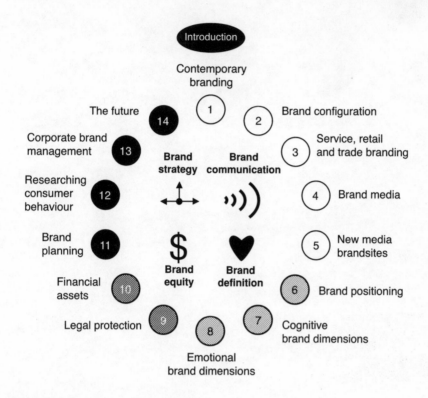

Figure 0.1 Book navigation guide

THE AUTHOR

Iain has over 10 years' international experience living and working in Japan, Hong Kong, the Netherlands and the United States as a brand marketing strategist for blue-chip companies. He is a leading strategist at the consulting firm Prophet. He has led award-winning international projects for clients including BT, Vodafone, Swiss Airlines, Guinness World Records, Philips and the LE Group.

His extensive psychological and sociological knowledge have shaped corporate strategy and customer-focused propositions that increase revenue. This approach has proved equally effective for delivering internal brand campaigns that motivate and educate employees.

Iain is a regular press commentator on strategic marketing and branding issues for *The Economist*, the BBC and numerous trade magazines. He is a frequent speaker on marketing, innovation and communications. He also occasionally lectures on the MBA courses at the London Business School (LBS).

Iain is a Member of the Chartered Institute of Marketing (MCIM), a Member of the Marketing Society and a Fellow of the Royal Society of Arts (FRSA).

Prophet is a strategic professional services firm committed to building and growing great brands and businesses. If you would like to hear more about how it can help your business, please contact Iain at iellwood@prophet.com.

ACKNOWLEDGEMENTS

The author would like to personally thank the following marke-teers, business owners, colleagues, clients and friends for their insightful ideas and for their constant encouragement: Liza Bingley, James Cockerille, Charles Colquhoun, David Cox, Richard Crighton, Alastair Kingsland, Graham Moore, Jeremy Myerson, Ian Woodhouse, Grant Usmar, Madelijne Vermeij.

Thanks are also due to those who were kind enough to be inter-viewed for this project and are quoted in the text:

Michael Abrahams, Abrahams Design
Anneke Elwes, brand planner
Gary Lockton, North Creative Consultancy
Celia Lury, Goldsmiths College, University of London
Will Maskell, PI3 Ltd
Jane Merriman, William Grant & Sons
Joanne Wallace, McVities
Simon Waterfall, Poke Consultancy
Professor James Woudhuysen
Peter York, SRU Ltd

Thanks to Victoria Groom at Kogan Page for those interesting lunchtime discussions and patient waiting for the final draft. Finally, many thanks to my family – Rob, Jan, Andrew and Peter – for all their care and encouragement.

INTRODUCTION

The brand is one of the most valuable assets that any business possesses:

* Branding provides the key communication with customers.
* Branding creates critical differentiators in the marketplace.
* Branding shapes internal company culture.
* Branding leverages the intellectual assets of the business.
* Branding generates increased business performance.

Yet despite all these benefits, branding is still too often seen as a mere tactical tool rather than a business strategy. There is a huge financial potential for businesses that can maximize their brand equity. The excellent Return On Investment (ROI) of any branding programme can be seen with brands such as Orange (mobile phones), Unilever, Jaguar and Disney.

Brand creation and brand management are essential for success and profitability in the business process. This book provides a holistic overview of the essential leading methods of brand analysis, brand creation, brand development and brand management. It is a hands-on guide for marketing and business professionals and those in higher education.

Readers gain an insight into all the components of brand management including a wide range of business models and techniques that help to build strong and effective brands in the marketplace. Illustrated with specific examples, it provides a toolbox of proven techniques on how to analyse and choose the most successful combination of brand dimensions on which to develop brands. It is a companion resource for the management of all brand issues.

The terms 'brand' and 'branding' have become over-used during the last few years and have become devalued as a result. This book revalues all the management concepts of branding by dealing with each in a distinctive chapter. The book therefore covers all the essential components of brand management but ensures that they are described and illustrated with clarity.

Who the book is aimed at

This book is aimed at everyone who comes into daily contact with brands, products and services. It is for use by those within industry and business responsible for the marketing, visual communication and management of brands and their expression through all media types. The CEO is the ultimate brand manager but everyone in the organization is responsible for delivering the brand vision.

The task of managing brands is as important to niche entrepreneurs as it is for small business owners and large corporate businesses. The increasing professionalization of charity work means that it is equally pertinent to non-profit organizations as those who are quoted on the stock markets around the world. Any group of people who provide a product or service to others need to communicate the availability and benefit of that proposition to all stakeholders. A strong brand acts as the source and the medium for that communication process.

How to use the book

The book is divided into four key components to make it easier to find the material you need. Each component is easy to locate by the titles at the top of the pages. Each chapter within the four components relates strongly to each other but is also interrelated to all the other chapters. Those with less knowledge may wish to start at the beginning, while those more advanced will proceed directly to the relevant chapter first. The glossary at the end of the book will help to define all the terms that are used in the book and the industry.

Brand communication

Chapter 1 introduces the concepts of brands and brand management and explains why they are so important for a business. It demonstrates the connection between the current business model of a market and an approach to brand management. This chapter illustrates the role of a brand as the key communication tool between the business and all its stakeholders.

Chapter 2 describes the methods of brand management in the context of other marketing and business disciplines. It demonstrates the characteristics and structuring of sole brands, validating brands, range brands, line brands and product brands. This chapter illustrates the use of brand extensions and their hierarchies reflecting the business organization.

Chapter 3 emphasizes the unique characteristics of service, retail and business-to-business brand management. This introduces the issues that impact on the branding of intangible services like time-based brand delivery. It also covers the use of complex decision-making units (DMUs) within an organization and emphasizes the need for a brand to reflect compound values and dimensions to different audiences at different times.

Chapter 4 describes the methods of communication between business and customers. It analyses the advantages and disadvantages of different media types, including above the line and below the line media. There is an in-depth look at packaging and especially its function in FMCG brand communication. Finally, as media are often a bought-in service, there is an introduction to the best way to approach and use agencies.

Chapter 5 analyses the emerging new media of the Internet and digital television and their impact and opportunities for brand management. It illustrates the strategic development of new media brandsites and highlights the key tactics for brand communication. This chapter also introduces the business model of e-commerce, intranets and extranets.

Brand definition

Chapter 6 describes how the brand DNA, the essence of a brand, is created and refined. It identifies the areas of greatest potential for specific brand imagery and identity. This chapter describes the positioning and development of the brand proposition and personality. It also demonstrates the tools for brand name creation and assessment, together with the process for the creation of a corporate identity, logos and trade marks.

Chapter 7 defines the cognitive or rational dimensions of a brand proposition and emphasizes their use in communication. It illustrates the strategic and tactical uses of cognitive dimensions and tools for brand management. It also introduces Maslow's hierarchy of needs and demonstrates its use in defining customer needs.

Chapter 8 describes how the pleasure principle can be used to define and measure deep customer satisfaction. It characterizes the emotional dimensions of a brand and their ability to fulfil consumer needs. It also illustrates the strategic choices for emotional brand dimension development.

Brand equity

Chapter 9 clarifies the legal definitions that a brand mark and intellectual property can use for protection. It characterizes the differences between a trade mark, copyright, a design patent and trade dress. It describes the application process for gaining trade mark protection and illustrates the use of design elements to increase protection.

Chapter 10 describes the increasing use of a financial evaluation of intangible brand assets on the balance sheet. It describes the current key valuation methods including the multiple criteria often used by leading accountants. It introduces the topics of licensing and royalty agreements as another type of financial performance evaluation.

Brand strategy

Chapter 11 describes the brand planning process and introduces essential methods and tools for effective brand management. It analyses and compares a range of strategies and tactics for brand creation and development. There is an explanation of key brand extension strategies and portfolio management tools.

Chapter 12 introduces the research processes needed for understanding and categorizing consumer needs. It illustrates the advantages and disadvantages of primary, secondary, exploratory, descriptive, causal, quantitative and qualitative research approaches. It also illustrates a large range of strategic and tactical research methods and media.

Chapter 13 demonstrates why the real brand manager is the CEO and the importance of internal brand communication. It illustrates the internal brand culture and its effect on productivity. This chapter describes why and how all employees are responsible for and can be motivated towards the delivery of the brand vision. It demonstrates an effective internal brand communications programme.

Chapter 14 informs about the new rules for brand management in the new economy. It illustrates the opportunities for new business models that create better customer buy-in and satisfaction with a brand. It highlights the importance of an integrated approach to new and traditional media in brand communication.

The Glossary provides a useful quick guide to check terms used throughout the book and industry. The Bibliography references works mentioned in the text and suggests works that will be invaluable for the brand manager who wants to develop further in all the specific areas of brand management. Finally, the Index provides a quick finder for essential topics, people and processes of brand management. It cross-references topics throughout the book.

BRAND
COMMUNICATION

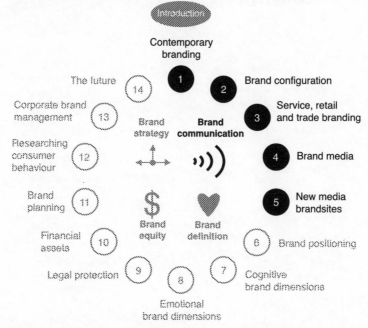

Figure 1.0 Brand communication

This first of the four parts in the book introduces the standard operating procedures for brands across key business models, market categories, media types and new virtual media opportunities. It covers all the important issues of current brand management thinking and introduces new techniques to maximize potential gains. It includes:

* introduction to brand management;
* brand hierarchy and configuration;
* service branding;
* retail branding;
* business-to-business branding;
* communication media;
* above the line media;

* below the line media;
* packaging;
* Internet branding;
* digital television branding.

CHAPTER ONE

CONTEMPORARY BRANDING

Branding, marketing and the business environment

This chapter introduces the concept of brands, the scope of branding and brand management and contextualizes the material of the later chapters. Key definitions and perspectives on brand management will be introduced to frame the subject and its underlying drivers. The history of brands will be illustrated together with their relationship with business models throughout the past, present and future opportunities.

Branding is now recognized as the core tool that connects all the business stakeholders through all the media channels. These will be briefly introduced to map out the connections between the later chapters.

Objectives

- Demonstrate why brands are important to every business and consumer today.
- Define the nature of a brand and its relationship to a product or service.
- Illustrate the connection between business models and brand development throughout history.
- Clarify all the stakeholders and media channels available to brand managers.

Why branding is important today

A survey last year by the Henley Centre revealed that the public trust brand names such as Kellogg's, Heinz and Marks & Spencer more than Parliament, the police and the legal system (*Sunday Times*, 'A can of worms is a bad diet', 5 April 1998). This research highlights the importance of the relationship between consumers and key brands; and shows that it has strengthened to such an extent that it is now healthier than the relationship with our social structures. This is evidence of the power of consumer culture and the liberal free market economics of the westernized world. Three trends support this belief:

* Individualism: westernized societies recognize the fragmentation of our personal and social identities and this encourages self-identity construction through the consumption of material goods and services: you are what you buy.
* Globalization: individual consumers are becoming a smaller part of a much larger world and need to find easy and quick ways to guide them through that world.
* Symbolic experiences are increasingly in demand. Consumers are buying experiences rather than commodities whose contents are largely image driven, intangible and symbolic.

The combination of these three trends has led to a shift away from producer or sales led marketing towards customer focused and customer driven business models. This means that understanding what motivates and satisfies the customer is the key to successful modern business practices. The brand acts as the logical and primary connection and mode of communication between the producer and the consumer. For brand managers, this prioritizes the modelling of a brand personality along the format of human relationships, since customers already have the skills and experience of how to relate to other people.

Definition of a brand

There are many definitions of what a brand represents and to which audiences; the simplest are the following:

Product/service + Aura = Brand communication
Product/service + distinctive value = Brand equity

The distinctive value is the rational and emotional added value that employees and customers feel is part of their consumption of the proposition. This creates a price premium for the business and adds equity to the balance sheet.

The aura represents the communication of the signifying and differentiating characteristics of the proposition.

At the core of all successful brands there is always a successful product or service. The product or service can be imagined or visualized as a hard, white golf ball, while the brand is a translucent, multi-coloured ball of gas the size of a large balloon surrounding that golf ball. The balloon's membrane is the flexible personality that can be squeezed and changed to different accents of personalities, while the central golf ball remains. The consumer's decision to buy a specific brand is mostly based on the character of the balloon, while the underlying use is often based on the character of the golf ball.

The brand therefore acts as a kind of flag, waving to consumers, creating awareness of the product and differentiating it from other competitors. This communication function is the core of brand management for a business. The extent to which brands can communicate a message with the consumer is still under debate. Celia Lury, sociologist at Goldsmiths College, University of London, defines a brand as a marker: 'A marker is very different from a message in the sense that the content of a marker is much less, but nevertheless the fact that it points to something recognizable is as important as the meaning in a message.'

Other commentators (Campbell, 1998; McLuhan, 1968) argue that brands have a more significant role as the message itself. Both viewpoints stress the role of a brand in embodying shared meaning between the producer and the consumer. This shared meaning is the aura the brand has developed in consumer culture over time. It is the recognizability and differentiation that allows consumers to make detailed choices between goods and services that are virtually identical.

Peter York, founding partner of SRU Ltd, stated, 'A brand should ensure a long-term and forgiving relationship with its audiences.' The emphasis on the long term is crucial for the ecology of a business: it is easy to dilute a brand's equity by selling down. Any advantage would only last for a short period before the brand was reduced to a commodity with little or no differentiation in the marketplace, relying on a price as the key purchasing driver. The sensitivity of a 'forgiving relationship' focuses on the one-to-one relationships that consumers have with specific brands. It is a relationship in human terms and as such can have a flowing character rather than one that is flat but steady. The strength of a brand is shown when it retains customer support through a difficult period.

How business models have driven brand development throughout history

The visible marking or branding of goods is a practice that is over 2,000 years old. The Greeks and Romans, with their sophisticated economic and commercial enterprise, developed 'maker marks' to establish the origins of specific goods. This was required because the Roman Empire had expanded, creating a great distance between producer and consumer. Previously, the producer and consumer would have had a personal relationship in the same village or town, and a personal bond of trust existed. The increase in distance, and greater import and export trade issues, meant that that level of personal trust was impossible. The consumer had to rely on the evidence of the maker's mark to reassure them that the goods they were purchasing were of the same quality.

The trade in goods also required the marketing of those goods in a fledgling competitive environment. This meant the distinguishing of specific regional origins and master craftsman for the consumer. These early marks related to the types of goods on sale: a butcher's mark, a spice merchant's mark or a carpenter's mark. These marks were often little more than a visual representation of the goods provided – a hog's head or a hammer and chisel of a carpenter. They were the first representations of a brand mark, literal depictions but also characterizations.

The second important origin of the brand mark was the signature applied to a piece of work, on the base of an earthenware bowl, or a manuscript or a carved statue. They all represent the identity of the maker and act, as with any signature, as an assurance, a personal recommendation and guarantee of the goods. The signature also helps to establish the quality of the goods in comparison with other makers or merchants in the same field. Where the symbol of the goods, such as a jug of wine, establishes the type of goods, the name establishes the origin of goods (most names at that time reflected the type of work the person did, like John Carpenter or David Butcher) and the style or quality of the goods as well. The combination of these two create the tangible brand marks that we recognize today. Celia Lury suggests, 'Brands are a kind of marker of exchange between producers and consumers. As such they have a long history from heraldic devices to guild marks or family firm marks where the mark acted as a kind of guarantor of quality.'

The practice of hand-marking goods continued throughout history at a similar pace until the 18th and 19th centuries when rapid economic and industrial expansion generated mass-produced items. This, combined with the expansion of distribution channels for the increasing numbers of goods, led to die-stamping and imprinting, printing of word marks and brands on goods.

It has often been stated that the 1890s were the first golden era for the modern brand mark. It was during this time that some of the world's most famous brand names were created and advertised to the consumer. The growth in advertising has always been closely linked with the growth in visible branding. The following were already leading brands during the 1890s:

American Express travellers cheques
Avon cosmetics
Cadbury's chocolate
Coca-Cola drink
Colgate toothpaste
Financial Times newspaper
Gillette razors
Heineken beer
Heinz baked beans
Ivory soap
Kodak photographic paper
Liptons tea
McVities biscuits
Pears soap
Philips electronics
Quaker's oats
Steinway pianos
Van Houton's cocoa
Wedgwood pottery

This list emphasizes the importance of a long-term commitment to the brand and business. Brand management must therefore be seen as essentially a strategic tool to business development and profitability.

Most of these original brands were the name of the inventor or founder of the business; as Professor James Woudhuysen, Seymour Powell Forecasting, confirms, 'King Gillette, Mr Gillette was around about a hundred years before Bill Gates and Microsoft. Not only did the brand personify the corporation, brands were themselves personified by individuals.'

As the 20th century developed, these original founders and their businesses grew to such an extent that they became large corporations. The founders retired and a board of management replaced that single vision. This shifted the emphasis from a single person to the product and the newly emerging service industries. The product became the hero of the brand's story and its technical (rational) performance was the key element of the advertising and marketing. The business model of the early to mid 20th century was based largely on fast-moving consumer goods (FMCG) and the growth in brand development was largely championed by this sector. The list below highlights the leading brands throughout the 20th century:

Coca-Cola
Colgate
Disney
Goodyear
Guinness
Heineken
Heinz
Hershey
Ivory
Kellogg's
Kodak
McVities
Persil
Ray Ban
Schweppes
Wrigleys

Once again, longevity and reliance on a strong core vision have kept these and many other brands at the top of the consumer's preference list.

Contemporary business models and brands

The current phase of new media technologies brings with it a range of new business models that influence how brands are developed, how they communicate with their customers and how they are bought and sold on the financial exchanges around the world. Leading examples of this include Amazon.com, which has grown logarithmically in the past couple of years. Its online bookstore has widened its remit to travel, Zshops (clothing, toys, stamps and antiques), auctions and home improvement. The brand drives customers to the site based on the Amazon attitude, not the product category. Similarly, lastminute.com sells almost everything you would like to buy, from holidays to gifts. Freeserve.co.uk is an Internet service provider that has cornered the market for small business and home users by offering free access (apart from phone costs). What is significant about these new businesses is that their brands are based entirely on an attitude rather than a category and most of the new e-commerce brands have yet to make a profit. Their strong IPO and stock quotations are all based on speculative future earnings. No other business model would have supported the growth of these brands. Chapter 5 analyses these in more detail.

Brand stakeholders

The brand's role as the core of stakeholder attention has become increasingly important as the level of goods and services on offer increases and the breadth of media communicating with consumers expands. Figure 1.1, from Bernstein (1991), shows the extent of the different audiences and media channels that communicate the brand.

The nine media channels can also be split into above the line and below the line variants. Television also has multiple channels, with satellite and cable companies offering up to 300 channels in some parts of the world.

All of these stakeholders need to be addressed and informed about the brand at different times of the year, whether they are quarterly financial results or daily customer impressions. Obviously, not all the media channels will be suitable for all the audiences, but often they will provide integrated solutions. This inclusive approach emphasizes the holistic nature and value of a brand and leverages its strength to maximum effect. Doing so can provide further revenue

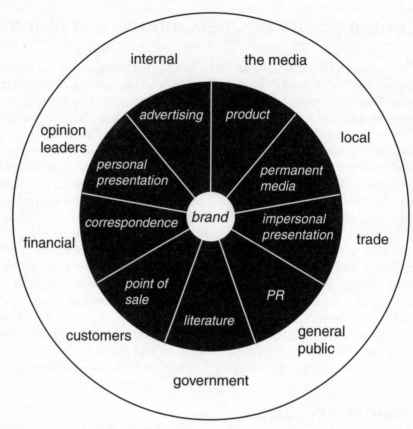

Figure 1.1 Communication channels and key audiences (Source: Bernstein, 1991)

streams and create a stronger fortress against competitive and market pressures. Clearly, in this model the ultimate brand manager is the CEO, who is finally responsible for the performance of the business. It is the CEO who is also charged with defining and ensuring the long-term strategic direction of the brand. It is the responsibility of all employees to deliver that vision whether they work in marketing, logistics, production or administration.

Brands and customer loyalty

As we have seen, customer loyalty is the key to the long-term success of a brand and business. The promise that the brand offers must be supported by the product offer in use, otherwise the brand will quickly be recognized as a superficial gimmick. Keeping the customer happy is the core of any business vision, but it is only now in the 21st century that technology can really deliver one-to-one marketing. We can now hope to regain the business model of the Greek and Roman times when consumers had direct contact and a dialogue with the maker or merchant.

Customer loyalty is based on delivering a product or service that people would like to buy and enjoy using. The role of the brand is to increase awareness of that product offer and to present its benefits in a way that is appealing to the consumer. Human nature changes very slowly, and as Maslow's hierarchy of needs (see Chapter 7) shows, there are clearly defined stages to our mental progression. The underlying business proposition can therefore retain longevity – men still need to shave their beards every day; we still want to drink tea or coffee; we still need to wear warm clothes. However, the technique of presentation of the goods and services needs to match the *Zeitgeist* to be culturally relevant to the target consumer. This is the role of a brand, and the brand personality needs to be

Summary

- Brands are important because they act as the communication tool between increasingly globally separated businesses and consumers.
- Business models have always driven the brand development model, from the early Romans, through the Industrial Revolution, to the current new media businesses.
- A brand is the aura that surrounds a product or service that communicates its benefits and differentiates it from the competition for the consumer.
- There are nine key stakeholders of a business: internal, the media, local, trade, general public, government, customers, financial and opinion leaders. There are nine key media channels to reach those stakeholders: the product, advertising, permanent media, impersonal presentation, public relations, literature, point of sale materials, correspondence and personal presentations. This approach emphasizes the holistic nature of brand management and reinforces the view that the CEO is the ultimate brand manager.

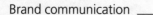

continually monitored and updated to ensure the closest match between consumer expectations and the brand's promise. It is the combination of the two that creates and sustains brands like Coca-Cola, Gillette, Disney and American Express.

CHAPTER TWO

BRAND CONFIGURATION

Structuring the brand and the organization

This chapter examines the relationship between branding and marketing within companies and the consumer's mindset. Working through examples of the 'seven Ps' of marketing, we can see how branding complements marketing and in some cases is the major part of the marketing plan. As we have seen, contemporary branding has a broad function and works best when it is the responsibility of everyone in the company. Therefore, marketing can be defined as a focused part of that organization – the externally looking and acting part of the company.

This chapter introduces the usable subdivisions of brands within a corporation. This will cover the corporate or eponymous brand, line brands, product brands and brand extensions. It highlights the most appropriate use of these brand management tools in several case studies. This chapter will also explain some of the dangers involved with sub-branding activities.

Objectives

* Illustrate the connection between marketing and branding.
* Explain the different types of brand architecture.
* Identify the different levels of branding.
* Analyse the use of brand extensions.
* Assess the balance between global and local brands.

Branding and its relationship to marketing

Whatever the size of the corporation, everyone should be focused on creating and delivering the product or service that customers want, at a price they are willing to pay. However, in modern organizations the function of marketing has often been delineated from that of product development. This can lead to a loss of focus by the internal product development team by relying on the marketing team to do all the brand management. While a balance is acceptable, a one-sided approach that leaves attention to brand values too late in the product creation process is not acceptable, as it will not maximize the potential profitability of the brand.

Brand management, as practised in the traditional Procter & Gamble model, was a fairly junior marketing function: brand managers were responsible for the delivery of market communications for a specific brand or sub-brand. They were used more as a marketing assistant who dealt with only operational issues and was responsible for maximizing revenue of one brand in a portfolio. Large FMCG companies such as Unilever require several brand managers who can individually develop a specific product brand such as PG Tips tea. Such managers may be in competition with another Unilever brand manager responsible for developing the Brooke Bond tea brand. These kinds of corporations seek to grow the market size and maximize their overall share of the money we spend, in this case on groceries.

Product managers are often the people who implement innovation in product development, so they need to work closely with brand managers to ensure any innovation is aligned with the brand personality. For example, the Persil brand unwittingly started a shift in brand perception when a new product was introduced. It had been recognized as the brand for 'caring mothers', but the new biological action used an aggressive enzyme that ate not only dirt but also parts of the clothing and created dermatological problems. Within a couple of washes, some clothes were in shreds, not the kind of thing that a caring mother would expect or want. Persil withdrew the brand and reformulated the product innovation to regain its brand position.

To ensure that product development reinforces the desired brand proposition it's wise to coordinate and communicate the mid-term brand vision with that of the technical development group. This can also be done at the kick-off meetings of major product development: by including all members of the creation chain they can anticipate the impact of innovation on the brand and vice versa.

Advertising managers play a role in the management of information from marketing to (usually) external agencies. They have a good understanding of what the internal brand vision is and are better able to match those needs with an appropriate agency. Corporations often have a roster of agencies they work with for several projects, ensuring continuity of expression that allows the agency to develop a deeper understanding of the brand. Some of the top have large brand planning departments that assist internal staff or develop the formation of brand strategy.

The advertising manager needs to coordinate the international expression of the brand, which could include securing famous local celebrities such as Candice Bergman for Sprint in the USA or Johnny Vaughan in the UK. The advertising manager needs to ensure that the translation, in visual terms, of the core brand values is appropriate in each country, possibly without developing country-specific solutions.

Market research managers must similarly coordinate the responses from regional markets to pre-launch materials through to post-launch dissonance surveys. Again, interpreting and translating the meaning of the data (rather than simply the letter of the data) needs careful attention. They may also need to research and analyse competitive brand footprints in home and overseas markets to monitor differing brand propositions in separate regions.

Sales force staff can be a valuable expression of the brand and a useful source of direct customer feedback. The behaviour of sales people needs to be totally informed and aligned with the brand if they are to be successful. Cosmetics salespeople at the counter of large department stores need to express what is distinctive about their brand in a highly competitive and emotional marketplace. In this case they deal direct with the public, so they can quickly find out what people expect, like and want from the brand. There needs to be a strong feedback mechanism in place, to transfer that information back to marketing managers.

The seven P's of marketing

1. Price
2. Product
3. Promotion
4. Place
5. People
6. Process
7. Physical evidence

These seven topics, shown in Figure 2.1, outline the core tasks and concerns of the marketing mix for most companies. The original four – price, product, promotion and place – were developed by McCarthy (1987) for the durable goods and FMCG industries. The later addition of people, process and physical evidence highlights the shift in western economies towards service industries, although I would argue that business-to-business or product industries also need to pay close attention to the latter three. The appropriately specified product should be seen as part of a continuing dialogue with the consumer and needs to be delivered, by people, in a timely and well-supported brand execution. The following sections analyse each of these elements to show how brand management can maximize their effect at each stage.

Price

Product price should not just be an addition of development costs, marketing costs and profit margins. The perception of price is critical

Figure 2.1 The seven P's of marketing

to the perception of the brand, as consumers tend to compare prices within a field of goods or services at the point of purchase. They develop an expectation (whether accurate or not) of what quality they can buy for what price, which includes how much extra they are prepared to pay for a premium branded product. Careful brand management of pricing policy is critical, so that products are not undervalued or overpriced in the marketplace.

Strong brands can create a 'price premium' above their competitors. This is the additional price the organization can charge for the 'brand'. It is a sign of the customers' appreciation of that brand that they are continually willing to pay for this brand extra. The return on investment in a brand is transparently paid back though this price premium. The Sony brand has always been able to charge typically a 5–10 per cent premium compared with similar goods of other brands. This is directly related to the brand equity in the customers' minds.

I believe that some companies price their products too low and the resulting effect is to devalue the brand in comparison with similar high-quality products. Although it is a difficult decision to make in a highly price-sensitive market, it is crucial to the maintenance of an 'A brand' proposition. For example, Philips Domestic Appliances produces a range of excellent-quality coffeemakers for the mass market. Its competitors mostly fall into two categories and are following two different product strategies – first, other high-quality European brands such as Tefal and Braun; second, the lower end of the market has brands like Princess, although the price points for these two segments are close together. The Philips brand attempts to offer the same quality as Braun and Siemens at a lower price, while competing well against the lower segment by offering higher quality for the same price. The general market reaction has, in my view, been to devalue the quality perception of the Philips brand from a leader such as Braun into one that is a middle brand, just above the imported brands. It is easy to understand how the consumer might think that the Philips brand is an expensive version of the low-quality, imported brand and offers lower quality than the Braun brand. This situation can arise through trying to reduce prices too much, leading to an unnecessary cut in profit margins as well. If you have invested in making a high-quality product, don't allow the price level to be fixed too low, otherwise people will not believe that such a low-priced product could be of high quality. The damage to the brand in the longer term is difficult to repair, especially as shrinking profits reduce investment and quality. It becomes a downward cycle that is likely to be self-ful-filling: as profit is reduced, so are investment and product quality.

Product

Some companies may only have one product to brand, such as Apple Macintosh. Others may have a collection of sub-brands and brand extensions to manage as a large portfolio. Both these types of companies still need to choose whether to focus on the product brand or the corporate brand, and we will discuss these later in this chapter.

If the product is your chosen brand vehicle then it can be a pow-erful tool. The design of the product and the design of the experi-ence of using it are the key ways of expressing your brand. The Apple iMac is a good example of how a company can reinforce its brand image through product design. The company brand values focus on humanizing technology by simplifying products and func-tions. It developed the graphic user interface so that people could put things in their desktop Trash bin, for instance, instead of typing programming language to achieve the same result.

Good design can play an important role in translating brand values into product attributes that enhance the brand experience. The colourful design of the new iMac is a complete change from the traditional beige computer box. The use of translucent, brightly coloured plastic reinforces the shift away from a serious technical feeling to a fun and relaxed approach. Apple has emphasized ease-of-use and accessibility-for-all, with a 'You can be online in 10 minutes' tag line. It points out that you no longer have to be a com-puter geek, but computers can be for everyone at home. The market reaction has been fantastic: it has revived the profits at Apple com-puters and the translucent, bubblegum-coloured machines are the best and most striking expression of its brand. Testimony to this success is that there have been many imitators in the PC market, but because they superficially copy the external attributes, they do not reflect the true internal culture of those businesses and are therefore unlikely to retain substantial benefit from these actions.

The biggest advantage of using a product to focus brand values is that people often use a product every day or even all day. This means that the product brand experience is effective all day and every day, reminding consumers about the benefits of the brand. We may wake up to Sony (alarm clocks) every morning; have breakfast with Tefal (toasters); drive to work with Saab (cars); Microsoft (computer software) welcomes us to the office each day, and so on. The value of a daily reminder that Microsoft makes computer software is tremendous for its profile and brand management.

The downside to this kind of brand activity is that you have to be sure that your product is fit for the task the consumer wants to achieve, that it won't let people down. If this happens, then of course the consumer gets a daily reminder that your brand is not good. They also have time to build up a list of reasons why they will never buy your brand again. They may even tell their friends about the poor brand experience that they've had to endure.

Promotion

Promotion is often the core of brand management activities, and may involve marketing, public relations, sales promotion and advertising. All these tools and many others should be used to persuade the consumer to believe in your brand. It is important to make sure that the core message is on-brand across all these media. This does not mean that they have to be identical (although this is one strategy) but they do have to complement the brand values to their chosen target audiences. For example, a print campaign in a national newspaper will need a different tone from a TV campaign. The strengths and weaknesses of different media need to be carefully balanced and managed. The advantages and disadvantages of these varied media types will be expanded on in Chapter 4.

Place

The place where a consumer buys a product should also help to reinforce your brand values; this means the location as well as the type of store. These range from the simple warehouse approach of Ikea superstores to the highly evolved Nike Town or the Disney stores. Retail sites engage the consumer in a carefully staged brand event, but they are one of the most underused tools for brand development. It is not just a matter of making sure that the interior colours match the corporate identity: there is a huge opportunity for the consumer to experience the brand in a multidimensional, multisensorial ambience.

Brands that sell through other retail outlets use point of sale (POS) or point of purchase (POP) materials to define their brand message clearly amongst many product offerings. Larger concessions can be found in department stores where the Chanel brand will have a dedicated counter to create its own brand experience. Packaging in FMCG goods often has to deliver that brand experience and sense of place on the shelf of the supermarket.

In certain sectors, the location or address of the retail site is often crucial to the perception of the brand. Leading fashion brands know they must have a store on Bond Street in London or Fifth Avenue in New York, otherwise customers will not take them seriously. Brands can use the connotations of a specific location to enrich their brand, so it is important to choose retail locations carefully.

People

People are the greatest asset for any company: if they can be encouraged to express the brand at all levels, the business will benefit enormously. This is especially true in the service sector, but even business-to-business branding is conducted via people.

People who often have to deliver a service directly to the customer need to be aware of how they represent the company brand. They are in effect goodwill ambassadors for the brand and special training sessions will help maximize this potential. For example, the attitude of Post Office staff affects our perception of the Post Office brand, as does the FedEx person who delivers business packages.

Process

The organization of business processes can help your brand, for example by reinforcing brand values through timely delivery of the service. The entertaining way that Virgin Atlantic delivers its airline service is very different from the cheap and cheerful approach of easyJet and the elegant and calm manner of British Airways. Virgin staff have an entertaining attitude, realizing that travellers are bored on long-haul flights, which is very different from the 'butler' or 'waitress' approach of some airlines. Richard Branson, the company's chairman, presents himself as a highly entertaining personification of the brand through PR activities.

Physical evidence

The physical elements that go to make up your product, retail, business or service brand need to be aligned to your brand personality. This means that packaging, POS materials, even documentation should all be harnessed to support the brand. All these elements will be examined later in Chapter 4.

Corporate brand

A corporate identity is the visual representation of the structure of a brand or company. It defines the relationship between elements of the brand, product or service. (This is explained further in Chapter 6 in the segment on corporate identity.) Corporate identity specialists tend to segment companies into three types of structure, emphasizing the differing level of interaction between the organization of the company and the expression of the brand:

1. sole identity company;
2. validated identity company;
3. branded identity company.

Sole identity company

The sole identity company represents an organizational structure that has a single brand proposition and personality throughout the portfolio of products (see Figure 2.2). Large conglomerations that

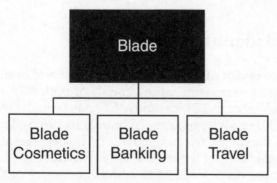

Figure 2.2 Sole identity company structure

typically acquire and merge with other businesses rely on their umbrella brand to maintain a strong identity. These are often large capital businesses like the Hanson group or large consumer durable groups such as Panasonic, which may have originated as one business but, as acquisitions have grown, moved into other sectors.

The strength of the sole brand is that even as the company's underlying businesses change, the brand personality remains constant for customers. This is especially important when launching new products, or entering new markets: the global brand recognition will reduce risks in both cases. All the products should benefit from the sole brand personality as an initial point of customer recognition. However, each new product or category must match with the expectation that the corporate brand suggests.

There are weaknesses to this approach. When the list of business extensions increases, the goodwill of the brand may not stretch far enough. The crucial question is whether the consumer will accept that a company that makes excellent televisions will be good at making microwave ovens or bicycles or carpets, as in the case of Panasonic. If the qualities of those new products match with the corporate brand personality, then they are likely to be accepted. For example, when Virgin produces a range of clothes, they match with the fun, alternative lifestyle image of the airline and the record stores.

Branding activities for a sole brand usually focus on awareness campaigns, intended to remind customers they are available, competitive and strong. When British Petroleum advertises, it is simply to keep its brand at the top of the customer's mind, rather than selling a specific product. Large corporations may well have to combine this kind of branding activity with more focused, country- or product-specific promotions.

Validated identity company

This is a convenient method for large product and brand portfolios to be managed to maximize the benefits of both sole and branded strategies (see Figure 2.3). In the FMCG markets, the manufacturer Unilever validates a large range of brands including Domestos, the bleach, and Persil, the washing powder. The best use of this kind of endorsement is during the introduction and development of a new brand. In those early stages, the added guarantee of the Unilever brand provides a further safety cushion against consumer anxiety.

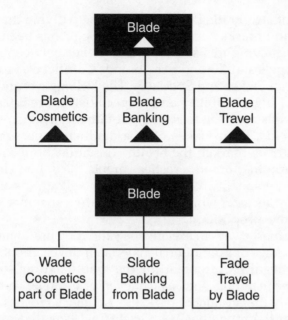

Figure 2.3 Validated identity company structure

Later in the brand's lifestage, the sub-brand may become more widely recognizable and trustworthy. This means that the size and placing of the two brand marks should not be static and needs constant management to maximize the value of both. Often the core brand is reduced to simply a name and address on the back of the packet, but still acts as a guarantor for those about to try the brand for the first time.

In other sectors, the core brand is retained as part of the total brand execution, and may even form part of the brand name execution. Hasbro, which now owns Spears Games, has a long tradition in the toy market, and effectively uses this to endorse both new and old games. So the word game Scrabble also has a prominent Spears logo on the front of the box, which supports the idea of a family of high-quality games in the Spears portfolio. But individual games like Scrabble also retain a strong identity and promotional material targeted towards their consumer group. The Hasbro brand has a strong portfolio of other brands including children's favourites like Play-Doh, Action Man and Monopoly. Each one has its own brand identity and positioning in the marketplace, but they are all underpinned by the Hasbro brand giving added reassurance to the consumer.

The use of a validating brand can also help divide the tasks that the two brand marks need to fulfil. Kellogg's has been very successful in achieving this split of brand values between the parent brand Kellogg's and the endorsed brands Cornflakes, Frosties, Rice Krispies, Bran Flakes and Special K. The Kellogg's brand provides an image of high visibility and a specialist in breakfast cereals, giving the consumer the reassurance of quality and expertise. The sub-brands like Bran Flakes offer a distinctive personality that targets a narrow market: the health-conscious, fibre-eating adult consumer. Another brand, Frosties, targets the young child with a fun cartoon personality. With this strategy Kellogg's is able to take advantage of its size, while still offering the consumer a targeted and distinctive proposition.

There are many ways to execute the validating brand name on the product, package or promotional material. It can be unobtrusive, if it is a purely legal requirement for the manufacturer's name and address to be included, such as Unilever, or it can be co-positioned on the front of the product or pack, like Kellogg's Frosties. Copy can suggest that the range has been exclusively created for the consumer: 'selected by Harvey Nichols', for instance. We will discuss the advantages and disadvantages of these later when we look at how changing brand names can be managed.

Branded identity company

Other corporations, particularly FMCG groups, may use a portfolio of different brands to represent different brand propositions (see Figure 2.4). Unilever, for example, is relatively unknown as a

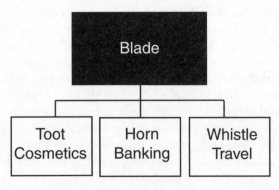

Figure 2.4 Branded identity company structure

company brand, but we are all familiar with the Flora, Oxo, Bachelors and Bird's Eye brands that it owns. Again, many of these will have been acquired during its corporate history, but there has been a strategic choice not to combine or lose their brand names. Pillsbury is another brand that has a large portfolio of products under the Pillsbury name as well as other brands like Green Giant Vegetables and Old El Paso Mexican food ranges. In the finely segmented FMCG markets, the expression of choice towards the consumer is a strong reason for retaining separate brand identities.

These brands usually have their own individual brand manager who is responsible for its identity and development, with brand managers often in competition with each other. While cannibalization of each other's sales is an issue, the branded approach is one way of maximizing total market share and corporate efficiency, and ensuring competitive and creative brand building.

Products like margarine packs are relatively small in size and content, and are visually indistinguishable from one another. However, through the use of branded identities and good packaging design it is possible to create clear identities that the consumer can differentiate between and choose. This is particularly important since we don't often get the chance to have comparative tests of products before we buy; we rely on its brand personality to convince us. The key elements used in FMCG branding are the graphics, packaging and promotional advertisements to create a unique selling proposition.

The advantage of these types of branded identities is that they can be finely tuned for niche markets and target consumer groups. Some brand personalities simply do not travel well, so selling the same product in another country may benefit from a different brand name and brand personality, while sometimes the consumer's goodwill towards a country-specific brand should not be wasted by changing to an umbrella brand. Philips, the Dutch consumer electronics giant, still sells under the Walita name in South America, where it often achieves a number one position in sales. Until that situation changes it is unlikely and unnecessary to alter to the (relatively) unknown Philips brand. The disadvantage of this type of approach is that each individual brand requires its own branding effort and promotional budget. These offer little cross-benefit for the rest of the portfolio, so success in one brand is not easily transferred to another. Obviously, bad publicity does not spread across the group either, but this is a defensive strategy only.

Range brands

The critical reason to introduce range brands is to help organize and structure a large number of products under one brand proposition. This kind of proposition may often be an ideological belief or top-level idea that precedes the individual product type. For example, Lean Cuisine clearly targets those who are weight conscious whatever meal they plan to eat. Similarly, Marks & Spencer's organic range of food targets those who are worried about the naturalness of food, again, preceding any specific choice of food.

In the retail environment, the structuring principle of range brands can help stores to plan effective displays of the products. They also create a large, visible trading block on the shelves where individual product brands would be lost in the competition. Distinctive brand executions and packaging are used to reinforce the power of the range.

The use of range brand strategies is increasing as companies attempt to cross-sell to loyal customers. They allow a range of goods or services to be expressed through a single brand proposition that already appeals to an audience. It has often been associated with the rise of lifestyle segmentation, where a company attempts to fulfil consumer groups' needs, from the cradle to the grave. The range brand helps to narrow the choice of the consumer from the vast array of brands and products on offer. The Holiday Inn chain from Six Continents hotels uses the range concept to clearly differentiate its product offers for customers. The core brand Six Continents has four key sub-brands: Crown Plaza, Intercontinental, Staybridge Suites (a Holiday Inn validated brand) and Holiday Inn. The Holiday Inn has the range brands Holiday Inn, Holiday Inn Select, Holiday Inn Express, Holiday Inn Sun Spree Resorts and Holiday Inn Family Suites (see Figure 2.5).

This loyalty is effective so long as all the products are excellent and their innovation keeps pace with consumers' expectations. Once a consumer has been attracted to a product in the range and is satisfied, he or she is very likely to want to buy other products in the range. For example, someone who likes Pepperidge Farm's American Collection Nantucket cookies is also likely to try its Sausalito cookies from the same range. The range brand American Collection becomes a convenience navigator for shoppers in a hurry, allowing them to pick any item from the range, knowing that they will all fulfil their needs.

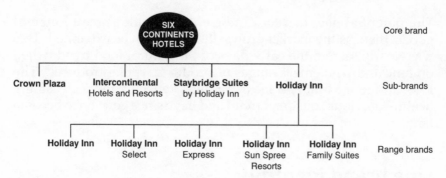

Figure 2.5 Holiday Inn range brands

This guarantee effect means that it is much easier for a company to introduce new products into the range as they are already supported by the range brand. This is effective in the mind of the consumer and the trade buyer, both of whom trust the new product. This should reduce any resistance in the supply chain and make the cost of introduction correspondingly lower. The payment by the brand to the retailer of slotting fees for shelf space means the brand manager must carefully analyse the total portfolio to maximize profit.

Range brands can collect and combine differing products that make up a total brand concept for consumers, like the Gillette range of male cosmetics. The range includes shaving foams, skin moisturizers, deodorants and aftershaves, all backed by the same brand proposition and promotional materials. In this case the focus of communication is the shaving cream, while the other products are sold as supporting elements to the total story. Again, the secondary products require relatively little introduction effort and cost and the whole package is strengthened by the enlarged brand proposition.

To build a successful range brand it is best to understand consumers' mental maps of their needs and how they would like to purchase groups of products. Reflecting their own conceptual model of the goods will make it easier to satisfy them and encourage them to buy-in to the whole range. This is especially true in the male cosmetics industry, where consumers are notoriously reluctant to experiment with new products. Consumers appreciate the implicit guarantee of the known and trusted range brand and this encourages them to try out new products across the range.

The range brand concept is a reduced risk method to introduce a brand concept that picks up on a new lifestyle trend in the market.

The potential new market can be entered with a small range of goods, then, as the market grows, the range can be expanded. This was clearly seen in the early days of the natural food trend, when organic and wholemeal ranges of products were introduced. The low-fat, reduced-fat and fat-free ranges reflected the increasingly health-conscious consumer trend and have since gone on to become large, mainstream ranges.

Line brand identity

The concept of line brand identity is similar to range branding but deals with products that are functionally closer. These are often new flavours added to a range or new variants on an existing product concept. Sainsbury's olive oil was originally introduced as a stand-alone product, in several size versions. Later its line was extended to differentiate between olive oil, virgin olive oil, extra virgin olive oil and peppery olive oil. The total brand image has been strengthened with minimum extra brand-building effort, and consumers appreciate the range differentiation that allows them to match a product closely to their needs.

The car industry has been successful in using a line brand strategy to sell variants of its cars. When consumers decide they want to buy a Ford Focus, they are then offered a choice from one line of Fords that can include many subtle differences. These are badged with a series of letters and numerals on the rear of the car: 1.1L, 1.4L, 1.7L, 2.0L, GL, GX or Ghia. The badge structures both the mechanical and the price differences in the mind of the car trader and the consumer. They can perceive the bottom of the line 1.1L through to the top of the line 2.0L Ghia, in easy increments.

The retailer often welcomes the introduction of a line of closely related products, because the brand story is already clear. The visual presence of the line will provide a strong focus on the shelf that requires minimal brand support material. It also creates a stronger brand image in total that should help to boost sales.

The main disadvantage of line brand extensions is that it is too easy simply to continue introducing new product versions. The cost and risk threshold is low, but there is a negative effect on the total range, as it always needs to fulfil a single vision. Otherwise, the burgeoning line becomes incoherent and loses the distinctive proposition that was the attraction in the first place.

Product brands

Some of the most successful brand management examples come from product branding, where each product has its own brand, logo or trade mark, brand name, packaging design and brand personality. This means that each product brand is exclusive and distinctive in the marketplace, with the brand portfolio mirroring the product portfolio. Each of the marketing mix elements can be carefully tuned to maximize penetration in the chosen target audience.

Using a multiple product brand strategy can successfully gain a larger overall share of the market than is often possible with a single product brand. This can be witnessed in the detergent markets, where a manufacturer like Procter & Gamble or Unilever may well have several distinctive products in the same product category. The exact difference in the formulation of its margarine spread may be minimal, but the expression of the brand personality may vary widely. For example, Flora is the premium brand in vegetable oil margarine, which offers consumers the ultimate in healthy caring for all the family. Its 'I can't believe it's not butter' brand offers consumers a healthier margarine that attempts to duplicate the taste of butter, but without the perceived negative health risk. Its third brand, Olivio, presents a Mediterranean version of a healthy spread, using olive oil as the health and taste accent. All three offer themselves as versions of a healthy spread, but they address different target audiences in a different tone of voice. Consumers appreciate purchasing brands that more closely reflect their concept of themselves, and may not realize they are from the same manufacturer. The company benefits because its combined market share for the product is higher than would be likely with only one brand.

The candy and sweets market is often covered by product brand propositions like the Mars bar, the Snickers bar and M&Ms. These are all specific and unique products, although they largely fulfil the same need with similar ingredients. The added value of the product brand identity is so strong that consumers can make a clear choice between them and often remain loyal to one such product brand.

A product brand strategy is useful for companies that generate innovative products and create new categories, as they can position their new product or category without reference to other brand propositions. This is a higher-risk strategy than the previous ones, but one that can be extremely rewarding. It's higher risk because the new product will require investment in its own branding and promotional materials. But it can also avoid any downside to the core brand if the product launch is not successful. In the minds of the consumer it is only that particular product that has failed and not the company itself.

Brand managers need to assess whether the product is sufficiently unique to warrant an individual brand or if it could be better branded through a line, range or corporate proposition. Factors that will affect the success of a product brand include: the advertising spend, the uniqueness of the product, the quality of the pack design, the conceptual big idea for the new brand and how closely this matches with consumer desires.

There are many successful product brands in the market and one of the common elements is their improvement over time. Even a successful brand launch will not guarantee constant profitability: both the product and the brand personality need to be updated regularly. This may emphasize new features or simply be an update of the brand personality to match with contemporary target consumers. Snickers, Mars bars and Coca-Cola are all strong product brands and maintain their added brand value by being modern and drawing on their heritage to create products as brand heroes. Using the heritage of a long history of quality and innovation can be a strong tactic to get customers to switch brands if their usual brand is not available. This is often presented as the 'legend' of the product brand, with stories that build up the brand personality. For example, Coca-Cola prides itself as the brand that went to war with the GIs in World War II, Korea and the Gulf War. It associated itself with the space programme by announcing to the returning Apollo astronauts, 'Welcome back to Earth, home of Coca-Cola.'

All these additional brand milestones can be organized and managed with a little effort and creativity. Think about special events in the coming year that will fit your brand personality and try to ensure that your brand has some connection with them.

Brand extensions

Brand extensions are one of the most discussed topics of brand management, since there are many conflicting viewpoints. Before deciding to extend a brand, you need to ask, 'How far can I profit from extending my brand without damaging the core brand proposition?' (see Figure 2.6). It is a continuum of opportunities: there are

Damage to brand

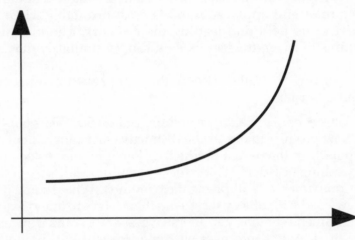

Level of brand extensions

Figure 2.6 Brand extension model

many variables for each individual business and these do not stand still over time. But there is frequently a negative relationship between the ability to extend a brand and the elasticity of profitability that is reflected by the growing stable of products.

At one end of the scale there is a single product brand like Mars bars, that remains successful and is constantly optimized. At the other end is the vast range of goods that fall under the Pierre Cardin brand, which has been stretched too far and has now been devalued. In a similar move the Gucci brand is extending from luxury clothes to household items like oven gloves, cooking aprons and dog toys. Following these poor examples, it can only be a matter of time before the greed of the brand strangles the market and it loses its shine.

However, some brand commentators believe that we are entering an era of potentially endless brand extension opportunities. They cite examples like Virgin, which sells everything from records, to airline travel, to cola drinks, to wedding parties, to clothing, to cosmetics and computers. This brand has the ability to connect directly with the consumer to convey a set of values. If consumers buy into those values then the logic is that they will appreciate any or all of the Virgin brand products. Virgin has become a true lifestyle brand, with people adopting its values as a convenient way of reflecting their own aspirations. Whether this is the dawn of a new era is difficult to say, but for the majority of brands it's likely that the current game rules still apply. A brand is most profitable when it is an expert in its field and leading the category. The more fields it attempts to cover, the less likely it can continuously master all of them.

According to Tauber (1990), there are seven distinct types of brand extension:

1. Same product in a different form, eg Fun Size Mars bars.
2. New product that uses the distinctive taste, ingredient or component of the parent product, eg Persil Liquid instead of Persil washing powders.
3. Companion or complementary product. Where some products are used with others, these lend themselves to brand extensions, eg Gillette shaving gel, aftershave, shampoo and shower gel.
4. New product that uses customer franchise of parent brand. Marketeers develop different brands to sell to loyal customers.
5. New product that uses some expertise gained in producing or marketing the parent brand. Brands are extended into areas where customers believe the original brand has connotations of special knowledge or experience, eg the Swatch car with flexible customization following the success of Swatch watches.
6. New product that uses a benefit, attribute or feature owned by the parent brand, eg The Body Shop and green values.
7. New product that uses designer image or status, eg Porsche-designed luggage set.

These may all be possible for a brand, but again, it's important to balance the desire to extend with the impact on the core brand. Peter Lynch, the Wall Street broker, calls the negative diversification of brands 'di-worsification' to emphasize that not all brand extensions are suitable or desirable. Jolley (1988) has suggested there is a two-way process involved in a brand extension: there is the flow of connotations from the core brand to the extension, and there is the flow of connotations from the extension reflected back on the core brand. The exact nature of these depends on the prominence of the co-branding and they can be positive, negative or neutral. To maximize the benefit of brand extensions it is important to define their relationship based on the mindset of the consumer. It may be advantageous to have a distant relationship, or it may be better to have a strong connection between the two brands.

Advantages of brand extension:

- Lower introduction costs for new products or lines. The creation of awareness in both the trade and consumer group will have a correspondingly lower cost.
- Lower risk on investment in new products.
- Increased opportunity for customer trial and use, through the variety of products on offer.
- Once a company has a large market share in one product, it will be easier to gain share in an associated market than further increase the original.
- Leverage brand name in the market, especially against competitors.

Disadvantages of brand extension:

- Reduction in the total brand value if any of the products are lower quality.
- Dilution of the brand proposition and personality. Will the brand personality stretch to cover increasingly diverse product offers, targeted at different target groups? Or will the brand become too indistinct for the consumer to be attracted to it?
- Will the extended products have negative qualities that can damage the core brand values? Brand extension is not risk free; there will always be some change in brand perception.

Extending brands always works best in a top-down direction, from a position of strength. It's relatively easy to bring out a brand extension of a cheaper brand product line or a smaller unit than the original. Ralph Lauren has been successful in extending from luxury clothes to selling jeans, bed linen and even branded paint. It is, however, much more difficult to attempt to move your brand in the other direction, turning a basic brand into one that has a premium proposition. It would be almost impossible to believe that the paint company Dulux could sell luxury clothes, yet the Armani clothes brand creates the strong position, while many will buy the cheaper Armani jeans collection. It is important for the board of management consciously to direct branding activities to specific brand levels rather than accept all forms of brand/sub-brand combinations as equally valid.

Global versus local brands

As global consolidation takes place, there are huge financial incentives to buy up strong brands in fields where a company is weak, rather than developing a new brand from scratch. Many of these brands were originally companies in their own right before being swallowed up by larger groups. They had their own corporate culture and were able to offer a distinctive proposition to the consumer. As part of a larger group, it may be important to retain that brand distinction in order to be successful.

Alternatively, a large company may wish to incorporate these brands to build a stronger, single brand proposition. This has the advantage that as the group grows larger, the cost of presenting the brand on the global stage is amortized across more products. There is also a great deal of goodwill to be gained when entering new markets. In North America, the German company Braun uses its own brand name to position its shavers as a premium European brand (even though it is owned by Gillette). This allows it to charge higher prices and to be sold through more exclusive channels than other generic brands. It expresses its European heritage through its simplicity of design and the superior quality of its products. The Dutch brand Philips has taken a different brand structure for North America and promotes its shavers under the well-known American brand name Norelco. This proposition relies on the consumer feeling that the Norelco brand is part of American culture, rather than an imported brand. Its Christmas branding campaigns are legendary; I have even heard people say that they don't feel it's Christmas until they've seen the Norelco Santa on TV.

These are two very different approaches to entering and managing global brands with products that are both identical to their European versions. The Braun brand uses the imported concept, promoting itself as a premium foreign brand that remains separate from other American brands. It uses all the icons of Germanic engineering quality and precision to help build its brand personality. The brand speaks of the ideological brand pleasure of owning a German product with connotations of BMW or Mercedes cars. The advantage of this approach is that global branding helps to make this brand more successful through association with a larger entity. It also consolidates the Braun brand proposition as a single, powerful personality in the mind of global consumers. This can be seen negatively as less focused on American needs, by some consumer segments.

Conversely, the Norelco brand relies on integration and association with the local American culture. It is the brand that is or has become part of American daily life, the brand your father has always bought. This has the advantage that the brand is non-threatening, especially in times of economic uncertainty. But it also means that it is more difficult to position the brand in a premium category as it is clustered with the other American brands, Wahl and Remington. The brand is not seen as part of a larger global group with its inherent strength, but it can be seen as catering more closely to the local needs of Americans.

For both companies there is a risk of ignoring or alienating a certain segment of the population. They need to accept this risk by being clear about their expectations for size and growth of their market share and the potential movement of market opinion. As globalization increases, it is more likely there will be benefit from consolidating single brand names, especially if the product is identical across markets. Where the product is customized for a particular market or consumer group, it may be more worthwhile to retain separate identities.

Summary

- Branding activities can be found throughout the business chain, while marketing is restricted to the external delivery of the product or service.
- There are three broad types of brand architecture for a business: the corporate, eg Barclays Bank; the endorsed, eg Eternity by Calvin Klein; and the branded business, eg Snickers bar (Procter & Gamble).
- The product or service may have a range brand, a line brand, and a product brand, eg Apple Macintosh, Powerbook and G3.
- Brand extensions need to balance leveraging the brand equity with the dilution of the core values.
- Increasingly, there is a consolidation towards global brands with local brand personalities.

CHAPTER THREE

SERVICE, RETAIL AND TRADE BRANDING

Effective strategies for different sectors

This chapter examines activities in three branding domains that are additional to standard product branding. We will look at service branding, which is especially important in developed economies and affects the newly deregulated business environment of privatized utilities, airlines and social services. Key similarities and differences that distinguish service branding will be explained and analysed through the tangible effects of their intangible service brand qualities.

This chapter also looks at the increasing influence of retail branding and the issues that own-label branding faces in the marketplace. Staff-customer relations involved in retail branding are analysed as an expression of brand personality. It also looks at how the nature of retail sites can form a total brand experience, going beyond the reproduction of visual merchandising. Business-to-business branding requires different techniques, but these activities are still underpinned by person-to-person relationships. There is a specific examination of the role of the decision-making unit (DMU) within the business-to-business buying process. All three alternative branding domains draw on the framework of the seven Ps described in Chapter 2.

Objectives

- Understand the specific characteristics of service branding.
- Examine the ways in which people deliver brands.
- Understand the specific characteristics of retail branding.
- Analyse the use of own-label brands.
- Understand the specific characteristics of business branding.
- Understand the decision-making process in organizations.

Service branding

Service-driven economies

Current business thinking suggests that there are three important elements to service brands. First, companies in the service sector deliver that service through the physical attributes of several elements. For an airline it's the seats, the price, the food and the in-flight entertainment, suggesting that it is the combination of these elements that produces the service. Simply recombining these standard elements would therefore produce another level or type of service.

The second issue is the current focus on customer or consumer driven marketing. This would suggest that all brands are serving the customer whatever their requirements. This is a reason that relationship marketing has developed in place of the more traditional production or financially driven marketing approaches.

Third, western economies now rely largely on service industries for employment. The workforces are more mature in understanding the need to be service oriented, and have also become more demanding as service customers themselves. These experiences also mean that they have become more knowledgeable and sophisticated about service brands. The privatization of many previously state-owned utilities has clearly developed a model of service branding in the social sector. Telephone companies, railways, universities, health authorities and gas companies have all had to develop a distinctive brand personality from a previously uniform institutional persona.

Information technology and innovation have created many new service industries. The Internet may run on personal computers but there are a large group of industries that have rapidly grown to service this communication network. These range from search engine companies such as Yahoo! through online booksellers Amazon.com, to companies such as AKQA that design Web sites. The financial turnover and staff employed by all these companies are now significant in the national economies of many western nations.

Service brand processes

Intangible benefits

First, the brand is itself intangible, despite the physical nature of its constituent components. It is the experience of the performance of the combination of those elements in a particular context and time that expresses the brand personality. This is unlike product or package brands that rely on the tactile and often repeated use of an object to develop the brand's personality. Service brands need to convey brand personality in action and during a specific time only.

A customer's lack of experience with a service means that brands must develop new opportunities to express themselves. Customer recommendations are often strong advocates of a particular brand, as a satisfied customer is a loyal customer. Loyalty cards introduced by supermarket chains help retain customers in a competitive retail environment, and the information gathered through them can also be used to refine service parameters. Free demonstrations, a reduced first rate or free gift can help introduce new customers to your service. Financial services often use free bags, T-shirts or calculators to entice new customers to begin using them, especially with target groups like students or the young.

Time-based brand experiences

Because service brand experiences are time based, they are unrepeatable. They may only happen once in that form. This means that individual customers may experience slightly different brand personalities. Later in this chapter we will look at staff relations and experiences that can help to build consistently correct brand experiences.

The ordering, buying and use of services often take place at different times, so brand experiences need to manage this time chain.

They need to remain relevant throughout this process, eg buying an insurance service contract for your home. The ordering or buying may happen years before you actually need to use the replacement service that you have bought. Customers need to be reminded about the brand personality by reinforcement at regular intervals. This could be as a yearly update, corporate branding on television, or sponsorship of sports events.

Brands that provide services need to cope with shifts in demand, and they must deliver the service when the customer requires it. However, since they cannot build up inventory of stock they must develop strategies to cope with these fluctuations. This highlights the importance of continuous planning, reviewing and updating of service delivery schedules. Brands that are best able to match these shifting demands are often perceived as leaders in the marketplace. Airlines attempt to offer a fixed schedule of service, so sudden changes in passenger flows can cause long delays, leading to a negative perception of the brand. Negative perceptions easily occur when customers are already in a high-stress situation, eg flying or dealing with lawyers or medical matters. The added stress can multiply customer satisfaction or dissatisfaction enormously.

There is elasticity to the length of time that customers will wait for a service. Depending on the particular service it may be a few seconds (telephone answering services) or a few hours (flight delays) or a few days (furniture delivery). Brands can distinguish themselves by performing best in their class. They can also develop a trust that the bandwidth of service times will always be met. Courier parcel services or railway operators rely on this kind of distinction to retain business. Usually, keeping the customer informed of any changes should help maintain brand integrity. Service brands can also divide their service categories into first class, business class or economy to represent different expectations for their customers.

People-to-people services

Services are generally delivered by people to other people. Service providers must attempt to deliver the same quality of service to all customers all the time. This is a difficult task given the nature, diversity and spread of the population. Companies must choose the bandwidth of their brand personality in the global market. They could enforce rigid uniformity as McDonald's does, where every staff member in every country should greet and treat customers in the same prescribed manner. Or they could develop an acceptable range of local behaviour that will allow for local conditions. The advantage for McDonald's is that one system can be continuously refined and spread easily across the world, as internal communication is standardized. Customer acceptance of your service can be a problem where there is a strong native culture. Staff using standard rules works fine when conditions are acceptable, but if the service provider has to work under unusual pressure then staff may not be able to cope well going outside the rules. In these cases, staff who are trained in a more flexible manner are more likely to be successful.

Different service sectors have different levels of customer interaction. Legal services are often bought by individuals, so the relationship between staff and the customer needs to be more intimate and personal. The customer's experience of the brand will generally be based on their opinion of the service provider. Airlines have to deal with a much larger group of customers, so their brand will be experienced through the relations of many staff and the customer. But it will also be based on how customers perceive the behaviour of other customers using the same service. When we go shopping we look at the other customers to gauge whether they are similar people to us, as they also reflect the brand position. This can be extreme in the case of chic restaurants where some potential customers are put off by the presence and behaviour of other customers. The service brand needs to manage both these kinds of customer well to maintain a consistent brand personality.

Staff training and attitude are a key element to expressing a strong service brand. Staff should be well trained to deal with the processes involved with the service, as this will ensure that an acceptable level of service is always provided. Training should, at some level, include all staff, even secretaries who answer the phone or those who deal with suppliers. The golden rule in service brands is that all staff belong in the marketing department. Excellent internal corporate communication is therefore vital if staff are to understand and contribute to the brand personality.

Staff attitude is a more difficult element to control, but it is often just as important. Customers are sophisticated and do not appreciate being patronized or obviously treated impersonally. It is no good simply repeating the corporate procedure to a customer if it is done insincerely. Motivating corporate staff to live and breathe the brand personality must start at the top of an organization. Well-motivated teams who are eager to please customers are an invaluable part of the total brand experience. Staff–customer relations should become collaboration, as the customer is often involved in generating the service result. A service is only a service when it has been experienced, therefore a brand only becomes a brand experience when it has been ordered, bought and consumed.

Retail branding

Retail branding has risen along an ever-increasing path of influence over the past 30 years. This section looks at the shifting balance between producers and their brands and the retailers and their own brands. This resonates with the more general shift in society from a focus on production to that of consumption. It expresses the change in how consumers understand and develop their own identity. We will examine the increasing use of retail sites as a form of brand experience, and look at how staff–customer relations can contribute to effective brand management.

Consumers now spend a large part of their leisure time shopping, and retail sites should take more advantage of this in the way they present the brand. There are several distinct elements to retail brand experiences that can help to reinforce the brand:

* advice;
* service;
* trust;
* social;
* entertainment.

Advice
The nature of advice will depend on the type of business you are in, but the tone should be carefully matched with your brand personality. For example, an upmarket perfume brand should have knowledgeable staff who can really advise customers which fragrance is best for their skin type. An 'A brand' sports store should have real athletes helping to advise consumers about product choice, reinforcing their commitment to sporting excellence. The level of advice required will determine the choice of personnel and the level of training given to them.

Service

The level of service in a store should match the brand quality. Tesco supermarket has defined its checkout service as no customer having to wait more than five minutes, otherwise it will open another checkout to cope with the overflow. For a luxury cigar store this level of service is clearly unacceptable: the retail brand site should always match or exceed the consumer's expectations.

Trust

The layout and design of the store can help to suggest trust to the customer by reinforcing known cultural connotations of safety and security. This is particularly important for institutions, banks and medical centres, as people are unlikely to trust a bank that has a scruffy interior or a medical centre with unhygienic staff. In the same way that design can help to organize an interior so that it is easy to navigate, it can also help express the brand through distinctive shelf systems, banners, point of sale materials, shopping bags and ticketing. It is the combination of all of these, presenting a coherent image, that will ultimately generate the best brand response from customers.

Social

It is well known that many shoppers, if not all, require, expect and enjoy some type of social interaction from shopping. By targeting customers, brand managers can develop specific events and social patterns to encourage customers to visit the store and experience the brand.

Entertainment

Equally, most customers like shopping to be enjoyable, whether this is as simple as muzak in the mall or more clever entertainment like video walls, competitions and events.

Power retailing

In the United Kingdom and the United States, retailers in many sectors have become successful and powerful. Part of their success has been achieved through their management of generic label goods/own-brand labels and manufacturer's branded goods. The rise of retailers can be seen as part of the economic boom of the 1960s. In 1964, resale price maintenance was abolished in the United

Kingdom and this allowed retailers to set their own pricing policies independently from the suppliers' recommended retail price. Self-service shopping became successful and allowed larger stores with fewer staff to develop. During this time the car became available to more households and this meant that they no longer needed to shop at the corner store. Consumers also appreciated the ability to buy all their goods under one roof simultaneously. Retailing is now part of the leisure industry, as consumers like to spend their time as well as their money browsing through stores. Michael Abrahams suggests, 'When people go to Bond Street, they are buying the atmosphere and the environment as much as the clothes.' There has also been a tremendous consolidation of the retail market, with most town centres now looking similar, with a homogeneous set of retailers appearing on every high street. These factors greatly affected the smaller stores, which were less able to compete. The spiral effect of this continues to squeeze the smaller players – although conversely, the development of small niche shops was the success story of the 1980s.

Retailers and manufacturers addressing the balance

There are two processes at work in the struggle for power between the manufacturer and the retailer. One of them is an upward spiral benefiting the retailer's brand, while the other is an upward spiral benefiting the manufacturer's brand. These opposing processes sort out the strong from the weak brands. However, manufacturers and retailers must work together to manage effectively the consumer driven economy. Clearly, the manufacturers have a greater significance in the research, development, production, advertising, branding and distribution of the product. They often have a larger, more general view of the market as a whole. The retailer has detailed information about precise products and consumption at specific dates and times and can therefore understand the buying process better than the manufacturer. Retailers have strong comparative data for analysis and can take corrective action in the short term.

Retail marketing

There has been a shift in western service-based economies from an emphasis on production towards consumption. This privileges the retailer. Previously the manufacturer would develop and produce goods sold to the trade and then on to the consumer. It was the manufacturer who decided what should be made and how much it should be sold for. This has now changed and the retailer increasingly holds the balance of power. It is the retailer who increasingly specifies the type, quantity and delivery conditions for the manufacturer. This has caused a fragmentation in the power of manufacturing brands and strengthened the retail brands.

Supermarket multiples are an excellent example of how retail power has increased in the business chain (see Figure 3.1). Their grip on the general grocery market has tightened with a few key brands such as Sainsbury's, Tesco and Waitrose dominating the UK market. They can use their superior buying power to reduce costs and generate profits, which in turn squeezes the supplier still further. The supermarket multiple as a brand has generally moved from a low-price, low-quality operation to that of high quality at good value.

The business management of supermarket multiples has become much more sophisticated in comparison with the manufacturers. Their stock controls and just-in-time supply networks mean that fresh goods arrive at the time required, thereby reducing stock costs. The merchandising of goods has developed from simple shelving to innovative promotional packaging and bright, clean, wide aisles in stores. The introduction of loyalty cards has helped competitive multiples define and protect their territory and the shopping data gathered from these cards is enormous. For the

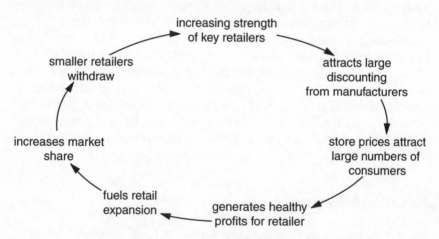

Figure 3.1 Spiral of growing retailer influence (Source: de Chernatony and McDonald, 1992)

average shopper, the reward of extra points or money-off purchases far outweighs the inconvenience of the store gaining access to their personal shopping habits. Stores can use this information to predict and redirect stock, promotion or seasonal trends. Currently, consumers have only one card per store but it cannot be long before they develop a more sophisticated programme of bronze, silver and gold card versions to segment their shoppers further. Potential fast-track checkouts for gold cardholders are a seductive concept for those with little time available.

Manufacturing marketing

Manufacturers need to develop their customer branding (towards the retailer) alongside their consumer driven branding (see Figure 3.2). Consumers and the retailer will want to know what your unique selling proposition is in comparison to their own brand product. This process should help the manufacturer to strengthen its brand against the retailer's own-brand labels. If this is not done then the manufacturer brand may weaken and become simply a supply brand for retailers.

All the normal consumer marketing tools should be used with the retailer. Think about how the retailer plans its stores and how it perceives your brand in comparison with itself and competitors.

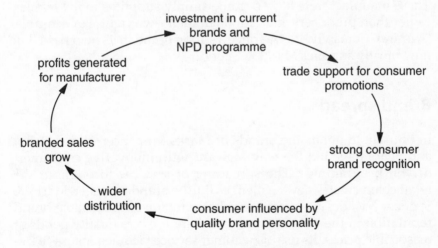

Figure 3.2 Strong manufacturer's brand response (Source: de Chernatony and McDonald, 1992)

The following is a list of key segments used by retailers (in Randall, 1997):

* Essentials. These brands are leaders in their field; they are often heavily marketed and will draw people into the store.
* KVIs (Known Value Items). These items are used daily. The price and quality of leading brands are well known.
* Brand leader. The number one or two leading brands that most consumers expect.
* Profit brand. These brands use high volume or value to generate excellent profits.
* Variety/choice brands. Brands such as Grey Poupon Dijon mustard provide variety and offer niche solutions for consumers.
* Fighting brand. Retailers can also carry lines that offer value for money. This may be carefully balanced with their own-label brands. But if there is no own-label brand in this category then a price fighter will be included.

Corporate ownership and own-label brands

Retail brands have become so strong that their parent corporations are now powerful. Retailers have generally moved to a position where they can dictate terms to weak manufacturers and brands. These manufacturers have become simply suppliers to the retailer, rather than producers and brands in their own right. For example, 'A brand' Coats Viyella was once a strong brand in its own right, but now mostly supplies Marks & Spencer.

Brand spread

In household goods the brands of Marks & Spencer, Home Depot and Sears have led the way forward with innovative consumer-driven programmes. The spreading of services throughout the retail chain creates new challenges for the brand manager. Marks & Spencer has, despite recent problems, retained an enviable brand reputation in the clothing market where it offers quality goods at reasonable prices. Its use of customer service facilities ensures a tradition of high consumer trust. It has now been able to transfer this trust into the premium prepared foods sector. Despite having very little history in the food sector, its foods are widely regarded as the top in the market. These brand extensions continued into financial services where the trust of the consumer has translated into a profitable pensions and PEPs business for Marks & Spencer.

Retailers' own-label brands have now come of age and express the high ownership level of the retailer's brand in a market category. During the mid-1970s, own-label branding was characterized by cheap, poor-quality items. The packaging often emphasized simplicity, with monotones, simple names and basic text designs. They were supposed to attract budget-conscious buyers who could not afford premium brands. However, the increasing affluence of shoppers and the psychological barrier of purchasing these own-label brands meant that they were not successful.

The following 10 to 15 years into the early 1990s saw an increase in quality, innovation and promotional activities (see Figure 3.3). The top-branded supermarket multiples' own-label brands are now better quality than many manufacturers' brands. It is only the true 'A brands' that offer better quality at a higher price than the supermarket own-label brands. This is a form of physical evidence of the superior brand perception of the supermarket multiples. Own-label brands now account for almost half of the stock in a typical supermarket. They use the attraction of leading brands to draw shoppers

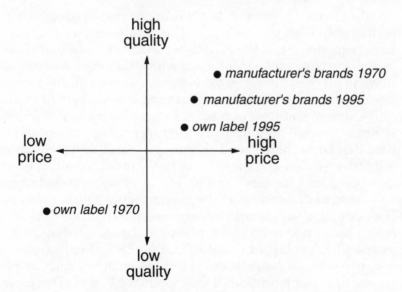

Figure 3.3 Relative changes of own-label and manufacturer's brands (Source: de Chernatony and McDonald, 1992)

into the store, then place next to them their quality own-label branded goods. Leading brands understand this dynamic relationship and generally see this as part of the competitive environment.

Own-label brands

Supermarkets use own-label goods to offer the consumer reasonable quality for a reasonable price. Strategically, they can be used to build and express the brand values of the multiple by wide use of own-label branded goods throughout the store. This enables them to differentiate themselves from competitors' supermarket brands. This was critical before the introduction of loyalty cards when supermarkets tended to stock the same brands. Own-label brands can form a lower level of price fighter within the store since they are generally appreciably lower in price than the leading brands. Supermarkets claim this is because they do not need huge national marketing campaigns, but it is easy to understand that they prefer the larger volumes the lower priced goods generate.

Retail sites as total brand experiences

Retail sites are one of the best opportunities for developing a brand relationship with the customer. They can be used to maximize a brand experience that has a symbolic space and time dimension. By having total brand experiences, consumers are more likely to be fulfilled in all their sensorial perceptions. These will help generate extremely positive memories of the brand that will be hard to change.

The design and style of retail sites have become more important in recent years. This reflects the ever-increasing amount of leisure time that consumers spend shopping. A well-designed store can fulfil the cognitive and the emotive needs of the consumer (more on these needs in Chapters 7 and 8). The carefully managed cognitive and emotive dimensions of the brand should satisfy these needs. For example, a supermarket's cognitive brand dimensions are generally concerned with convenience and ease of shopping. The store's physical layout should therefore be self-explanatory and easy to negotiate. A supermarket brand's emotive dimensions may emphasize sophistication or cosmopolitan values. Therefore the store should choose colour schemes and materials that confirm and enhance these perceptions.

There is an old retailing truism that says that the longer the consumer is in the store, the more likely he or she is to buy something. This suggests that retailers should now consider themselves not only in the service industry but also the entertainment industry. They should develop expressions of their brand dimensions to satisfy this consumer need for leisure activities. Certain stores such as Nike Town and the Disney Store are already doing this. They use the space in the store as a retail outlet, but they also use the space as the mythical home of the brand. Not all the space is used for immediate sales; some of it is devoted to developing the brand–consumer relationship, with TV walls, music, entertainment and advice clinics.

Staff–consumer relations play an important part in developing retailing as a total brand experience. The staff must express the values of the brand with each other and with the consumer. Well-trained staff who are motivated to express the brand are an extraordinary asset in retailing, as they are in service brands. The Disney Store for instance has no checkout staff but casting agents, while the Nike store has different coaches for each department, eg the football coach. This shift in attitude creates a changed relationship with the consumer: it is no longer simply one of buyer and seller, but one of mutual respect and friendship.

Retail sites are the culmination of the brand experience as they involve all the elements of the product, the service and the retail experience. Using the model of the theme park, we can develop retail sites that are better able to fulfil the brand promise through total brand experiences. That is not to say that all retail brands need to be as humorous and exciting as a roller coaster. But they can maximize their potential for a complete brand experience. Even a bank can offer a more comprehensive brand experience by using TV walls to reinforce TV advertising messages. Banks could create a symbolic brand space that emphasizes their brand dimensions over competitors. They could offer rain covers over their cash point machines. Retail banks could show that they are thinking about how to please customers by offering them coffee and music while they wait rather than allowing bus stop-size queues to prevail. It is the combination of elements of time, space, staff and style that generate the most successful brand retail sites.

Business-to-business branding

Compared to product and service brands, business branding can be considered underdeveloped. The first two have always had a user or consumer focus that generated an interest in the cognitive and emotional side of the buying process. In business there was a feeling that the buying processes relied purely on cognitive factors. It is generally appropriate to suggest that business processes and organizations act in an objective manner. But we must not forget that all organizations are made up of individual subjects. It is the professional and personal characteristics of these organizations that influence buying decisions. Purchasing managers also consider the goals they have set themselves within their sphere of responsibility when they make a buying choice. This means that improvements can be made in developing the business-to-business buying process. Many techniques developed for service and consumer brands can increase the effectiveness of organizational marketing. However, there are still several distinct characteristics within the business buying process that need addressing.

Managing complexity

Technical
Business-to-business buying is still generally about technical appliances or services, whether they are paper clips for the office or the latest electron microscope. They all have to do a job that fulfils a target specification often based on information from many experts within the organization. Each department will have a technical criterion that it needs fulfilling from the equipment. For example, a computer network may have to be accessible to product designers who are relatively non-technical *and* the highly technical computer or engineering departments. On top of this there will be a financial target that the system must meet in terms of capital costs and training costs. The reason that these are often formalized specifications is that from an organizational point of view they should be personnel-independent. This is a key difference between business brands and consumer brands, although it is rarely as simple as that.

A business purchase is usually larger than a single consumer purchase and that means that the amount of risk involved is also much greater. The risk is not just the cost of capital but also the cost of opportunity. A company needs the product or service to enable its own business to grow and be more profitable. This added risk means that more managers within the organization will be involved in the buying process. It also means that the process will take much longer and be more carefully considered. Branding can play a key role in reducing the perception of risk involved with purchases. This can be especially true for first-time purchasers or new brand entrants into a market. Decision makers will want to know that they are buying a brand that is recognizable and therefore relatively safer than an unknown brand.

People

In organizational buying there is often a key difference between the purchaser and the user of the equipment or service. The person who actually uses the product must therefore explain to someone else the important features or characteristics required. For larger purchases there may be a whole team of experts who give information to the purchasing process. The brand must therefore communicate to and appeal to a much wider and diverse audience. Brand managers must identify these personnel within the organization and target specific and distinctive communications towards them. Within organizations it is more likely that the buyer would like to build up a long-term relationship with a supplier and therefore reduce risks still further. This offers the chance of strong brand loyalty as the threshold for change is also raised significantly. This also means that it is much more difficult to break into a new business account and develop a fresh personal relationship with the buyer.

Time

The length of time for selecting, auditing and processing business purchases is much greater than for consumer purchases. Brand support must therefore continue through this elongated process. Brands may need to address different audiences with slightly different messages at different times of the buying process. To be eligible for short-listing, the brand should initially support a general level of competence in the field. Later in the process the brand should express more detailed values. These could be reliability to the service department, or quality to the quality control department, or low running costs to the financial department. Each dimension of the brand should be carefully targeted towards a specific interest area within the purchase process.

Organizational buyers will want the business relationship to develop over time and they may even want to develop business jointly. This means that brand managers must be prepared to think about the development of another brand with their own. Software suppliers such as Microsoft must also think about processor suppliers downstream such as Intel, and upstream clients such as Compaq.

The buying process

A buying process for business brands is more complex than for consumer products. One person may take the actual decision but they will rely on a large number of experts to manage the buying process (see Figure 3.4). These will include:

- *The user.* The person who will actually work with or integrate the product or service.
- *The influencer.* This may be a technical adviser who will know the field of the technology or service. It may also be the financial adviser who will attempt to control costs, both initial and long-term running costs for the purchase.
- *The decider.* This will be the person who actually makes the decision. It may be a line manager or a director, depending on the total size of the cost of the purchase.

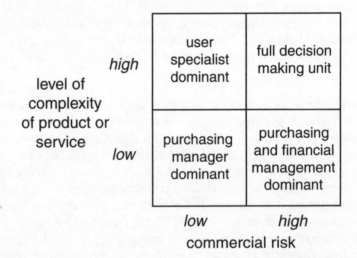

Figure 3.4 Matrix assessment of the decision-making unit (Source: de Chernatony and McDonald, 1992)

⊛ *The purchaser.* Once the purchase decision has been made the purchaser must organize the contracts, delivery and payment terms.

There may be other members who fulfil similar roles and the team may be large. Alternatively, the team may be small and the manager is also the influencer and purchaser. It is important that the total brand personality is used to maximize the effect on all the team. The buying process can be divided into several key steps:

1. Problem recognition.
2. Problem analysis.
3. Need definition.
4. Solution search and acquisition of proposals.
5. Evaluation and supplier selection.
6. Order processing and delivery.
7. Performance evaluation.

To simplify the complexity of dealing with a buying team we can separate buying into three categories: a straight re-purchase, a modified re-purchase and a new purchase. This will allow us to focus on the specific differences in branding that each situation requires.

Direct re-purchase

Direct re-purchase is the simplest kind of business purchase and may be done by only the purchasing manager of the company. They wish to continue using your brand of product or service at the same terms as previous purchases. They are happy with the level and type of service and delivery. In the case of the re-purchase, the brand needs to reassure buyers that what they are getting is the same as before. The brand must act as a badge of quality control and assure the buyer that this will be a trouble-free product. Branding here can focus mainly on the emotional dimensions of the brand. It should confirm the buyers' preconceptions that they have made the right choice. It can also be used as a reminder that the brand exists and is a valuable part of the business chain. The brand will help the brand manager to maintain presence with minimal effort.

Modified re-purchase

Modified re-purchase is a purchase where the brand has been selected but the individual product or service may need some refinement or development. Possibly the brand personality has deteriorated in the mind of the buyer or new brands have entered the market. The specification of the goods may need changing or updating. Brand managers should try to find out if the need of the customer has changed significantly. Perhaps the company goal has shifted, for example from safety to reliability. The process of re-purchasing will be extended to include the relevant but limited group of experts who need to reassess the specification of their needs and your brand. This type of re-purchase requires careful brand management. If the customer is not satisfied with your brand it could be the start of a change of supplier. A brand needs to express strongly the cognitive and emotional benefits of the product. It can also accent the good working relationship and co-development of previous projects. The purchaser needs to be reassured that the brand can grow with the company and that neither is growing apart on different trajectories.

New purchase

This kind of purchase will probably be the most complex. The brand has been chosen for short-listing against competitors or existing brands. This means that the distinctiveness of the brand should express how it is better than the competition. It will also have to gain trust from the purchaser. The longevity of a brand can help to minimize customer perceptions of risk. A full range of cognitive and emotional dimensions of the brand needs to be expressed. The extended process will incorporate many experts from both organizations. These negotiations should include technical experts from your organization to act as advisers for the marketing managers. They can also explain brand technologies to their technical counterparts in the buying organization. For example, nylon cloths often have patented processes and names per company; a different company may have a similar process and product by a different name.

Promotional activities

Continued service and delivery are the long-term goals of business brands. Because the purchasing is likely to continue over an extended period, business brands need to develop a long-term method of promotion. The corporate brand can be used to maintain a complete presence in the marketplace. It will also signal to prospective new clients which category they are prominent in. The emphasis here should therefore concentrate on presenting a sophisticated and competent corporate machine. After all, even if you have the perfect product, no manager is going to buy from you if he or she doesn't trust you as a business. The buyer's preferred way of reducing risk is to visit the sellers' plant and get a holistic sense of the brand. This suggests that they are interested in the general image and performance of the company as a whole, rather than only the specific product that they wish to buy. Companies who do not develop a well-perceived corporate image are unlikely to get even to the tender stage of a business purchase. Several promotional channels can be effective for business-to-business branding.

Sales representatives

The complexity and nature of business-to-business selling means that sales representatives are crucial in the buying process. Purchasing managers will often rely on the advice of colleagues, representatives and experts. The representative must therefore be able to express clearly the brand personality. This emphasizes training and brand awareness for representatives. They may not be the only people to meet the buying team, but they will be the most constant. This becomes particularly important over time where the long-term growth of the brand can be leveraged by a brand-adept sales force. Cold calling is an important sales technique, but it will receive greater consideration if it comes on the back of a global TV advertising campaign. The campaign will raise awareness of the brand, putting it on the mental list, and should also reinforce the brand values, making the proposition attractive to the buyer.

Advertising

This has a much smaller role to play in branding than in the equivalent consumer goods world. The branding of FMCG goods is largely developed and sustained through advertising. In the business environment the use of personal relations and advice is key to purchasing decisions, although sales people need to be supported by advertising. A company must know which other companies are in its product field to think about alternatives to its current supplier. Advertising campaigns are valuable when developing new markets and can focus on general awareness of the company brand and its products. A key role of most advertising is to communicate a message that should inform and persuade all stakeholders, including key members of the business purchasing team.

Large corporations such as Microsoft can afford to use TV advertising to maintain brand awareness. Global coverage of its user base also makes this the most cost-effective method of reaching them all with a single message. Even technical brands such as Intel have used television to create awareness of something on the inside of a product. The power of TV is strong and seductive in expressing a brand's personality. Companies that can afford TV advertising can already be considered strong and reliable in the minds of purchasers. They are above the threshold that separates companies that may not be secure enough for possible business-to-business selling.

Trade fairs and conferences both help to develop and promote industry sectors and they will often have seminars attached to the programme. Brand managers should develop papers that will attract business experts to new knowledge that will help present their brand in a stronger light. This can be emphasized by the sponsorship of an event or research paper. It is important that the trade stand and employees all reflect the company's brand values. Annual trade fairs are ideal chances to gauge a company's size and professionalism, and build up important personal relationships with suppliers and purchasers.

We have seen the distinctive characteristics that service brands, retail brands and business-to-business brands must develop. Service brands rely more on the branding of a process or a collection of elements than on any single product. This means that uniformity may be more difficult to achieve. It stresses the need for excellent internal communications and training of staff. Retail brands rely on the total brand experience. They can also use a collection of staff, product and retail sites to express a brand personality. Relationship-building brand activities should utilize the time spent by the consumer in shopping. Business-to-business branding relies on a series of elements that must fulfil the different targets of the different members of the buying team. It is important for the brand manager to identify the buying team members and their roles within the buying process.

There are clear commonalities across these zones as well. There is a continuing emphasis on the relationship between personal identity and brand personality. In service branding, a staff member who can create a very personal form of brand relationship often delivers experience. The sociological perception of a retail brand and buying behaviour correlates closely with the individual consumer's idea of his or her personal identity or aspirations. Business-to-business branding has a strong rational side to it, but it also offers opportunities for personal branding relationships to be developed. Again, staff training and expression of the brand personality are crucial.

Clearly, the people in your organization are one of the most important assets in developing business-to-business, retail or service brands.

Summary

* Services offer time- and people-based brand delivery, in which it is more difficult to create consistency.
* Services are often intangible, and therefore physical evidence needs to be used to confirm the quality of the service.
* Retail brands have become increasingly powerful; people may trust their supermarket brand more than the government.
* Own-label goods have shifted from being poor to high-quality, good-value items.
* Business brands are often bought by a person who is not the user.
* The complexity of business purchasing is greater and the brand will need to appeal to different types of people at different times in the process.

CHAPTER FOUR

BRAND MEDIA

Established communication channels and techniques

This chapter will introduce the methods of communication, language and meaning-generation for brand management. The role of advertising in brand execution will be explained through the need for awareness and favourability. Traditional media will be examined, including above the line media: the press, radio, television, cinema, outdoor and transport. There will also be an assessment of below the line media: direct mail, point of sale, exhibitions, print, sales media and all other forms of marketing communications. Packaging design and FMCG branding will be examined through the cycle of protection, identification, dispensing and disposal. Since many of these activities involve working with external agencies there will be a brief summary of how to choose, measure and manage an external agency.

Objectives

- Explain how communication and meaning are generated between people and objects.
- Analyse the advantages and disadvantages of advertising.
- Describe the characteristics of above the line media.
- Describe the characteristics of below the line media.
- Examine the role of packaging in brand communication.
- Describe the best way to work with external agencies.

Communication

Identity is only worth something to a business when it is properly communicated to its intended audience, and they recognize and acknowledge its value. This means that the process of communication plays as important a role as the images we may use. The model of communication between humans is the best analogy for developing a model of communication between businesses and consumers. This is because people understand and use the protocols of this type of communication. They have a long experience of manipulating verbal and non-verbal messages and deciphering the meaning behind those messages. They have become experts at developing a message and sending it out to the world, and at receiving messages and translating them into a coherent meaning that they understand. Crucially, they are experts at two-way communication. To be precise, communication must be two-way to be considered effective, but until recently many brand communications remained unidirectional and therefore relatively ineffective.

The two-way communication process clearly expresses the goals of excellent brand communication because it:

* develops over time, creating a biography of the brand;
* encourages feedback on performance and appropriateness of the message;
* encourages listening to the consumer;
* develops a one-to-one mentality to brand communication, increasing the personalization of the message.

The two-way communication process starts with the *sender* (business) determining what is the right message to send out to their consumers (this will be dealt with later in this chapter). This means deciding on the content of the message, the personality and the channel(s) that the message will be communicated through. The message is then communicated towards the *receiver* (consumer). As it is communicated through a medium, it becomes less controllable by the business. It then reaches the consumer, who must interpret the message's meaning. The words or images used are not always the same as the meaning associated with those words or images. The value of the meaning is determined through shared meaning in consumer culture (see Figure 4.1). This is why brands can sometimes find it difficult to manage their message effectively, once the message is sent, the consumer or interest groups can manipulate it to mean something else.

This shift in the *meaning* of a message is often referred to as 'noise', the interference that changes or diffuses a message as it travels through the consumer culture. This can be seen in the shift in the *value* of the message: sometimes a sub-culture will champion a brand, even though it may not be its intended target. This often happens with youth culture and pop music: the Kangol brand, which was previously a motorbikers' outwear brand, suddenly came to be understood as a trendy youth brand. The brand itself had not changed but its meaning in consumer culture had changed dramatically.

The context of use and the user can also dramatically shift the value of the meaning of a brand. The supermarket chain Tesco has started parallel importing Calvin Klein T-shirts and Nike training shoes to sell in its stores. It is able to sell them at a lower price than other stores and Calvin Klein *et al* have taken legal steps to stop this practice. They argue that the consumers' understanding of the meaning of their brand is one that is exclusive and has been created by using exclusive stores' service, branding and pricing policies. They suggest that without these layered messages of exclusivity the aura surrounding the brand is diminished and therefore the practice is harmful to their brand. The current legal ruling is that parallel importing is unacceptable. The reality is that the sale of exclusive goods in supermarkets will damage the long-term perception of exclusive brands; but it highlights the fact that the locus of meaning

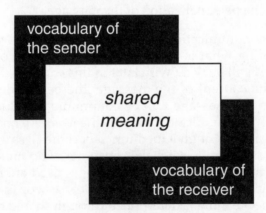

Figure 4.1 Zone of shared meaning between the business and the consumer

is not with the brand owner but in the consumers' mind and domain. This means that brand managers need to find ways to influence the consumers' perception; they cannot dictate their proposition to them and be successful. This also includes managing or anticipating the likely noise that their brand message is likely to receive or must pass through.

The most obvious type of noise is the language barrier, even in countries or regions that supposedly speak the same language. Regional dialects, phrases and accents can all cause confusion as to the true meaning of a message, although so can simple misunderstandings between people. The reality is that communication is never 100 per cent perfect. A great deal of modern communication relies on the receiver filling in the missing parts of the story, either through experience or intuition. In some media-savvy consumer groups this is a requirement: they actually enjoy the fact that only they can decode the message. They appreciate being associated with smart companies that use ironic messages to convey their brand meaning.

Consumer culture – the contemporary filter for messages

The modern consumer culture of westernized countries forms a filter to many of our daily activities and communication. There is a strong undercurrent of living in a 'to have is to be' society, where others judge us by what we have, rather than what we are, as we judge them by what they have. This may be used to interpret an initial encounter or a longer-term impression of people; they increasing rely on visible brand marks to help them negotiate their lives. As Celia Lury suggests, the brand becomes a marker to guide us in the choices we make: who to talk to in the pub, which restaurant to avoid, which people are most likely to be like us at the football match. It becomes a shorthand for our personality, and the expected personality of others we meet. This can represent the personality we have, or it can be the personality we would wish others to think we have – an aspirational image.

This means that we may see ourselves as:

I am what I drink – a Guinness drinker or a Heineken drinker.
I am what I wear – an Armani wearer or a Levi's wearer.
I am what I watch – a CNN watcher or a Sky Sports watcher.

I am what I listen to – an Abba fan or a Rolling Stones fan.
I am what I drive – a Saab driver or a Ford driver.
I am what I eat – a Ben & Jerry's icecream eater or a low-fat yoghurt eater.

Each of these brands helps to build us into who we are or who we wish to be and communicate this to others. Brands and visible brand marks have become the most effective tool in helping this process. Brand managers should see their job as enabling consumers to achieve this kind of recognition. This means they need to have a deep understanding of the social and personal identity needs of consumers. As markets become more globalized, these identities will reflect the change in consumer culture. Identities driven by New York street culture can influence Amsterdam teenagers and those in London.

Semiotics

The brand message that is received by the consumer is not just the words, but the cultural meaning that is associated with those words, symbols or images (see Figure 4.2). Ferdinand de Saussure (1966), Roland Barthes (1993) and Jean Baudrillard (1998) have developed the study of this kind of symbolic messaging in the study of semiotics. Their work attempts to map out the cultural connections that consumers make between images and their meaning beyond the text. It relies on the fact that the words and images we use have a cultural connotative meaning beyond their textual expression. The London consultancy Semiotic Solutions uses these methods to analyse consumers, markets and advertisements and build marketing campaigns. They deconstruct text, images and non-verbal communication on the basis of their semiotic meaning beyond the surface text. Semiotic analysis has proven very effective and one of its best features is that it can be applied across the widest range of media and technologies, providing a complete experience of a brand personality.

The meta-topics of consumer culture like gender, race and class have always had associative meanings beyond the text. To read *Horse and Hound* magazine describes a social position as much as an interest in equine and canine behaviour. To clothe a baby in a pink trouser suit and bootees conveys femaleness more than modesty or style. To listen to rap music suggests a racial dimension as well as an interest in syncopated rhythm. But even simple, everyday

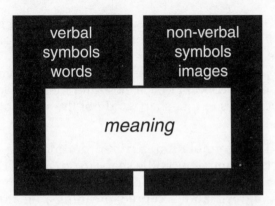

Figure 4.2 The combination of verbal and non-verbal elements create meaning

behaviour and attitudes can be expressed through the symbolic use of brands of the most mundane goods and services.

Brands and their expressive imagery have become the easiest shorthand for most of our daily reflection of ourselves and understanding of other people. Semiotics research and analysis attempts to define these rules of imagery and use them to promote specific meanings beyond the text. They also promote the use of multichannel communication with aural, behavioural, visual and other codes of use.

Barthes (1993) has described how we understand the meaning of an advertisement not just by its tangible content, but also by the symbolic meanings it implies and we as the consumer can read and understand. Semiotics is based on the relationship between the sign, the signifier and the signified (see Figure 4.3), which forms part of structural linguistics, the way we transmit and receive meanings from images and text:

* Sign – anything around us that produces meaning, images, objects, words, sounds, movements, animations, video, tastes, etc, eg a print advertisement with an image of a Mercedes car.

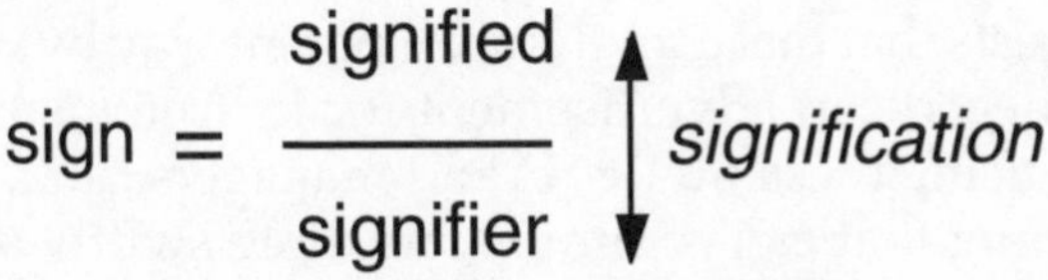

$$\text{sign} = \frac{\text{signified}}{\text{signifier}} \quad \updownarrow \text{ *signification*}$$

Figure 4.3 Relationship between language elements

* Signifier – the sensory impression of the sign, the mental perception of a sound or image on a page, eg the impression of a car-shaped image on a page.
* Signified – the abstract concept that the sign invokes in our memory, eg the concept of 'car-ness and Mercedes-ness' in our mind that relates to that shape and not the shape of a fish or a Toyota.

The signified is a connotation, a first-order meaning that we all agree connects a champagne bottle shape to our idea of champagne. There is a second-order meaning or denotative meaning that relies on generally agreed and accepted meanings, eg that Moët et Chandon is French and high quality. It is these denoted meanings, the generally accepted meaning of an image or word, that can be used as myths in brand communications. These myths can be as simple as our understanding that the French excel in epicurean delights or Japanese products are reliable. It could also be the use of words like 'royal' or 'gold' to suggest high quality or top of the range service on an airline frequent-flyer programme; we all expect that the gold card is worth more than the silver one.

Thwaites and Lloyd Mules (1994) have developed a semiotic system to decode and encode messages within images, text and narratives that can be used to build brand communications that are embedded with symbolic meaning:

* Define the key signifiers that are to be used on the page/video/sound (eg picture of a Mercedes A class car on a page).
* Define the range of possible signifiers for each of those signifiers (eg car-ness, Mercedes-ness).
* From these signifiers, define the social codes or connotations (eg transport, German-ness).
* Confirm the denotations that are likely to have become naturalized in society, the myth that has become accepted in general usage as the meaning for those connotations (eg safety, freedom, precision, reliability, smooth drive, luxury, good taste).

Barthes suggests that these myths are a potent way by which we can encode and decode an advertisement for its true meaning beyond the print. By using these myths, brand managers can tap into a rich field of meaning that can communicate more swiftly and precisely the intended message, than a lengthy article. To be successful they must use the codes that are shared by consumers – again, communication is only successful when it has been received and correctly interpreted by the target consumer.

Semiotics can help to define the brand personality in a succinct way by using the knowledge that is already freely available in consumer culture. In cross-cultural communication this can sometimes create misunderstandings, but in most cases the use of universally accepted signs provides a rich basis for brand personality. Professor James Woudhuysen describes consumer brands as 'a kind of installed-base-group-memory and behavioural reinforcement, which is realized though repeated, high-intensity interactions with say a Coke bottle.' The best way to do this is to draw on symbolic ideas and imagery that already exist in the consumer's mind and re-present and re-position your brand in relation to that symbolic imagery. Appropriate symbolism can be found everywhere in daily life, and by looking at the contents of the aesthetic codes found in Chapter 7.

Brand perception

Psychologically speaking, perception is the translation of the signals we receive from all our sensory organs (eyes, skin, ears, mouth, nose) into neural signals that form patterns in our brain (signifiers). These then need to be processed and translated into something that makes sense and has meaning for us (signifieds). It is this process of translating, interpreting and organizing our perceptions that allows us to understand and navigate our world. The way we organize these perceptions is based on experience, grouping and other techniques of pattern building.

Gestalt perception, according to Kassin (1995), is the ability to understand a larger meaning than the sum of the parts. It is the ability to see a pattern of dots but understand the shape and meaning they describe if we joined up the dots to make a shape or word we recognize. The key elements that help our gestalt perception are figure and background, and grouping techniques.

Figure and background

Figure and background refers to our perception of which objects or elements are more prominent in an image we look at. They are often universal, but can be personal as well; two people do not always understand the same meaning from a single image. They may be biased or drawn to focus on different elements of an image with different meanings. Typically consumers are more drawn to intense, unusual, loud, high-contrast, dynamic and startling elements. However, when the entire group of competitive brands on a supermarket shelf are vivid and colourful, then a quieter approach may also prove successful. Often advertisements try to attract by aggressive images and sounds but they can get lost, merging with all the other aggressive advertisements. A successful counter-attack can be to present a single quiet and thoughtful approach or a comedic approach against that visual pollution.

Alternatively, brand managers should try to ensure that the viewer or listener is directed towards one intended message, rather than others that may lie embedded in the image or group of images. By picking the most relevant symbolic image that corresponds closest to the consumers' expectations; the communication is likely to be easier and more effective.

Perceptual grouping

Perceptual grouping is our ability to make patterns out of what we see, even if the information is not complete. A pattern can be based on the proximity of objects to each other: we would understand two people who are stood very close to each other as having some kind of relationship. Brand images typically and successfully place their product consistently next to another object to signify a close relationship between them. Ralph Lauren uses images of upper-class society, horse riding, sailing and exclusive hobbies to connote that message about his clothes via the proximity of the two images. The sponsorship of events by brands is another form of proximity branding: by closely associating Visa, Kodak or Guinness with a global sporting event, these brands are confirming their global nature to consumers.

Consumers associate groups of brands by their proximity to their meaning. Sportspeople have a set of different brands that cover training shoes, tracksuits and equipment like tennis racquets or swimming goggles. Together they form a set by their proximity to their ideal type of these items, the cheapest for example, or the best quality, or the most fashionable brands in each category.

Perceptual similarity is another type of gestalt, where a brand portfolio might use the same pack, shape or colour to signify their relationship, enabling consumers to perceive the brand collection. This is also the way that consumers perceive natural categories of brands, by their visual proximity to each other. In order to redefine a brand as a new category it may be necessary to break with current proximity to competitors. This type of brand group is held in the consumer's mind as his or her perceptual set of possible brand choices. In order for a brand to be chosen it must already be part of that perceptual set or list in the consumer's mind; ideally it should be at the top of that list. Ries and Trout (1981) have examined this type of brand positioning in detail and expose many of the tools to help brands become top of a group, or start a new perceptual group.

Perceptual continuity can help a brand to build a brand narrative across media types and over time (narratives will be discussed in more detail later in this chapter). Consumers can build a flowing, continuous pattern from the separate elements of a brand campaign. This has been particularly successful in television advertising. The Oxo brand ran an updating family story for many years providing a sense of continuity of the brand for their consumers.

Perceptual closure allows consumers to fill in the gaps between elements of a brand presentation, even if they have not witnessed all of them. The long-running narrative of Nescafé Gold Blend advertising allows the consumer to pick up the story again, even half a year later. This is especially useful if the target audience is likely to have variable patterns of life or movement, such as shift workers, mobile workers and frequent travellers. Perceptual closure also means that brand managers do not have to spell everything out for the consumer; in fact many consumers appreciate brands that allow them to finish off the communication as a sign of their own sophistication. As consumers become increasingly media wise, they disassociate themselves from mundane and obvious brand promotions, seeking out ever more ingenious and mentally rigorous brands. These are often the brands that steadily increase the amount of closure they require the consumer to add to the communication. These consumers enjoy them in the knowledge that not everyone will be able to affect closure and get the message successfully.

The final element of gestalt perception is common fate, the sense that similar groups of brands have a similar trajectory in consumer culture over time. This can include which groups of brands are going out of fashion at any one time, or which are just coming into fashion. Consumers can also perceive which groups of brands are moving from narrowcast audiences to broadcast mass market audiences. This often occurs when youth or cult brands that are part of the look of a generation become very popular and then enter the mass market at the same time.

There is fantastic value in leveraging gestalt perception of a brand, since any single brand communication can then leverage the total brand value. The brand icon, brand name or logo is often the core of this brand perception. Seeing the Mercedes triangular badge drawn on a page has a greater meaning than the component elements of the black lines or the metal car. Our perception and understanding of the Mercedes badge already includes memories of the advertising, personal experience and codes from consumer culture. Building this kind of perception into a brand campaign is critical if individual elements are to invoke the whole brand personality. Successful brands like Nike have managed to reduce their message to the swoosh logo and 'just do it' without the Nike name, and still invoke 'Nike' in the mind of the consumer. The perceptual set of our experience can enable consumers to fill in the gaps in a brand communication, or guess the next phase without it ever being created.

Advertising

The added value of advertising

A definition from the Institute of Practitioners in Advertising is: 'Advertising presents the most persuasive possible selling message to the right prospects for the product or service at the lowest possible cost.' Advertising works because the message that is created is transferred to the receiver in a format that has a shared meaning. The role of advertising in brand management is to help generate awareness of the brand proposition and express the brand personality to a target audience for minimum cost. This awareness may be needed to:

* Launch a new brand on the market. This will express the brand personality to the targeted audience.
* Revitalize a brand that is losing market share.
* Protect a brand against a competitor's brand advertising efforts.
* Suggest new ways a brand might fit with a new target customer's needs and desires.
* Reinforce a brand's appeal in the market.

* To raise awareness of a brand for trade communication, stock-holder information and investor relations.
* Remind current customers of aura – the brand personality they have purchased.

The golden rule in advertising is to make the message both simple and short; anything else will not be well received or may not even be understood by the customer. This may seem obvious, but experience suggests that too many advertisers have been asked to convey too many brand messages in too much complexity. The net result is often an incomprehensible bag of messages that do not support the brand personality in the mind of the consumer.

Advertising approaches

Strong's (1929) AIDA model – Attention, Interest, Desire, Action – is one of many similar models that explain how advertising helps to transform a brand proposition into a successful brand advertisement.

The *attention* of the consumer needs to be attracted first; this can be through intrigue or drama or rational arguments. Once the consumer is alerted to listen or view, he or she must be *interested* in the message that the brand personality has to convey. This message needs to generate a *desire* to associate or be associated with this brand. Finally, the advertisement must convince the consumer to take *action* and buy the brand. This is a logical explanation of what in fact is often a subjective and irrational experience for the consumer. Advertisers have found that it is usually not possible to convey all four of these messages within one advert, so they formulate a series of adverts that when viewed sequentially form a credible and seductive story. They are usually parts of the same story that are told in different ways.

For example, the television advertising campaign for the Barclays Bank new B2 account ran a series of short clips on different weeks. Over the four weeks they explained the four different messages. First the attention was generated with a series of clips of a deserted tropical beach with sound and only the B2 logo appearing at the end. No explanation was given as to what B2 meant, or who the company behind the product might be; our attention was gained because of a lack of communication in the adverts. The next series of clips showed a man on the same beach counting stones out as though they were coins. The strapline asked us to question what would happen if our financial situation changed. The third clips used the same man with the stones and offered us an alternative to the way we normally bank to help avoid the problems suggested in clip two. The whole visual and metaphorical effect was to first intrigue us; we don't like not knowing what an advert is about. Second, our interest was gained by posing a question that we recognized but were uncertain of the answer. Third and finally they showed us a seductive answer that generated a sense of desire to go out and buy the product. By splitting the messages between adverts, instead of trying to accomplish them all in one, the effect was far stronger and clearer. The use of timed, sequential adverts works well on TV and in other media as well. The elements must gain wide enough coverage to ensure saturation of the individual parts of the message.

Advertising effectiveness

The effectiveness of an advertisement can be measured across several vectors, using a range of research techniques (see Chapter 12). These need to be clearly stated as the target at the start of the briefing process and can then be used as the measurement tool at the end of the campaign. Blythe (1998) defines these as:

1. Awareness. There is a high correlation between brand loyalty and brand awareness.
2. Liking. Likeability appears to be the single best predictor of sales effectiveness, since likeability scales predict 97 per cent of sales successes.
3. Interest. This clearly relates to likeability.
4. Enjoyment. This appears to be a good indicator in advertising pre-tests.

The attribute of awareness is essential if customers are to learn about the brand. The likeability, interest and enjoyment attributes all relate to how the brand personality fits with the expectations of the customer. This is the role of ideas and meaning in communication. Chapters 6, 7 and 8 all explore the component elements of a brand personality and the way it is conveyed to its target audience. The following sections look at how the choice of media types can help that process of communication.

To derive the maximum benefit from an advertisement, corporate identity or packaging brief, the core needs should be formulated in a SMART way:

Specific
Measurable
Achievable
Realistic
Time-based

Briefings based on these criteria should create results that live up to expectations and reduce uncertainty. They make explicit the added value that the project requires and how and when the results will be judged to match those needs.

Advertising must shift from monologue to dialogue

For the early history of advertising, the miracle of mass-market communication was a great success with businesses and the consumer, although the contemporary consumer wants to be addressed in a different tone and a different manner. As Giles Lury (1998) has described it, the childlike consumer, who was happy to accept being told what to do, has grown into an adult, and now demands equality of communication. The reality is that the previous type of advertising never was communication in the true sense, since it was an untargeted and one-way message. Mass media were used to broadcast open and unsolicited messages to an accepting public. It is for these reasons that many commentators have suggested the 'death of advertising' because it is unable to deliver the depth and precision of conversation that businesses would like to have with their customers.

Technologies like computer databases and narrowcast media have also played a part in enabling these focused modes of relationship marketing. The use of sophisticated database knowledge can pinpoint particular user groups with the precision of the surgeon's knife. The use of electronic loyalty cards lets retailers track customer movements and preferences on a single product basis. The development of the Internet, cable television and expansion of telephony have all added to the ability to target specific customers with specific brand propositions. The ability to achieve all of these is due to the massive increase in computing power that is available, even on a desktop model.

The result of these shifts towards selective and two-way relationship marketing is that traditional advertising has lost some of its power. The use of direct marketing has increased rapidly to fulfil the needs of business in the last 10 years. Database marketing is more targeted in terms of its message, its audience and its timing.

Furthermore, its effectiveness is more easily measured, and constant improvements are being made.

Media type selection

Depending on the target audience, the media type will need to be selected to convey the brand-advertising message. Each one has its own advantages and disadvantages that will help to make the appropriate choice. The proposed budget for advertising will also impact on the ability to use certain media types such as television. Although television advertising is highly seductive, in some cases it may not be the most appropriate tactic. For example, television is a mass-market tool, and if the brand is targeting a narrow group with an esoteric message, then most of the effort will be wasted. Jefkins (1994) provides a comprehensive analysis of all advertising media types, but this brief introduction should enable initial choices to be made in the light of their relative merits.

Above the line media

Five media – press, radio, television, cinema, and outdoor and transport – cover what has traditionally been recognized as above the line media: those that paid commission to advertising agencies. The 1976 Restrictive Trade Practices Act and the 1979 Office of Fair Trading ruling declared this artificial division uncompetitive and it is no longer a legal restriction. Below the line media are all other types, including direct mail, exhibitions, packaging, print campaigns, and various other media. They pay no commission, and are paid for by a percentage of the cost arrangement. Some agencies still use this division as a convenient segmentation of where their expertise lies and what kind of work they will do. Many new agencies see themselves as 'through the line', suggesting that they and their clients are now more flexible in their approach to media.

Press

The press can be split into the following groupings:

National newspapers
Local newspapers
Free newspapers
Consumer magazines
Trade magazines
Technical journals
Directories and anthologies

The press can offer detailed accounts of events, often combining many viewpoints on the same subject from either side of the issue. Magazines are particularly good at developing an enriched narrative that is often re-read many times, or even cut out and kept by the target audience. Each magazine or newspaper has a well-defined political, social class, ethnic or cultural bias that should be taken into account. This means that it is easy to segment and target consumers along these lines, although some target groups are particularly reluctant to conform to these groupings, and it may be necessary to adjust the tone of the message for different media. The circulation figures for the press are easy to collect and analyse for response rates, and the use of promotional vouchers encourages action after the advert has been seen. This can be repeated, forming a regular point of contact for the target audience, especially if the brand gets known for taking the back cover of a magazine every issue. Ralph Lauren once took all the advertising space in one issue of *GQ* magazine. Since this is approximately 60 per cent of the pages, it became more like a Lauren brochure, totally immersing the consumer in the world of Ralph Lauren.

Radio

Radio can have a local, national and international dimension to its message delivery, helping to target specific audiences. Radio advertising delivers short messages, often for only a few seconds, so they require immediate impact. They are also delivered by the human voice, which is transitory but strongly emotional; famous voices are often used to create a positive memory effect on the listener. One of the negative aspects of radio is that it is often used as a passive background sound rather than an active information channel, although it can reach large audiences, even around the world, with a single advertising slot. The style of the brand message must be tailored to fit with the other content that surrounds the advertisement; this means careful research of the target audience and their preferences.

Television

Television is the most expensive way of advertising your brand message and relatively few companies can afford it.

Television advertising also delivers a short message, which is repeated several times over a week. The message has to be instant, directing the consumer to other sources to discover the detail of the brand proposition, such as Web sites, telephone call centres, print or retail sites. Television has the advantage that it combines the elements of visual action, sound and animation, all of which are highly seductive and powerfully projected into the mind of the consumer. Due to the in-home delivery mode, audiences are receptive and appreciative of high-quality clips, although sometimes the clip survives in the memory while the actual brand message does not. Because of its method of transmission, television advertising is inclusive, using broadcast aesthetic codes rather than niche messaging. The balance of this is changing as more cable and satellite channels develop, leading to increased targeting opportunities, but with decreased coverage. This is also reflected in the way that consumers watch television channels. When they have 200 channels to choose from, they often enjoy surfing and zapping to avoid advertising or news breaks. This means that the attention span of the viewer has generally decreased in the last few years.

Cinema

The cinema is a larger, more seductive version of the television brand media but it has special characteristics as well. The brand message is still temporary, but can be longer than the 30-second television slot. The physical nature of cinema creates an impressive audio-visual brand experience that generates a high impact on consumers. The darkened auditorium and the demeanour of the cinema-goers mean that they are relaxed and receptive towards brand messages. The cost of developing cinema brand messages is much lower than for television; even the local restaurant can afford it. The cinema-goers often like the adverts as a prequel or warm-up to the main show.

Outdoor and transport

Outdoor and transport brand advertising are often used as a secondary or reminder message together with advertising in another medium. The brand message is almost always read by people on the move and from a distance, so instant impact is essential. These types of advertising are most effective in raising awareness of a brand, rather than specific communication leading directly to action by the consumer. The site-specific nature of outdoor advertising means that a regional or location campaign can easily be created and monitored. Ambient advertising on trains and subways can be extremely effective because of the captive and bored nature of the consumers: they will read almost anything.

Below the line media

These media types are generally printed communications including point of sale (POS), public relations (PR), direct mail (DM), in-store promotion and many other forms of communication.

Point of sale

Point of sale media act as a stand-alone salesperson, where there are insufficient sales staff, in hypermarkets and supermarkets for example. They help to identify new products to the market or a repackaged product offer. They are usually complex cardboard constructions with high-quality four-colour printing. They are relatively cheap and last reasonably well, so they can be used in large numbers across a region or country. They can be used to reinforce brand personality characteristics through themed executions such as *Star Wars* Darth Maul-shaped cutouts. They are most successful when linked to promotional offers or are interactive.

Public relations

Public relations is a separate category of marketing communications and, unless you are a natural, requires specialist agency skills. The benefit to the brand is its positive portrayal of the brand personality through press channels and live events. Good PR can help to build the brand heritage or hall of fame that captures the public's hearts. Sponsorship of sporting events, ethical concerns or industry conferences has been a successful way to use PR.

PR is also essential when the brand needs to admit it made a mistake, when it has misjudged the consumers' mood. The outcry in the UK about genetically modified crops shows how a negative situation can be turned into positive PR to help improve the value of the brand. Iceland, the first supermarket to declare its stock as free of genetically modified foods, gained an enormous amount of goodwill in the marketplace. The news coverage alone was a welcome unpaid advertisement that gave the supermarket a three-month lead on its competitors. This can be a risky policy, but if the action is aligned with the brand personality, then the message can be solid and confident.

Direct marketing

The growth of DM has been phenomenal in the past 10 years, allowing companies to target ever more precisely groups of prospects. Sophisticated computer databases with complex algorithms offer predictive success rates of market/lifestyle/demographic/geo-political combinations. Of course, many people still find letters purporting to be offering a personalized service, while managing to misspell our names or get our sex wrong, unacceptable. Quality of service is paramount when developing a one-to-one dialogue with the customer.

The rise in virtual businesses like phone banking with First Direct, or book-buying from Amazon.com, or catalogue shopping with the Cotswold Collection, means that our needs are increasingly being tracked on a micro level.

When the Häagen-Dazs icecream brand was launched, the company decided to concentrate on below the line promotion, rather than using an expensive TV campaign. As Joachimsthaler and Aaker (1997) point out, it chose this strategy because it believed that it would appeal to its target audience better than a mass media approach. It opened a series of exclusive icecream cafés where the brand presentation could be carefully controlled, and ran a series of print advertisements in the Sunday newspaper lifestyle sections. In both cases it was successful in quickly generating an exclusive and distinctive proposition of the brand. It used a brand personality of seductive self-indulgence, in contrast to its rivals, who still promoted their icecream as a cheap and fun event. The exclusivity of the brand personality was confirmed by the exclusive price, which was approximately a third higher than that of rivals. The target audience of young, affluent consumers were attracted to the desirable, sexy imagery of young couples fooling around with icecream in the print campaigns. It resonated with the images of Mickey Rourke in the film *Nine and a Half Weeks*: icecream had just become sexy!

Using creative promotional activities has helped many brands to generate leading market share results. The best way to generate these is to try to understand what kind of brand experience the personality would best fit. As consumers become more sophisticated, they are attracted to brands that can be clever in the way they present themselves. There is a certain amount of irony and self-interest in being associated with companies that dare to be different, especially those that show they have a better understanding of who the customer is and what they want, rather than simply repeating the tired formats of their competitors. The companies that are prepared to be bold and innovative in their promotional activities are likely to be the most successful. The ideal way to develop an innovative programme is always to test out the approach first on a target audience, preferably of lead users. If the new approach is true to the brand personality, then consumers will appreciate it; if not, then it may need refining; although it is important to stay focused on the core brand personality and not be too drawn by the research data.

Packaging

The original product packaging was simply for the protection and transport of goods. There were few examples of branded packaging until the late 19th century, when commercial competition started to grow rapidly. Companies such as Pears soap began branding their packaging to distinguish it from that of lower-quality unbranded competitors, while many goods were still packaged or wrapped in the shop, after a specific weight had been chosen. However, it was not until the 1960s that packaging design – what James Pilditch (1961) called the 'silent salesman' – began to be used as a form of brand expression. Because of the increase in self-service retail outlets the packaging now had to do much of the work of selling your brand against a large number of competitors with similar products. While this adds to the pressure on packaging design to perform, it cannot be expected to sell what is not there – the product itself must meet customers' expectations. Contemporary packaging design is now the crucial brand personality vehicle for most FMCG brands, particularly if they cannot support a TV campaign.

The pack design and graphics can help to create what Paul Southgate, of Brand House, calls 'total branding', where all the elements work to actively express the brand personality. Active branding is designing each element to add meaning to the brand personality, while passive branding relies on the meaning being added from external sources. Passive branding is therefore less controllable in terms of what the perception of the brand is, and usually takes longer to build over time. The first step of any new pack design is to decide whether it is a repositioning of an old brand pack or a new product development task.

A reposition requires the subtle refinement of the expression of the brand values in the pack design, possibly by making them more contemporary. This may also include shifting the balance of target customers across gender, age, political, geographic and socio-economic parameters. Brand pack refinement is often simply a graphic update, which is an extremely cost-effective short-term solution, as Will Maskell of PI3 Ltd confirms: 'Graphics has a much higher turnaround because the investments are a lot lower; and so you might find there would be a graphic update two or three times before the pack structure.' It is often surprising how much can be done with a small amount of change, that consumers are able to identify and appreciate.

New product development allows the pack to define part of the brand personality, and this is especially true for FMCG brands. Here the new brand values can be translated into a new brand pack, whether it follows a category style or it highly innovative. The parameters for this will be much wider, so it is important that the packaging designer and brand manager work closely together to reach a shared vision of the new brand pack. For example, if a new brand promises protection, this could be protection expressed as a bodyguard – masculine, sturdy and aggressive; or it could be a caring arm around the shoulder. The choice of expression will attract very different target groups.

The choice of *translator* of those brand values is the role of the 'big idea' in packaging design. This is where the brand planner starts to translate the words used in the brand proposition or personality into a series of images, metaphors and analogies that the design creatives can use. It is important that the brief is sufficiently open that there is space for creative freedom, but contains enough direction that the designers know where to look for their concept solutions.

Once the big idea for the brand pack has been generated and approved by the client, the role of brand execution becomes important. This is the style of the pack and its graphics, and again it can have a strong influence on the attraction of target audiences. Imagine a tea brand that targets working women and has 'relaxation' as its core brand value. The big idea for this might be 'Putting your feet up after a hard day.' The execution or style of this might be an adult cartoon, attracting younger women, or a watercolour style attracting older women; it may have an exclusive or value feel to it, all of which would attract different target audiences. It is important that the packaging designers understand the perception of these two, before they start. A conjoint analysis method of research should provide information about target audience preferences and tastes. This compares the elements of several propositions in random order to develop a model of which combinations are most preferred.

There are four elements in the cycle of effective packaging (see Figure 4.4):

1. **protect** – implicit quality;
2. **identify** – in-store brand navigators;
3. **dispense** – in-home branded use experience;
4. **disposal** – re-use or recycle and the environment.

The choice of what kind of packaging to use will depend on certain factors:

* what the product in the pack is;
* what the brand personality is;
* what the retail environment is;
* where it will be sold;
* how much sales assistance will be available;
* how much POS material will be provided;
* how it will be stacked on the floor or shelf;
* how it will be taken home;
* whether dosage size is important;
* whether it needs to be tamper-proof;
* whether freshness is important;

Figure 4.4 Four core packaging qualities

* where the packaging will be used – in the kitchen, bathroom, living room or bedroom at home, or in a commercial environment;
* whether the packaging is also the container for the goods.

Packaging design covers a wide spectrum, from a brown box that is simply used to protect the goods in transit, to a luxurious piece of structural and visual magic that coveys a strong brand personality. There are two basic types of packaging: protective packaging, which is a temporary cover protecting a product like a television set and is discarded once the product is home; and there is integral packaging for FMCG, which is a product container and is used until the product is finished.

Protect – implicit quality
Protective packaging is largely used for consumer durables such as televisions, toasters and telephones. Where the product is displayed on a store shelf, the packaging is usually a simple box for transport. The opportunity for branding lies in reinforcing the corporate identity and confirming the contents and variant of the product inside.

Current trends towards retail warehouse outlets and the reduction of sales staff mean that often the product is displayed in the box on the floor or shelf. This type of packaging is therefore required to sell the product as effectively as the sales staff might. It becomes an opportunity for a branded solution. A good box of this type should convey the brand name, the ambience of the brand personality or benefit and additional feature information. It should therefore attract the attention of the shopper, explain the benefit and added value and describe specific characteristics that are superior to the competition. In short, it should answer all the questions the shopper might have asked the sales staff if they had been present. This type of packaging is often produced with two or four colour-printed graphics, maybe a see-through panel or a completely transparent blister pack to show off the product. The choice of these elements should carefully reflect the brand personality. It is no good having an environmentally conscious brand personality and displaying your product in a heavily printed plastic box. Much better would be emphasizing the recycled nature of the box materials and using a minimal, basic graphic treatment. Similarly, if your brand were a luxury item, then the use of noble materials such as metal and glass would be appropriate. The iMac computer is packaged with a styrofoam protector, which is designed also to be a small table to put the cables and connectors on while the computer is assembled at home.

Integral packaging and FMCG packaging

Most FMCG packaging must not only protect the contents, it must advertise and sell the product and be used as the dispenser throughout the product's life. Will Maskell of PI3 Ltd separates the task of an FMCG pack into two segments: the in-store purchase process, which is mainly graphic; and the in-home use experience, which is mainly, structural. Pack shape, size and colour are also important to differentiate your brand proposition in store. These are not completely separate, as shown in Figure 4.5, but they do allow us to focus on different needs at different times of the process.

Identify – in-store brand navigators

The role of brand packaging in a retail store is to attract the customer's attention, identify the product brand and sell itself in an instant. The brand should guarantee the quality of the purchased product, whether it is a category leader or a 'B brand'. A key task of FMCG packaging is to get the customer to try the brand for the first time and/or switch from their regular brand. This means that the pack must communicate the added value of that brand in the best

Focus of activity

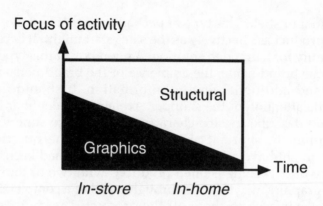

Figure 4.5 Packaging design emphasis over time (Source: Maskell, 1999)

possible way. Southgate's (1995) 'Total brand pack', where every element has been refined to express part of the brand personality, provides the best model of effective brand packaging design (see Figure 4.6). This is especially important in a competitive retail site where many brands compete for attention with very little difference in product quality and price. The use of POS or POP materials helps consumers to navigate stores and increases awareness of the brand at a place close to the product. They form a strong type of signage to increase the effectiveness of the brand pack. The key elements that contribute to a total brand pack are analysed separately below.

Shape, size and proportion
A pack with a distinctive shape that characterizes the brand personality is powerful because it identifies the brand and differentiates it clearly from the competition. This should help the brand to stand out on the shelf amongst competitors' offerings. The Jif lemon bottle in the shape of a lemon communicates the fresh lemon brand proposition, and clearly differentiates it from competitors. The classic Coca-Cola bottle, the Heinz ketchup bottle, the Orangina juice bottle, the Toblerone chocolate box, and many perfume bottles are all sufficiently distinctive that if you remove the brand label, the brand is still recognizable. It also makes the design of the shape patentable and therefore more difficult to copy. Depending on your product you may wish to follow the sector model for pack shape or, if you have an innovative product, develop an innovative pack to express this.

The size and proportion of a pack can help increase visibility on the shelf. When Pantene shampoo redesigned its shape, it moved

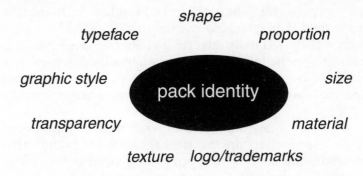

Figure 4.6 Packing elements that make a total brand execution

away from the waisted designs of the competition. Will Maskell of PI3 Ltd explains:

Pantene had been in the market several years now, but they really struck it when we helped create this wall effect in the supermarket. They used that to their advantage by making it appear bigger, you can find it straight away, and it has a very egalitarian feel: your Gran could use it or your sister could use it.

The innovation here was to create a pack that looked tall and square in front view, so that when stacked next to each other the packs completely filled the space from the top to the bottom of the shelf. This presents a large graphic area in a clear way to the consumer, and makes a strong visual statement from a distance. Since then many competitors have taken up this idea, but Pantene is still a strong leader.

Pringles were launched with a highly distinctive packaging concept for crisps. The product was unique: stackable, identical crisps instead of the usual jumble of shapes and sizes delivered loose in a bag. Pringles come in a cardboard tube, with a plastic top and foil seal, that was significantly more expensive than cellophane bags. This both protects the contents and creates a distinctive stand-out on the shelf, conveying the appropriate premium ambience intended. This was a good case of creative thinking in all departments: they managed to avoid the usual category icons and developed a truly unique value proposition.

Material and texture
The material and texture a pack is made from can also build up the brand personality. Premium brands often use noble materials to

express their superiority, while cut-price brands tend to use the cheapest materials available. Heinz ketchup still comes in a glass bottle, which is also used in its advertising. This achieves a unique brand personality in the mind of the consumer, although they may buy the plastic squeezable version, as it is easier to use. It is important for Heinz to retain its leadership position with a brand icon like the glass bottle.

The use of recycled materials is becoming increasingly important to consumers, particularly in the packaging field. Brands that support an environmentally aware proposition need to make sure their packaging is truly 'green' as these consumers are some of the most sophisticated in terms of product knowledge. It would be inappropriate for The Body Shop to use elaborate metallic finishes and printing techniques; its choice of simple shapes and plain materials is appropriate. The *grüne Punkt* or green dot mark in Germany ensures the credibility of the packaging as eco-friendly. The government establishes the recyclability of the packaging and this determines the levy that manufacturers must pay towards the cost of waste collection and recycling.

Colour and transparency
Often a category has a colour that dominates, which is usually derived from the category leader. The use of yellow and white in the margarine category is derived from the Flora brand, and the use of orange in the cream cracker category is derived from the Jacobs brand. Michael Abrahams confirms the importance of colour: 'Colour is the biggest thing that people recognize; it's often the start of an emotional connection with a brand.' Innovative new products should express this through choice of colour, but they may still have to conform to certain retailing rules, such as red for beef, yellow for chicken and green for vegetables. An alternative strategy is to purposely break the rules of the category to ensure the brand stands out from the competition. The Vitalite brand of spread uses a base colour of yellow for its pack rather than the category colour of white, which increases its visibility on the shelf.

Transparency on a pack helps to display the contents, which can be useful if freshness is a primary brand value. Crown paints use a transparent plastic case that differentiates it from the competition and allows the customer to see the real colour of the paint and compare, adding a further benefit.

Graphics
These need to be applied to the pack so that they promote the brand proposition and added benefits; they need to sell the product off the shelf, even to first-time buyers. Considering a large number of packs of different ingredients and brands are identical, the graphics have to work hard to convey the brand personality. First, the front face of the pack should be decided on; this depends on how it will be stacked on the shelf. The type of product and brand personality will help to determine the balance on the pack of brand name, product and other graphics such as logo or benefit images. Often, the larger the graphics panel, the cheaper the perception of the brand, while using a smaller print panel for the brand name conveys exclusivity. The type of product will also dictate the type of graphics: soap powder and margarine do not look good, so transparency would reduce the brand perception.

The packaging graphics should be used to build the brand proposition in the store, aiming to attract and convince first-time buyers. This needs to include the use of any corporate trade marks and logos, any sub-brands like the Healthy Cuisine range from Bird's Eye. The range colour, setting and typeface will need to be used to maximize the gestalt appeal of the range. Budweiser has a strong visual palette of red, blue and white that creates a distinctive identity on the shelf. A variant of this is also used for Bud-lite, transferring some of the equity across the range.

Dispense – in-home branded use experience
If the role of packaging in the store is to attract and identify the brand to potential customers, so that they try the brand, the role of the brand pack, post-purchase, is to generate loyalty, so that trial customers become dedicated customers. Ideally they should be so pleased with the brand pack that they use your brand as a navigation site around the store. Loyalty is a strong emotional connection that people feel when they have a satisfying experience and wish to repeat it. This is crucial in FMCG branding, since it is not possible or desirable to recruit a totally new customer set every week. The brand, product and pack must all live up to the customer expectations expressed by the brand personality. In the FMCG world, big money is to be made with loyal customers who continue buying your product hundreds of times in their life.

In packaging design this means adding value to the experience of using the product. Many of the packaging characteristics described above are equally valid in the home, although now consumers know what they have bought. The act of using one of these products happens often over time: it could be using a toothpaste tube twice a day, a coffee jar four or five times a day, or a washing powder once a week. That means they are going to experience the brand personality that many times, so it had better be good.

As Will Maskell of PI3 Ltd suggests, 'The best way to build added value in the brand pack is to start by designing the brand experience, then design the pack experience to match this.' This thinking could be applied to a coffee pack, where the desired brand experience in the coffee ritual may be freshness and aroma every time. To translate that into a physical pack may mean understanding where the coffee will be stored and used, and how frequently. It may require the redesign of a foil sealing mechanism, possibly making it re-sealable, choosing a glass jar shape that retains fragrances, and ensuring that the customer knows how to make coffee in the best way (communication advice). It is always best to start with the desired brand experience and translate that, rather than trying to find instant solutions, or use off-the-shelf solutions that may not be appropriate.

The structural design features of a pack are really important in satisfying the consumer through a branded experience. This may be a tamper-proof bottle cap on a bleach bottle, or an aroma dosage control on an air-freshener, or a grip detail on the side of a soft drinks bottle. They all build up the pleasurable branded experience in the mind of the consumer. If the brand personality is clinical, then the styling details should reflect this with precision markings and accurate pouring. In toilet detergents, Harpic was the clear leader for many years until Reckitt's created a new product and pack: 'What Toilet Duck did was it didn't actually solve the problem, it created a problem and solved it overnight. Which was these colonies of germs, living under your rim all the time. It was drawn to people's attention' (Maskell, 1999).

Packaging graphics need to also take into account the kind of category the pack is for, and the competitors they will stand next to on the shelf. The brand pack may be focused towards the buyer or the consumer of the goods, which might not be the same person. For example, the brand pack of an orange drink may target the mother who buys the drink by emphasizing the healthy vitamins inside, or it may attract the children with cartoon graphics and playful colours. In reality it may need to satisfy both these, but it is better to have a dominant theme and a sub-theme rather than try to sell these benefits equally. Gift items are often packaged for the consumer rather than the purchaser. Chocolates in a luxury display box are directed towards the brand experience of the user as they open and enjoy it, rather than the purchaser in the store who imagines the satisfaction of the user rather than themselves.

Disposal – re-use or recycle and the environment

In today's business environment it is not possible to ignore the environmental lobby; in fact many companies have been successful in harnessing green marketing. This is especially true in the packaging industry, where packs can often seem wasteful and unnecessarily bad for the environment. Companies have also to consider their own corporate responsibility towards the planet as well as their shareholders. There are two clear routes towards a more responsible packaging future. First, packs can be seen as an element of a system that can be re-used by refilling such as those available at The Body Shop, or they can be re-used in a new way, such as a Lavazza or Folgers coffee tin being re-used as a pencil jar, or a McVities biscuit tin re-used to store needles and cotton. The second route to responsible packaging is to make the pack as efficient and recyclable as possible. Given the complexity of green issues, this needs to be assessed case by case with a proper environmental audit. Examples are using recycled materials for production and encouraging recycling after use.

Legislation and customer and supply-chain pressure in several European countries are beginning to enforce green politics, particularly in Germany, the Netherlands and Scandinavia. Some brand categories are now required to accept responsibility for the return of packaging material from either the customer or the retail store. In high-volume goods this means large quantities of packaging material need to be re-transported back to the factory of origin. There are many opportunities for green branding as part of a holistic ethical brand policy and packaging is no exception.

Working with agencies

Many branding activities are often carried out by external agencies, but are controlled by an in-house manager. This may be a product manager, working with an external design consultancy, or a marketing communications manager working with a corporate identity specialist, or a marketing manager working with an advertising agency. This requires a different method and structure of communication than a purely internal approach. The external agency may be on a long-term retainer and therefore already know a lot about your business, or they may be brought in to provide a completely fresh outlook and therefore know relatively little. Either may be successful, but there will be a time when you need to choose an agency, brief that agency, work with them and judge the results. The reasons for using an external agency should always be clear to both sides from the beginning. It may be that extra capacity is needed to supplement internal resources for a short period, or to cover skills that are not worth developing internally. These approaches support the direction of the internal team. The alternative is to use external agencies to provide an objective viewpoint, bringing something fresh and different to the project. All of these things need to be carefully managed if the transfer of brand values is to be positive. There are positive and negative factors in working with an external agency.

Potential advantages:

* have external objective viewpoint;
* have broader sector knowledge from working with other clients in same sector;
* have no sector knowledge but bring valuable knowledge from a different sector, eg a service sector consultant working for an FMCG client on delivery systems;
* have greater specialist knowledge;
* free from internal politics;
* used on a project basis rather than structural cost;
* more creative at ideas generation.

Potential disadvantages:

* longer and more complex communication structure;
* may take time to understand the problem fully;
* work may be driven too much by creative ambition;
* may cause conflicts with internal staff members;
* require more time to monitor and advise;
* working with several agencies (design, advertising and public relations) may result in different brand personalities;
* potentially more expensive in the short term, but better value in the long term.

Choosing an agency

Depending on the core job that the agency needs to fulfil, there will be a group of companies that fit the task. The challenge is to find a match that generates enough passion and creative tension for success, without becoming aggressive. An agency that is too close to your comfort zone is likely to produce average work; an agency that is too extreme is likely to deliver something that is beyond your capabilities. That is not to say that agencies should not stretch your mind, but they should always remember they will be judged by the client and not at peer group award ceremonies.

The first issue is to decide whether you need a strategic consultancy or a tactical consultancy.

Strategic consultancy

* Operate as management consultants to the board of directors.
* Their people are highly trained as business/marketing consultants.
* They work on strategic business solutions.
* They are media neutral, not biased by any specific channel.

Tactical consultancy

* Operate as brand and design consultants to marketing managers.
* Their people are trained as visual consultants.
* They work on implementation of marketing campaigns.
* They often have a specific channel background such as advertising, print or face-to-face marketing.

Some agencies claim to offer both strategic and tactical advice, but it is a rare business that can be truly expert in both of these areas. It is usually better to separate the two tasks. First, research, analyse and generate the correct strategy. Part of this strategy should identify the preferred media choice and therefore help define the choice of tactical consultancy.

There are many ways to choose an agency, from informal conversations in a restaurant, to a formal competitive pitch. The best way is to look at the people in the internal team, and let them choose those that they are most comfortable with. Michael Abrahams believes in an intuitive meeting of minds between client and agency: 'You develop a rapport, you become part of the team, it's not a client–designer relationship any more.'

Others will want to have a more structured approach involving an audit of the agency's skills and experience. Often they will be given a formal briefing and then a paid pitch is worked out by a short-list of agencies. The resulting initial ideas give a very good flavour of how it will be to work with the agency; it also tests their understanding of your problem and their creativity in solving it.

As stated earlier in this chapter, there are some agencies that work above the line and some below the line, while others work through the line. The choice is often as much about whether one agency can handle all the client needs, one-stop shopping, or whether it's preferable to use a specialist in each field (advertising, design, DM, PR). I would advocate choosing specialists who are focused and dedicated to being the best in their specific field. The challenge for the brand manager is to get them to act coherently to build something greater than the individual input.

In some cases, large clients will prefer to work with one agency because they have a global network and can service all their regional needs. This is an argument, but only if the quality of that service is optimal for each region. It is no use having a coordinated service that is only strong in one of the selling regions. The other argument for using an integrated service is the chance to buy in bulk and reduce overall costs. I think there is a better advantage in paying for the highest quality and keeping agencies hungry for the work. If there is a need to use an external consultant, and their added value is quantifiable, don't waste your time on a cut-price one.

Summary

* Two-way communication processes need to be developed for successful brand management.
* Semiotic analysis can provide a rich resource for symbolic brand imagery.
* Consumers understand the meaning of brands on the basis of their perception of the collective imagery and text.
* Advertising increases awareness and encourages interest and potential sales in the brand.
* Above the line media – the press, radio, television, cinema and outdoor/transport media – are suitable for mass market brand campaigns.
* Below the line media – point of sale, public relations, direct marketing – are more suitable for one-to-one marketing.
* Packaging can be a strong, tangible expression of the brand.
* External agencies usually provide specialist knowledge and skills not found in-house.

CHAPTER FIVE

NEW MEDIA BRANDSITES

Strategies for the digital economy

This chapter looks at the increasing importance of digital media and its uses in brand management to form brandsites. These are a new method of building a more personal and interactive relationship with consumers. The use of digital technology and integrated computing power has realized a powerful new form of marketing that is rapidly becoming a cornerstone of any contemporary business scenario. There are several unique characteristics of both the Internet and digital interactive television that can improve brand communication. However, the central theme of this chapter is that brand managers cannot rely on traditional techniques: they must think of entirely new ways to maximize the effectiveness of these new media. This immaturity of new media brandsites can be felt in the profession and among the consumers who are eager to engage with the future. There are no set rules for these media: concepts for traditional, analogue media should not restrict your thinking – the media demand to be developed into a new era of total brand experiences. This chapter also briefly introduces a variety of media formats, such as intranets and extranets, to show how they can best be used for brand activities.

New media formats: Web site digital television or Web site?

Brand managers must now develop branding for two emerging brand media; both will become a significant part of the marketing

Objectives

* Analyse the new media formats of the Internet and digital television.
* Show the strategic development of new media brandsites.
* Illustrate the tactics for new media.
* Clarify the issues facing e-commerce.
* Explain the characteristics of intra- and extranets.

mix. It is important to understand the differences between the two and how to get the best from both. The industry is presenting them as a repeat of the VHS versus Betamax formats battle of the early 1980s. However, a deeper understanding of the issues suggests that there are similarities between Web media and digital TV. There will be room for both formats in the three- to five-year future period, depending on specific target groups and their needs. We will analyse the two and express the similarities and differences, so that individual branding propositions can be adjusted accordingly.

There are four key components (see Figure 5.1) to delivering new media brandsite solutions to the consumer:

1. content: the type of information or entertainment developed by a brand;
2. visual style: the graphic quality of the presentation of that information or entertainment;
3. interaction: this includes the quality of navigation around the new media;
4. technology: the types of formats and systems required to deliver the content to the consumer.

Commentators such as Gary Lockton at North Creative Consultancy regard the first two of these as offering similar value to a consumer via a Web site or through digital television formats. The quality of content and visual style rely more on the choice of agency developing them than anything inherent to either system. There are many small Web site developers who bring energy and creativity to the marketing mix. Television production companies are well established, but they are more expensive and may treat new media in more traditional formats.

Content needs to be complementary to the holistic brand philosophy of a company, bringing to light another facet to the brand

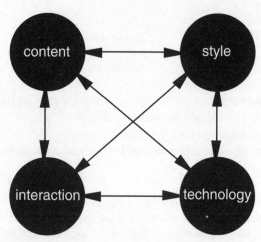

Figure 5.1 Four core components of new media brandsites

proposition rather than being online because we have to be. It also does not mean simply re-presenting traditional brand media in an online format. The biggest issue with both types of new media is the lack of understanding of the opportunities for branding in a new way, to develop new methods of targeting and satisfying consumers. This paucity of knowledge is in both the business community and the consumer domain; like any new media, it will take time to find the best ways to communicate among them. This accounts for part of the mystery and magic surrounding online brandsites, where curiosity and engagement are higher than with the TV ad-fatigued public.

Interactive opportunities should be similar in both new media, but as the underlying technologies are starting at different parts of the development curve this could influence the total result. Consumers may have a different expectation from Web media and digital TV that will have to be overcome. Television has traditionally been a passive form of infotainment: people simply allowed programmes to wash over them for a few hours each day. The amount of interactivity was limited to the choice of five channels (in the United Kingdom) and zapping between commercial breaks, both achieved with a simple control device. The Internet, however, is an active medium, where people have chosen to search with something in mind, with relatively complex control devices such as a keyboard and mouse.

The real differences between Web and digital TV are exposed in their formats and delivery systems. These vary enormously from country to country, so careful analysis of a specific branding activity is required. For example, there is a 94 per cent ownership of television sets in the United Kingdom, similar to most western countries, while approximately 42 per cent of people in the United Kingdom use the Net, compared with 58.5 per cent in the United States (Nielsen net ratings, January 2002). Similarly, the United States has well-developed cable and satellite networks that offer hundreds of channels, while the United Kingdom has an embryonic battle between another series of competing digital formats.

The hardware for the competing systems comes from different historical precedents. Televisions are usually renewed once every 10 years on average, while computer users expect to upgrade hardware and software every one or two years, allowing for rapid improvements to be implemented and enjoyed by the consumer.

The speed of delivery of the two types of media will play a crucial role in their take-up. Accessing high-quality multimedia with strong interactive capability may not be possible in certain geographic locations or at particular times of the day.

The socio-economic and lifestage analysis of consumers will also play an important role in the choice of media and its delivery format. Sports programmes are currently one of the key reasons for choosing a satellite or cable network, and they have a higher than average take-up by working-class groups. Investment in a home computer or access to one at work is similarly biased to those higher up the socio-economic scale. Obviously, younger people are also likely to be more computer literate than those in older generations, but detailed research should be undertaken for confirmation. For example, certain segments of the 'grey power' generation are some of the greatest Net users, highlighting the combination of surplus time and finance.

The software contents of the two media also start from different bases. Digital TV will be compared by the consumer with expensive TV advertisements and quality films and sitcom productions. However, the broadening number of channels has also seen a reduction in quality of a large proportion of the content on US cable networks (see Figure 5.2). Web media have grown out of a text-based system, so additional sound and graphics were seen as an advantage, and many new multimedia sites are often high quality.

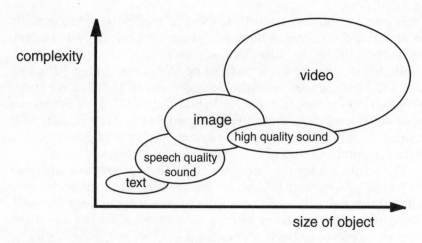

Figure 5.2 Media types and files sizes

The Internet

The Internet was first set up as an electronic link for the American military; it was intended to provide a command chain between centres, even if one of them was destroyed. This shift to the centreless network changed how we understand information exchange and communication. Information is no longer stored in a giant central storage device, but is scattered all over the world, and can be equally accessed from all around the globe. It has become a truly 24-hour global linking system that is relatively cheap and needs little expert training.

The first words sent over the Internet were 'Are you receiving this?' and they highlight the essential differences of Internet communication as compared with traditional television: those of personal messages and interactivity. It is these and other characteristics that have made the Internet a viable place to develop brand relationships with customers. The World Wide Web (WWW) has harnessed these opportunities in a format that is accessible and can be extremely effective.

Internet-generated revenue is expanding at a logarithmic rate. ActivMedia research, 2002, suggests that in 1998 only $73.9 billion worth of global revenue was generated. Four years later in 2002, this figure has risen to $1,233 billion (Figure 5.3) and it continues to grow rapidly. This level of growth means a great opportunity for brand activities to reach directly into the heart and head of customers in their own home.

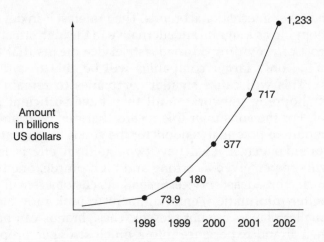

Figure 5.3 Internet-generated revenue (Source: ActivMedia, 2002)

The Web has become the new battleground for the computer- savvy generation. It has an ability to handle search processes, strong visuals, sound and a non-linear approach to information retrieval. A Web site is an address that locates a small parcel of information that relates to a company, institution or an individual. This unique address often has the same name as the brand name of the company, eg halifax.co.uk (Halifax, formerly a building society, now a bank), bmw.co.uk (BMW motor cars), economist.co.uk (*The Economist* magazine). This issue is important for brand names and will be expanded on later in this chapter.

Digital television

Interactive digital television (IDTV), digital television, computer-aided television (CATV), pay-per-view TV or home shopping channels – these cover all the variations that service providers will be offering in the near future. They highlight the shift to link television broadcasting technologies with computer-based intelligent and interactive communications.

In the United Kingdom, digital television has been launched relatively recently, and will gradually build up to offer a full range of services. It is broadcast through either satellite or cable networks and is a mass communication medium. The broadcasters will not only be BBC, ITV, Sky, etc, but also the Manchester United channel (MUTV) and companies such as Guinness, Cadbury's, Thomas

Cook and other international brands. Their interest is in developing home shopping as a significant alternative to the high street.

The cost of providing a broadcast service means that like TV advertising, only larger companies will be able to afford this medium. This will cause smaller companies to remain on the Internet shopping networks until they have sufficient growth potential. For the consumer this means that they will only see a small amount of potential vendors for the goods they want to buy. For the brand manager, it will have two significant effects. First, the brand will be perceived as strong and high profile, one that can afford such a broadcast service. Second, its customers will enjoy a much better information/entertainment to junk ratio since the many smaller players are not present. These brands can probably build their brand experience into a much stronger proposition without worrying about competing smaller sites, resulting in more satisfied and loyal customers.

New media brand strategies

In the United Kingdom, IDTV started later than the Internet, but there is no reason to separate the equal potential of both new media types in their ability to provide high-quality brandsites. For the rest of this chapter I shall refer simply to brandsites, meaning either a Web site or a digital television site of a company's brand communication.

Brandsites can offer a series of marketing channels that are ripe for brand activities:

* corporate, product or service identity and information;
* public relations management;
* defining and dominating a new channel of distribution;
* customer service;
* direct sales;
* customer and market research;
* complaints and helpline services.

Angehrn *et al* (1998) have characterized new media brand strategies into four distinct segments. They rely on a matrix developed from analysing the cross-relationships between the degree of sophistication of a brandsite and the degree of available customization of brand activities. Sophistication refers to corporate brandsites that show a high level of exploitation of the new media and their unique characteristics. The level of customization refers to the ability of brandsites to offer individualized services to individual consumers. We will look at the implications of each in turn.

The brochure segment is the most likely starting point for most brandsites, as they reflect a low-cost, low-commitment strategy. This will also offer the lowest return, as it works as an untargeted and unidirectional communication channel. There is little evidence that the rewards from this type of brochure site are any higher than for other types of marketing effort. They offer the consumer a simple repetition of information that they could get from other sources. They are clearly under-using the potential of the new media, and competitors who progress to more sophisticated sites will easily gain loyalty from customers.

The more sophisticated next step is a brandsite that offers a high-tech version of your brand. This would harness the power of the hardware and software to create presentations that are entertaining and offer learning and knowledge attainment opportunities. Multimedia brandsites quickly outstrip their rival brochure sites for preference by consumers. They also have the capacity to collect simple visitor data that can form a low-cost response loop for brand activities. Multimedia sites maximize the brandsite as a new support technology as part of the total marketing effort.

New media offer an outstanding opportunity for customization that has been under-used by brand managers. There must be a shift from broadcasting commercials towards leveraging the media to build two-way communications with consumers. This type of high-touch activity opens up possibilities for consumer loyalty that the first two types of brandsite cannot. The personalizing of a brandsite requires learning consumer preferences and adapting the information provided to fit those. These often rely on the consumer filling in a basic profile sheet concerning their habits, preferences and interests. Consumers who may feel they are intrusive can resent them, or see them as insincere when they carry messages such as 'Good morning, Mr Ellwood, would you like to read three new articles on Vietnamese cooking?'

Brandsites that progress beyond these simplistic approaches require high-tech high-touch brand experience. They use advanced technologies to generate 3D virtual spaces and are accompanied by sophisticated data agents that observe, learn and manage the flow of information you receive. The virtual store offers the perceptual cues that we have learnt to use while shopping in the real world. A sales avatar, a human-looking shopping assistant that is either human or computer controlled, may greet you. The agents also follow your journey through cyberspace, noting how often you return to a particular site or how long you spend there; they gain their knowledge through observation rather than intrusive questioning. The advantages of the natural movement, intuitive understanding and the sociability of such brandsites mean that they can generate clear customization and strong emotional attachment for the consumer.

The evolution of the new media brandsite

The banking sector has provided much evidence for the evolution of the strategic use of brandsites within a total marketing effort (Angehrn et al, 1998). The use of first generation brandsites such as brochure sites is widespread, and reflects the immaturity of the technology and its attendant uses. Sophisticated brands have now evolved these into second-generation sites that offer entertainment and information opportunities through high technology, while providing database knowledge for the company. A few sites have moved into the third-generation intelligent and fully interactive brandsites. The opportunities for building loyalty and leveraging brand positions increase strongly with the evolution of your brandsite along these paths (see Figure 5.4).

Using a brandsite will give your company the added brand quality of a leading edge company, although not for long. If you are the first in your sector this is something to shout about, but having an interesting, engaging and useful site that keeps customers coming back is worth more than being first. Creating a brand image of a leading edge company adds to the impression of a company that cares about its customers. It is a brand that cares enough to master an innovative technology in a way that increases customer satisfaction. For smaller companies, having a brandsite can also add to the perception of a company that is financially strong, stable and planning for the future. Not having a brandsite is now unacceptable for most companies: it shows a lack of interest in innovation or improvement in service-oriented communication. Financially it could also result in a great loss of custom to competitors who are willing to move forward with the times.

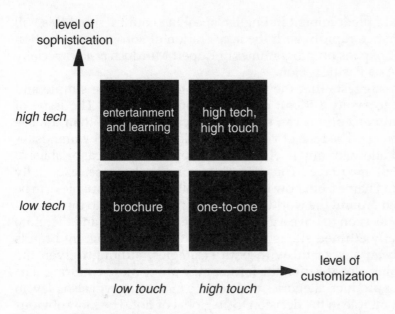

Figure 5.4 New media development strategies (Source: Angehrn *et al*, 1998)

Global branding issues

The global nature of the brandsites crystallizes some of the global versus local branding issues a company faces. Different companies have addressed these in different ways. A brandsite lowers the barrier of entry to the world of global brand communications. Previously, only companies of significant size could dream of connecting with customers on a global, round-the-clock basis. The Internet and IDTV have changed all this: for only a few thousand pounds a company can buy a computer and set up an online brandsite that is as accessible as those from corporate giants. There are two fundamental issues connected with this move towards global communications: the use of language and its cultural perceptions, and the use of global or regional brandsites for the same brand and the associated global pricing policies.

The Internet is currently dominated by American/English language sites. This is, however, changing and the fastest-growing Internet markets are in China and India, where language-specific sites are needed. By the end of 1998, there were more people outside the United States using the Internet than internally (*Internet Magazine*, November 1998), which suggests that a careful analysis of your target audience should be considered. Digital television is currently predominant in English-speaking countries, but this will also change rapidly with the acceleration of software production and the expansion programmes of Rupert Murdoch *et al*, especially in the Asia Pacific region.

This suggests that the form of any text should be simple and direct, to avoid difficult communication problems. The issue of cultural perceptions can be more difficult to control than the use of language. The tone of voice or honorific form used by brandsites should allow for any likely religious, spiritual, political or abusive forms of language. This has always been the case, especially for brand names, but now that even smaller brand companies can be accessed around the world they need to pay attention to this issue.

The decision to have a global site or region-specific and therefore culturally attuned site is more difficult to take. Different brands have been successful with both strategies, although given the increasing globalization the former may prove more enduring. The types of product categories that you are marketing will also play an important role in the decision to go global or not. The most obvious negative side of a global selling brandsite is that prices will have to be harmonized. Current large inequalities in prices between American and European countries, including the United Kingdom, for a large range of goods mean that this decision should be carefully considered. It is not just the loss of cash that is important, but the perception of your brand could be shifted from highly sophisticated to comparatively middle class or a low-end bargain brand. A review of competitors' pricing and global policies should help avoid drastic changes in brand perception.

Brandsite tactics for new media

One of the key tactics is to recognize that online media are different from traditional media. When segmenting your branding effort it is important not to try simply to reproduce the same experience in all forms of media. Bell Atlantic Corporation discovered that its real-world tactics were not working in the virtual world and has shifted the focus of its online brandsite. As Leonhardt (1998) describes it, 'A brand is the emotional shortcut between a company and its customer.' However, the best way to leverage that brand in the virtual world may not be to use the strong emotional message that would be appropriate for a TV campaign. There are several examples of companies that have deliberately chosen to use their emotional brand message in the real world, while using the rational brand message in the virtual world. This type of online behaviour has been termed *rational* branding and reflects the difference in use of TV and the Internet. Consumers usually watch television passively for entertainment, while Internet consumers have a more active search for practical or rational benefits.

Brands like MasterCard can benefit strongly from separating these two approaches into the two media. Its TV campaigns can generate attention and interest in the product, while offering little factual data or detailed information. Its online brandsite can then be used to cover all the necessary background that consumers need to make their choice, but this crucially happens *after* they have been emotionally sold on the idea of MasterCard. This approach will work well for service brands, but is not so good for FMCGs such as soap or detergent, since these products are not really useful in the virtual world and there is a low interest in their physical differentiation. Most consumers choose shampoo on the basis of the emotional value of a particular brand, so here it may be better to concentrate on an emotional brandsite offering advice and clinics with top stylists.

Here are 20 ways that branding online can offer added value, with some examples you could view:

1. Develop brand loyalty, through downloadable gifts or discounts. (www.disney.com)
2. Offer your company's product or service by a new and unused method. FedEx customers can now print barcode labels and track packages online. (www.fedex.com)
3. Go global – even small companies can now reach large global audiences for a low cost.
4. Develop online hotlinks with partner organizations. Anyone interested in a travel books site should also be one click away from a travel agent such as www.lastminute.com.
5. Use offline media to promote your online brand activities, engaging new converts. easyJet recently offered a series of discounted tickets in an online sale; many respondents heard about it in offline media and became Internet converts. (www.easyjet.com)
6. Regenerate your brandsite regularly. Online media is progressing at a staggering rate: every couple of months, you need to revisit your brandsite to keep ahead of the competition.
7. Use sound to improve memorability. Sound can add to a brandsite's impact and link it to other media. Direct Line insurance could use its tag sound to open its brandsite. (www.directline.com)

8. One-to-one communication: find out your customers' preferences and keep them up to date via e-mail. (www.amazon.com)
9. E-commerce security perception: make sure your brandsite encourages a perception of security for e-commerce. Only 0.1 per cent of UK users trust net security, yet it is safer than many other forms of credit card payment.
10. Creative promotions: online media are new and can leverage your brand in new, unthought of and exciting ways. Don't stay with traditional methods. (www.hulahoops.co.uk)
11. Generate online advertising revenue by selling space on your site, or indirect promotions.
12. Lead the way. Particularly within your category, it is important to be seen to be innovative. (askjeeves.com)
13. Search engines can develop personalizable search engines that can deliver what customers want, avoiding spam and endless net fatigue.
14. Make it entertaining. Use the knowledge developed for TV game stations and other media to entertain customers while at your site.
15. Brandsites are only part of a total marketing package. Do not rely solely on new media to develop your brand.
16. Use the 3D, time-based opportunities of multimedia. No other medium can compete for the total experience of a brandsite.
17. Make it fast. Consumers don't like to wait long for downloading pages. Keep them occupied while they wait or they will go away and never return. (www.yahoo.com)
18. People-to-people communications. Use your brandsite to show that you are a company of people and not robots. Include photographs of personnel of the month, or of the factory floor.
19. Use online virtual tours that help explain your product or service. Customers can 'try before they buy', giving them greater satisfaction. This has been especially successful for selling houses, as buyers can 'walk though' the property without ever travelling to it. It has been equally successful with theme parks and attractions. (www.edenproject.com)
20. Don't sell on your site unless it is appropriate to your brand image. Paul Smith, the fashion designer (www.paulsmith.co.uk), believes it is inappropriate for his customers, who actively seek out personal service, but it is appropriate for Amazon.com.

Proactivity

Proactivity is one of the key differences between new media and traditional television. Watching TV has generally been accepted as a passive experience, requiring little or no attention or acknowledgement of the content. For branding this meant that even seductive and carefully planned messages were likely to be poorly consumed, since the receivers were in a passive state of mind. Proactivity on new media brandsites falls into two categories: the company must proactively address the customer and the customer must proactively find the company site.

The company must make it easy for the consumer to find the brandsite by using a domain name that is identical to the brand name or as close as possible. Consumers will find it difficult to find a site if the site name is vastly different from the brand name, even with a search engine. So www.cocacola.com will be easily guessed by most of its consumers; however, www.flybmi.com is unlikely ever to be found without heavy searching. The current suffix .com may be further expanded to generate a range of domain-specific suffixes such as .shop for interactive shopping. The brandsite address is the start of the new media branding experience – those brands that are difficult to find are already condemned in the users' mind as brands that are unhelpful or not user-friendly.

Navigation

There are three basic questions to helping the customer find your brandsite:

* Where is the site?
* Where is the information I'm looking for within your site?
* Which is the right product for me?

Company proactivity is crucial to finding your brandsite among the millions of competing sites. Because they are all virtual or hidden, the navigation to find your site and navigating around your site become more crucial. Search engines such as Yahoo! or AltaVista help with the first problem by narrowing down similar sites. Digital television uses Electronic Program Guides (EPGs) to offer a similar search function that can also be customized for preferences. It is important to define brand keywords that are likely to be understood from a user perspective, rather than a corporate one. Try to think how customers would like to think about and find you, which is in itself an exhibition of customers' attitudes towards your brand. In a virtual world that has millions of possible addresses or sites, it is important that you help customers to navigate through this with the strength of your brand name. They will understand that brand names are the quickest method to navigate the jungle of the Internet.

Once customers have found your site the structure and method of navigating all speak strongly about your brand. It has been a common mistake of marketeers simply to transfer pages of their corporate brochure into brandsite format. This is as ineffective as applying the same corporate brochure to television advertising: you wouldn't do it there so don't do it with new media. Some sites have an entertainment approach to navigation that is in keeping with their quirky brand, such as the fashion brand www.paul-smith.co.uk. Sophisticated sites still require sophisticated software and hardware to run properly; downloading freeware such as Shockwave will enable your advanced site to be viewed as a 3D-multimedia experience.

Setting up hotlinks between your site and others can provide easy access and suggests that your brand is both substantive and acknowledged by trade authorities, such as the design agencies whose sites are hotlinked to the Design Council Web site. They can also hotlink several company or brandsites in different virtual locations, or connect with relevant events. For example, connecting a management consultancy Web site with the *Financial Times* newspaper site suggests that you understand who your customers are and how they think. Again it is the added value of your brand-site that improves the customers' brand perception.

Interactivity

Interactivity offers the opportunity for the company to move beyond the brand message to delivering brand experiences by developing a truly one-to-one relationship with the consumer over time. The brandsite can be used to develop a real sense of space in its virtual site, which can then be explored and enjoyed by the consumer. Without this, the consumer will feel that the brandsite is simply a flat and uninspiring place to be, especially compared with other sites that offer higher levels of satisfaction. This can parallel the lack of brand experiences found at some retail sites, while others such as Nike Town or Ralph Lauren offer a total sensorial experience. Interaction is the key advantage of the new media brandsites over other forms of traditional media, and it can improve the customer's impression of brand value. This means that customers must feel that they are getting information rather than that it is being given to them; users are actively pulling instead of having data pushed on them. MIT research associate Michael Schrage (in Sterne, 1999) says, 'The real value is in the interaction... real interactivity isn't about giving people more content to choose from. It's about letting people create their own content. The new media challenge, then, is how do you create content that creates content.' The balance between effort and reward in finding information is an important brand attribute. If it's too easy, the customer will probably not value it as much as if they have had to search for it a little; however, if it's too difficult, the customer will decide the information is not worth the effort.

Personal communication

New media brandsites are personal in the sense that they are private and individual, but they also open access to socializing across the world. The balance between these two has to be well managed if a brand is to generate excitement, intrigue, curiosity, satisfaction and confidence. These can be understood as parallel to the kind of behaviour between a real life customer and service personnel in a restaurant. The brand relationship will need to be built up over time, and will also need to develop and improve over time. This means that the brandsite must be updated regularly, or offer new items on a regular basis. These may be new competitions, or the latest press releases, or virtual rooms containing new concepts or ideas. McVities developed its Jaffa Cakes brand with a range of virtual collectibles, the online equivalents to Tamagotchi pets, to help build long-term relationships with its target 10–15-year-olds. Customers can download the characters and play, teach, exercise and feed them. Crucially, an element of continued interest is developed through the regular introduction of new characters with new functions. The characters must also be fed with downloadable virtual Jaffa Cakes, which means regular trips back to the Web site to collect them. McVities also placed the Jaffa site in the children's section of AOL UK online, rather than as part of an enormous McVities corporate site. Again, thinking like a user, here a 10-year-old or younger, helped with the success of the site and encouraged a long-term brand relationship through an extended brand experience rather than simply an informational site. This approach highlights some added benefits of branding in new media that are difficult or impossible to achieve in any other medium.

Online socializing has developed with online communities such as dungeons, multi-user dungeons (MUDs), user groups and chat rooms (see Figure 5.5). Brands can use a chat room on their brand-site to support a theme of personal access and sociability, while also using them as a vital proving ground for ideas and personal opinions on the topics of the community. Kozinets (1998) has described how these can be understood by analysing their social structure and the group activity focus.

An MUD is a controlled virtual environment that allows social games and fantasy play to be experienced. These environments encourage the building of a set of collective values that the brand manager can use to target those consumers. These are often consumers at the forefront of online media and they regularly generate new forms of addressing, linguistics and symbolic communication. Brands that wish to target those consumers need to be aware of these, although they should be used in a non-patronizing way.

Rooms offer a looser social structure than MUDs, but still encourage large-scale social interaction. They are organized along theme lines so they are ideal for targeting user segments and special interest groups. These can range from religious denominations, gender, political affiliations, and educational subjects such as bio-genetics, graphic design, or important issues such as cot death syndrome. Because these consumers are pre-segmented, they are a rich source of information for brand managers and can be used to link or circle similar issue groups that all strengthen the connectivity and authority of your brand.

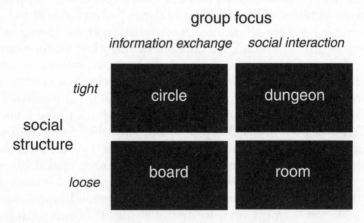

Figure 5.5 Online socializing development opportunities (Source: Kozinets, 1999)

Boards offer an interest-specific notice board that can be used and updated by its members. Their use of simple sorting techniques such as date of posting or related sub-topics means that they respond to the changing needs of the interest group. It is important for brand managers to follow boards that relate to their category, as they can suggest new trends that are on the verge of breaking into the mainstream. They can also become powerful allies progressing a viewpoint, although users are extremely sensitive to commercial pressures.

The importance of all of these differing groups is that they can influence perceptions of a brand through their online consensus. They also represent the fragmentation of consumer tastes into ever-smaller segments. It can be useful for the brand manager to survey these to understand the shifting attitudes of target groups as one boundary is broken down and another splinter group is created.

Interactive games as part of a brandsite are an excellent way to develop customer interaction. These can take the form of pure entertainment, competitions, or infotainment that combines enjoyment with reinforcement of brand values or product attributes. The new VW Beetle site (www.newbeetle.co.uk) offers a chance for customers to repaint the Beetle in their own choice of colours and graphics. This not only creates a brand perception of a listening company that is interested in the customer's viewpoint, but also gives VW access to possible new colour trends in the marketplace.

Product demonstrations should also encourage interactivity by developing a total sensorial experience with 3D graphics, sound and stunning computer-generated images. The beauty of multimedia is that it can often express ideas that are impossible to communicate easily in the real world. Companies can show live images from their factory, or offer a test drive of their latest car concept before it is even built. Comparative tests between older models and new concepts can also help express a brand's innovative dimension.

Feedback

Feedback from customers is a crucial advantage of new media brandsites over other forms of traditional brand media. Good brandsites should at least offer the opportunity for customers to get in touch either to complain or to comment. As with all consumer complaints, they should be treated as an opportunity to learn what might be wrong with your product offer and to satisfy a consumer. Research has shown that consumers who receive appropriate attention to their complaints are more likely to be even more loyal to that brand than if they had no complaint in the first place. Sites can also offer the opportunity for online market research, although this can provide many responses, and not necessarily from the people you are targeting. These online surveys will also require adequate analysis and responses that can be time-consuming. They do, however, signal that the brand is an active brand and willing and open to listening to customers, and you might gain some interesting perceptions of your brand.

The success of your brandsite can be measured in terms of how much two-way communication has evolved between yourself and your customers. These can be opinions, or entries to competitions, or direct sales, depending on the category and purpose of your site. If you are generating relatively little feedback, then you are underusing your brandsite, or treating it as just another type of one-way advertising medium. You need to reward your consumers for having found your new media brandsite, but you also need to keep them coming back repeatedly, so that you can build up a strong one-to-one relationship. The ultimate goal is to be bookmarked – only sites that offer sufficient current interest or reward will be on a customer's bookmark list. If you are not and another brand is, then the customer is unlikely to go through the trouble of re-searching for a second site on a particular product or service.

E-commerce

Many brandsites are also being used as a virtual retail site for goods and services. The opportunity to purchase over the Internet offers enormous convenience in certain product categories and target groups, whether the product is a commodity like milk or bread, or the consumers have little time or are old and infirm. Your brand can gain an excellent reputation by developing a convenient, low-cost alternative to shopping in the real world.

The most important issue concerning e-commerce is currently the security of transactions. As mentioned earlier, only 0.1 per cent of UK surfers buy over the Internet, largely because of concerns about credit card fraud. The situation in the United States is much better, where consumers are also more used to buying with credit cards over the phone. While the early transaction software was open to abuse by tech-wizards, standards have improved. The latest software, SET – Secure Electronic Transaction protocol (www.setco.org) – has been developed by Visa, MasterCard and others and is more secure than giving your credit card number to a stranger over the phone or in a shop in the real world. The SET uses an electronic wallet to contain your card details. When you buy something, your wallet communicates with the vendor's payment system for you. It encrypts your card details using the card issuer's public key and sends it to the vendor. The vendor then sends it on to the card issuer, who decrypts it using its private key. If you have enough credit, the card issuer generates a payment authorization using the vendor's public key and sends it on to the vendor, who then knows that the payment is guaranteed by the card issuer and confirms the sale to you. The beauty of the system is that at no point does the vendor know your card details, which means it cannot store them, unencrypted or otherwise, to be hacked into at a later date. It is a complex system that also requires digital certificates to be issued to banks and card issuers, and currently few vendors have SET capability. However, given the huge mistrust among UK consumers, any brandsite that is serious about generating sales should invest heavily in secure payment systems.

The perception of security of a brandsite can be an important factor in the consumer's mind. A site that clearly states how the user's personal information can and will be used in saleable databases will benefit from positive appreciation by consumers. The graphic layout of the payment site can also encourage the consumer to trust the brandsite, particularly the choice of words used and the tone of the messages provided. Consumers are well acquainted with virtual financial brands such as First Direct bank, but they need the physical evidence of security at the brandsite to ensure they progress beyond browsing to buying.

Intranet and extranet

The uses of intranets and extranets as types of brand activity have been under-researched. However, there is a growing body of knowledge that suggests that intranets could have a strong impact on internal brand communications. They are often used as a sales data transfer site between departments and for extranets, with suppliers or consumers. Because of this they have to standardize forms of identity and brand activities, often on a global scale. The access to this centralized, clarified internal brandsite has had three major effects. First, it has ensured that the story behind a brand and its essence has been clearly defined and expressed in the same way to all internal departments. This has led to increased clarity of purpose and message in and between these departments with the resulting benefit of a stronger and more committed brand. This increased commitment has also resulted in the second benefit: activities on the intranet/extranet have affected the corporate behaviour of employees by directing them towards a more harmonized brand attitude. The range of employees connected has also ensured that even back-office departments such as R&D and logistics have now become better informed and more on-brand in their daily activities.

The final major benefit was the one intended by the intranet builders: that there should be easy access of information across departments and locations. This has resulted in less duplicated work and swifter access to corporate knowledge. In the age of knowledge management, it is difficult to underestimate the value of an intranet/extranet for certain product or service categories. British Telecom has suggested that it saved £400 million in 1998 alone, through sales staff communicating through its intranet.

Summary

* The Internet and digital television are different but also have many similarities; both will be successful alongside each other.
* Four key components are needed for a new media brandsite: content, interaction, technology and style.
* New media brandsites can be strategically developed for low-tech, low-touch; through low-tech, high-touch; low-touch, high-tech; and high-tech, high-touch approaches.
* Tactics for new media brandsites are proactivity and navigation, interactivity, personal communication and feedback.
* E-commerce's current greatest issue is that of a lack of trust by the consumer.
* Intranets offer a company-wide access database and communication channel; extranets allow suppliers and third parties access to that knowledge.

BRAND DEFINITION

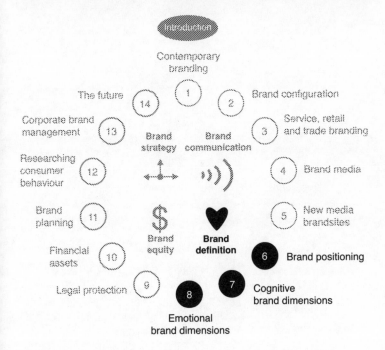

Figure 6.0 Brand definition

The second of the four parts of this book introduces the components of brand creation, from identifying the core values to the proposition and expression of a brand personality. It emphasizes the need for a deep understanding of the consumer mindset and the benefit of using both rational and emotional triggers in communication. It includes:

* brand creation and DNA;
* brand proposition;
* brand personality;
* corporate identity;
* logos and graphic style;
* strategic and tactical cognitive brand dimensions;
* hierarchy of needs;
* strategic and tactical emotional dimensions;
* brand pleasure.

CHAPTER SIX

BRAND POSITIONING

Creating a strong core DNA for a brand

This chapter demonstrates how to build a strong brand by developing rich content for the brand DNA, brand themes, brand names and brand identities. Drawing on the brand custodian blueprint it structures the process of the development and redevelopment of brand identities. The brand DNA as the essence of the brand is the crucial starting point to any successful brand and these elements are examined in detail. An illustration of the brand themes and narratives that characterize the brand DNA key words follows this. The expression of the brand will be clarified, ranging from the simple and immediate brand images to the complex and rich retail and narrative brand events.

The creation and definition of the brand name as the focus of the brand identity is illustrated in detail. The definition of the brand identity is explained and its expression across media types are described. This includes the description of brand logos and typefaces as an embodiment of the brand identity. The specific expression of the corporate identity is illustrated, comparing the differences between that and the brand identity.

Objectives

* Illustrate where the brand imagery can be developed from and how to choose the most successful.
* Demonstrate the definition of the brand DNA.
* Describe the development of the brand proposition and brand personality.

* Summarize the creation and development process for new brand names.
* Outline the process for the creation of logos, trade marks and corporate identities.

Aesthetic codes

Aesthetic codes are the images and symbolic meanings of a brand that are derived from all fields of consumer culture, including the examples below. They all provide a rich resource for building brand DNA, brand imagery and the symbolic meaning of the brand personality. Brand managers should decide which area(s) are the most beneficial for the brand proposition, then analyse and audit the most appropriate specific symbolic imagery to create a campaign. The list is a starting point of rich areas to mine for symbolic imagery; additional, relevant areas can also be examined, depending on the product, service or brand category:

Geography	Technology	Fashion
Science	Sports	Religion
Law	Societies	Monarchy
History	Art	Philosophy
Education	Popular culture	Finance
Cuisine	Animals	Rituals
Language	Identity	Humour

The symbolic aesthetic codes these represent are generally universally accepted by consumer groups, and specifically used by relevant interested target consumers to build and communicate their identity with themselves and others. Brands should similarly use these codes to communicate their value to these targeted consumer groups. By using their communication paths, brands can speak the same language as the consumer and encourage rapid consumer buy-in to the brand personality. The following examples show how specific aesthetic codes have been used to build a brand personality:

* The American Express card brand draws on the aesthetic codes of famous people and the concept of *membership* as the resource for its continuing brand personality.

* The Andrex brand of toilet tissue has consistently drawn on the animal aesthetic code of the puppy to *personify* its brand over the years.
* The Mercedes car brand has drawn on the geographic and language aesthetic codes of *German-ness* to present its brand personality.
* Ikea, the furniture retailer, draws on a *classless society* aesthetic code to develop its brand personality.
* The Jack Daniels whiskey brand uses the aesthetic codes of *history* to carefully present its heritage to consumers.
* Ben & Jerry's premium icecream has drawn on the aesthetic codes of *the 1970s American hippie culture* to express its brand personality.
* The Guinness drink brand draws on the aesthetic codes of *philosophy and humour* for its sophisticated black humour advertising. Peter York, founder of SRU Ltd, confirms why Guinness is so successful: 'People like to buy, to be wooed in clever ways, they like to have relationships with clever companies.'

These symbolic aesthetic codes provide a rich source for building new brand personalities around their corresponding themes and core brand dimensions. For example, a brand might wish to revitalize its proposition by drawing on its long heritage and history of successful innovation. A new brand may wish to use historical imagery to build a heritage it never had: by linking its brand to recognizable historical codes it can achieve the same result. The three-year-old Stewart Formula One motor racing team successfully branded itself with the Stewart tartan as part of its identity. While the team may be very young, its use of tartan conveys a symbolic sense of Scottish strength and permanence to its brand.

Brand custodian blueprint

The following blueprint structures the process of developing new brand names, identities and experiences expressed through all media types (see Figure 6.1). The benefit of this approach is:

* The brand DNA is a single source of reference for all branding and marketing activities, both internal and external.
* This approach makes managing several different external agencies less complex.

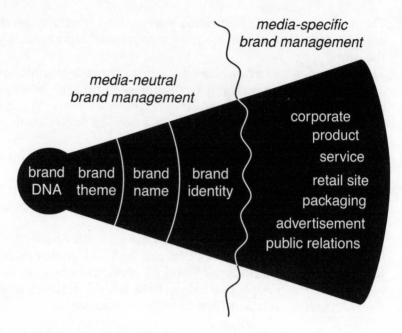

Figure 6.1 Brand custodian blueprint

- It reduces the risk of brand dilution.
- It increases the coherence and potency of the brand.
- It ensures greater longevity of this potent brand essence against dynamic internal and external forces.
- It provides a language for negotiating changes to the brand.

Brand DNA

This is the essence of the brand that summarizes both the internal and external benefits of the brand across all media types to all stakeholders. It should be guarded closely: each time a change is made to the brand DNA it should be done against a risk assessment. The value of the brand is directly related to the consistency of the brand DNA and its expression as a brand personality. The message of a brand should be as concentrated, succinct and powerful as possible, so that it can survive intact as it is communicated across media types; lengthy or vague brand DNA will become bland and unrecognizable to the consumer. Like human DNA, a small replica of it

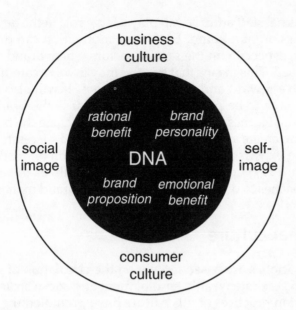

Figure 6.2 Brand DNA model

should be incorporated into each brand expression, whether it is a retail site, an advertisement or an internal marketing programme. The force of the brand is therefore increased by the alignment of all these brand expressions.

The brand DNA model in Figure 6.2 shows the relationships between and the building elements of a strong brand DNA. It can be used for new brand development and revitalizing or repositioning a brand in the marketplace. Depending on the nature of the brand and the business environment, some of the elements will be more prominent than others.

Business culture

The first input is the one that expresses the business culture of the brand, or the preferred business strategy. This can be the underlying business practice of the category, such as the soft drinks category, with incredibly low margins and high volumes. It can also reflect the strategic choice to milk the brand as a cash cow, or an innovative product development programme. Different business cycles and risk assessments per category can also influence the choice of business strategy for the brand.

The internal staff attitude can play a large role in the development and expression of a brand. Employee motivation can drive brand alignment, especially in the service sectors where brand delivery is people-based. This means that success may involve careful planning of employee reward and incentive schemes. It will also mean that staff will have to be properly trained to exude the brand in their every action. Harnessing people power to leverage the brand is not easy but can create a huge advantage if achieved successfully. One of the leading experts in the field is Kevin Thomson of MCA; his book (Thomson, 1999) on emotional capital crystallizes the arguments and approaches to developing staff buy-in to brand management.

Consumer culture

Western societies are based largely on the circulation of goods and services to generate wealth, employment and social structures. The consumption practices of this culture have promoted the use of the media and elements of image to influence consumers in their patterns of thought, education and decision making. Brand development must take into account the nature of those influences on people in everyday life. These are the aesthetic codes, which are the basis of most of our information gathering and processing activities. The material and dematerialized things that surround us are the things that shape our lives, and brands need to tap into the language of that consumer culture if they are to communicate effectively. It is an extremely rich source that can generate exciting and qualitative brand experiences for consumers. Consumer culture is the framework for the brand's biography as it flows from the past, through the present into the future.

Consumer culture is the field of competitor brands that the new brand will have to overcome in order to be successful. A careful audit of the competition using a SWOT analysis (see Chapter 11) should reveal which elements of consumer culture are increasing in value and which are decreasing. By mapping the brand's footprints against elements of popular culture, the white space, empty of market combinations can be discovered. It can also show the direction in which competitive brands are moving and how fast they are able to develop. It cannot, however, tell if a new brand is about to be introduced to the market, especially from another sector, which is increasingly the case in the merging of markets and product technologies. Threats can arrive from a much wider field than ever before, with supermarkets in the United Kingdom about to start selling cars, only three years after they started their own banks and pensions businesses. Left-brain thinking techniques and other projective tools should help to expose potential threats from this wider field of competitors and the increasingly wider geographical field of businesses.

Self-image

No longer can businesses afford to remain with a product or technology driven business plan; the consumer should be at the core of all business decision making. This means that finding out what the consumer wants and exceeding those wishes are imperative if the brand is to enable and enhance consumers' lives. One part of this issue is that consumers want to create and maintain their own self-image through the consumption and use of brands. Will Maskell of PI3 Ltd says, 'Brands should protect your identity, to make you feel comfortable about who you are.' This means that we can begin to segment consumers by their purchasing patterns. Segmentation is the easiest way to define sub-groups of the population with related needs, although these should be specific to the task and narrow enough that they are not generic. Consumers increasingly manage their self-identity through the explicit purchase and use of branded goods that coincide with their personalities. This is not the same as creating brand personalities that simply mirror consumer groups' personalities. Some brands can be successful by being respected or even held in awe by the consumer; brands that use a superhero-type brand personality rely on this kind of adoration. The Lara Croft cartoon advertisements for Lucozade represent an imaginary and entirely unattainable brand personality, but they are successful because of this high goal setting. Aspirational brand models are often highly successful, as they encourage consumers to raise their position in society through an attractive proposition. Wherever on the social strata a consumer is situated, they would rather feel they are moving upwards, however slightly, than be reminded of their present position.

Consumers need to be satisfied that their self-image fits with their own life goals, and one way of achieving this is to use branded goods to structure and build that position. Using the emotional dimensions described in Chapter 8, it is possible to discover and filter useful brand associations that will motivate and exceed consumers' self-image needs. In order to build a strong brand DNA these needs should be carefully researched and defined for the target consumer. This should ideally be a personal audit, but careful segmentation can lead to excellent and efficient results in understanding consumers' self-image motivations.

Social image

The other end of that identity spectrum is the social image that we all portray to our friends, family, work colleagues and others; this can be the same as our self-image, but the latter is usually reserved for our closest companions. In order to manage our personalities, we need to be able to project subtle variations of our image towards different target audiences. This may be more formal for work colleagues, more relaxed towards friends and more obedient towards parents or elders. Brands that understand how people manage these multiple selves will be more successful than those that pretend we are static and mono-dimensional.

To build a strong brand DNA, the social needs of the consumer target group need to be understood and used as input to the brand proposition and brand personality. How these represent and enable those shifting multiple social personalities will be crucial to the brand's success. Group membership is one of the key elements of our social world.

The sense of social self is not just directly with other people; it can also be the fictitious other we have in our heads. So our choice of toothpaste brand may not be exposed to the public, but we still have a sense of what others would think about us if it were public knowledge. This invisible peer pressure is no less influential on affecting brand purchases than that of real friends or relatives.

Rational benefits

The brand DNA must be a combination of rational and emotional triggers and benefits, satisfying the heart and mind of the consumer. Simple work sessions can help to define what those benefits are and what their priority is, in terms of primary and secondary brand values. Again, it is better to focus on fewer benefits and satisfy them well rather than attempting to satisfy many benefits less well. By prioritizing the benefits, it helps to structure the brand message and any communication materials or roll-out programmes.

Rational benefits are those benefits that speak through logical reasoning to the consumer in a cognitive framework of ideas (these are developed in detail in Chapter 7). For a retail outlet these could be:

* the brand that offers the widest range of products available;
* the brand that offers the best value for money;
* the brand that has 50 years' experience in sports retailing;
* the brand that caters for women (men/young/old/students, etc).

For FMCG brands the rational benefits could be:

* the biscuit brand that fills you up;
* the shampoo brand that makes your hair healthier;
* the toothpaste brand that makes your teeth whiter;
* the washing up liquid that kills germs.

For a service brand the rational benefits might be:

* we deliver in 24 hours, worldwide;
* we offer a quiet ride;
* we have a large network;
* we have a fast access time.

These are all rational benefits that can be justified and are easily accepted by consumers because of a reasoned argument. Because they are rational, they are repeatable and can be easily copied or matched by competitors, or they can be a brand in an area of low possible innovation, or a mature technology brand.

Rational benefits often provide the entry conditions to interest a consumer, without which they will pass the brand by. These are the implicit qualities that a brand needs to form part of the list of likely brands that a consumer will consider for any purchase. If a brand cannot make it on to the list of possible brands then it is almost impossible to convert that interest into purchase action. Following the examples above, consumers will usually only consider shampoo brands that make your hair healthier, or airlines that have a large network of routes. Once the brand has made it on to the consumer's entry list with an implicit rational benefit, the choice between brands will then be made based on the emotional benefit that differentiates brands that have identical rational benefits.

Emotional benefits

Emotional benefits are those that satisfy the heart and soul of the consumer, beyond the reasoned argument of the rational benefit. They can build on the rational benefit as an explicit differentiator, or they can be the immediate attraction that wins over the heart of the consumer through its pure emotional charge. In certain categories the emotional benefit can create an impulsive desire that is then post-rationalized by the consumer through the rational benefit.

The emotional dimensions are discussed in more detail in Chapter 8, but briefly, they speak to the humane, intuitive side of the consumer. They are expressed through ideas and images that are irrational yet compelling and often aspirational and inspirational in nature. Michael Abrahams distinguishes between the direction of the emotion:

> Damien Hirst's sliced cow, 'mother and child divided', may be a good idea, but it sucks out your emotions, it takes them from you. Truly great ideas, in my opinion, give emotions back to you, there is an important difference in the direction of the flow of the emotion.

Examples of emotional brand benefits might be:

* Tiger Woods-endorsed golf clubs.
* The washing powder for the caring mother.
* The face cream to make you beautiful.
* The sexiest clothing brand.
* The most exclusive car brand.

These all offer promises that are almost impossible to justify, but they persuade consumers by their suggestion that perfection can be attained. The most used and successful themes are those based around sexuality and status, core psychological desires of the ego and id according to Freud.

The emotional benefit is also often the theme that generates the *aura* around a brand that makes it special, and this can be heavily leveraged to persuade consumers to buy. Because this aura is unique it provides an excellent defence mechanism against competitors who may be able to replicate the rational benefits of the brand. Brands often have cycles of popularity where their aura shines brighter than other brands; careful brand management can help to lengthen those periods and reduce the downside of cyclical consumer tastes.

Brand proposition

This is the succinctly expressed summary of the rational and emotional benefits of the brand. It should include the target consumers, benefits, the desired action and the criteria for attaining that brand and those benefits. For example, it could be:

For sporty teenage men in urban areas, brand X is the most accurate watch available that delivers the superior performance and precision they need. This enables them to quickly develop their physical condition and impress their girlfriends and social friends for a medium price.

An alternative format could be:

Brand X promises to deliver the most accurate watch, which is important to you to help develop your physical condition and make you more successful at work. Brand X can deliver this because they are world leaders in time-keeping and are used at major sporting events. You can experience this accuracy by watching the Olympic games, or while racing, rushing to meetings or just walking the dog. To summarize, you will never be late for a meeting again, or lose a race because of faulty time-keeping. You can gain this kind of accuracy for the price of a good shirt, or less than £50.00.

The key elements are:

* the promise, clearly stated;
* the relevance and salience to the consumer;
* the believability or proof of claim;
* the range of opportunities and ways to enjoy the promise;
* the summary of the promise;
* the criteria to attaining the promise, either comparative or factual.

These can be written for any brand, and they help to organize what the brand is really offering, to whom and in what format, and the criteria for access. The process of writing brand propositions should be iterative: they need refining and editing ruthlessly to sharpen them and make sure that they offer something truly new and distinctive. The brand proposition can be tested with colleagues or in the more formal environment of focus groups, often comparing them against new and existing competitor propositions. It is worth being highly critical at this stage; too often the propositions fall into known formats that offer nothing special to the consumer, which is disastrous at this early stage, as they are unlikely to improve with age. It is better to develop fewer qualitative propositions that have been refined, than large numbers of superficial propositions in the hope that a winner will emerge.

Brand personality

The brand personality is the chosen character that best communicates the brand proposition to the target audience. As Paul Southgate, Brand House, has highlighted, it is not the personality of the target audience, it is the personality that is most likely to draw their attention, interest them, and encourage them to take action and buy the brand. A single brand proposition could be expressed through many variants of a brand personality to present a different voice to the consumer; it is important to choose the one that is most suitable from these possibilities. For example, Heineken beer has had a consistent proposition of 'Heineken refreshes the parts other beers cannot reach.' The brand personality has changed many times from videos of television celebrities changing their character from sad to happy; to cartoon comic strip characters whose body parts change in response to drinking the beer. One brand personality will appeal to a different target audience from the other, but all are based on the same underlying brand proposition.

The brand personality should be treated very much like a person or character, as this format is easiest for consumers to understand and accept. This is because consumers have a vast experience of dealing with human relationships and the nuances of differences in personalities. They are able to distinguish between subtle differences in brand personalities and build up their own loyal or disloyal relationships with them. Celia Lury, University of London, suggests, 'These relationships may be phatic relations that communicate general sociability, eg, "Good morning, how are you?" without the necessity, interest or expectation of a reply.' This view of brand–consumer relationships emphasizes a brand's ability to oil the wheels of communication rather than enabling any specific grammatical or dialogue function.

Brand personalities are often characterized by their analogy to other people, objects and services:

◈ If brand X were a car, what kind of car would it be?
◈ If brand Y were a sports person, what kind of sport would they play?
◈ If brand Z were a person, what sort of clothes would they wear? Are they male or female? What would they drink? What TV programmes would they watch? Where would they go on holiday?

Michael Abrahams explains, 'I often think about brands as people, because once you know that person, you can go and do the shopping for them. What sort of tie suits them, if any, what sort of clubs they go to or newspaper they would buy or food they might eat.' This kind of role playing is one of the best ways for brand managers to truly understand how their brand will behave and what kind of relationships it is likely to have with different consumer groups. He goes on to suggest that this type of analogy can help you to understand how the brand will grow up, or cope with a mid-life crisis. It offers a set of physical, intellectual and emotional dimensions with which to make judgements about the health and direction of the brand.

By analogous example it is possible to deconstruct and reconstruct a brand using the known symbolic codes of other objects and brands as the currency of that explanation. Once you are able to achieve this kind of closeness with the brand, it is possible to define how the brand would grow, react to negative and positive changes to the market and defend itself against tactical brand attacks from competitors.

Brand themes

A brand theme is the conceptual driver that all of the elements of the brand message can be connected with. Successful brands are able to develop all types of media and dimensions of the brand to align with the brand theme; it is the expression of the brand personality. The whisky brand Glenfiddich has developed a strong and distinctive brand personality whose brand theme is the Highlands of Scotland. This is a rich basis for building the brand personality, since it can be tuned and re-tuned to emphasize different aspects of that culture depending on prevailing trends. The Scottish theme could be:

◈ Pagan. A pagan brand personality is a raw and basic Celtic personality that evokes druids, early wizards and magic. The

Celtic aesthetic has strong, recognizable patterns of intricate detail showing early interlocking organic designs. The materials are rough straw and wood with dark earthy colours. The narrative would include territorial fighting with swords and bloody wars involving powerful men. The emphasis on familial clans, mottoes and totemism would be strong features.

* The natural beauty. This narrative would evolve around the enchanting scenery of the Scottish Highlands, the bright colours of the valleys in autumn; the majesty of the snow-covered winter mountains. The seductive scenery of green and the blue of the lochs would be emphasized. The freshness of the mountain air and water can be felt and tasted. There's a general healthiness to the beauty.

* The craftsman. This theme emphasizes the craftsmanship involved in whisky making, through a narrative about carving furniture, hand-making fishing flies and shooting gear. They show attention to detail, the richness of materials, and the patience of the maker. They show the reward for this as the perfect, beautiful finished object.

As Jane Merriman, new brand development manager, William Grant & Sons, says:

> The Balvenie Single Barrel whisky proposition is a quintessential esoteric malt. It is crafted, very traditional, its production process is crafted more so than any other whisky. Every element is crafted; it's even bottled by hand with individual batch numbers.

Each one of these can be used to emphasize a particular aspect of Scottish life while still retaining an overall sense of Scottishness. This means that the narrative can be enriched by reference to all the others and use all the channels of communication to build a complete story.

Brand narrative

Successful brands develop their personality over time; they do not remain static, because, as Peter York suggests, 'What happens to brands is experienced over time, so brands develop a social history.' Their brand proposition may remain constant, but its expression as a personality needs to be updated to remain contemporary in a changing competitive environment. A narrative is the story that a brand personality follows as its flows through consumer culture. As a story, the brand personality then belongs to a chain of events that can be traced backwards to the past, in the present and forward to the future. This helps consumers to align themselves with the brand as it reflects changes in consumer culture. Some brands rely on the narrative of their founder, such as Bill Gates of Microsoft, to personify the changes in the brand; as his focus and personality mature, so do the brand's. Other brands use a fictitious family or characters to play out a changing story, like the two Oxo families, whom we watched grow up over a period of 15 years of TV advertising.

The power of a narrative is that the brand personality can also look forward and backward in a nostalgic or ironic manner or look forward with an optimistic feeling. This sense of time closely relates to how we witness our own growth, creating joint memories at distinctive points of the narrative between the brand and us. This means we associate specific events in our lives with the expression of the brand personality at that time, creating a deeper sense of relationship and therefore loyalty to the brand. We remember our enjoyment of our first bike brand, car brand, the first beer brand we drank, the first condom brand we used and the first hotel brand we stayed at. These all form pivotal moments in our lives and the memory is intrinsically associated with the brand.

The brand narrative often uses the tools of icons, totems, clans and badges to reinforce significant moments along the story line. These could be the graduation ceremony, a wedding, the birth of your first child, etc. The brand that can conclude each of these events will be always available in the mind of the consumer. When they look at their child or partner they may be reminded of that event and which brand was there with them.

Brand experience

The best way to generate a successful brand personality is when all the elements combine to create a total brand experience. This means choreographing a performance of brand identity, in a branded space, with branded service and resulting in a branded memory. By creating a memorable experience, something that has actually touched the consumer's heart and mind, a brand moves on to a level of deep brand satisfaction for the consumer. The interaction of time and space in creating this memory is crucial since it places the consumer at the centre of an event in a specific time and specific place, not a generic activity that they may forget. They provide branded moments that can be captured as an activity that only one brand can provide or fulfil. The *whisky moment* at the end of an evening has often been the source of a branded experience. A specific brand is closely associated with providing that branded moment and the connection affords excellent protection against brand switching.

Retail sites are one of the best opportunities to develop this kind of brand experience, since they offer a carefully organized experience in a deliberately controlled environment. Everything from the light and sound levels, to the movement of people through the store, unfolding the brand story as they go, can be tailored to express the brand. This is retailing as theme park, an entertainment and leisure space as much as a commodity exchange space.

The key to defining successful brand experiences is to create a story that will satisfy the consumers' desires without resorting to the tired clichés of current market thinking. New concepts of people moving in spaces and enjoying the submersion in a total brand environment can be created, that break the mould of traditional service provision, retailing and communication channels. Brand experiences help to generate the brand mythology that a brand needs to develop its personality beyond the two-dimensional.

Brand name

The brand name is often the most highly visible and long-lasting connecting element of a brand for the consumer. It should crystallize the experience of the brand in a single word or phrase that is transferable around the world and can be protected. It should form an impenetrable barrier against competitors and define the position of the business in the mind of the consumer.

Our own name is the first thing that identifies us as who we are, which family we belong to and, usually, our sex. Brand names have a similarly important role as the first and often most memorable piece of the total brand identity. While all other elements are reviewed and updated over time, it is likely that the brand name will be sacred. Only in times of merger or acquisition does the brand name come up for revision. The name of the brand is often the majority element that a company buys during acquisition. This is particularly true for service and FMCG goods industries, where the capital assets like factories or machines are relatively small compared to the value of the brand.

The brand name of certain companies is more valuable than the capital assets they own (the factory buildings and machines, etc). We will look in Chapter 10 at how these are calculated and evaluated. FMCG industries particularly have a higher brand value to capital asset ratio. As the brand is valuable, it becomes evident why brand managers need to protect the goodwill associated with the brand name.

Given the responsibility and value that the brand name has, and its necessary longevity, it must be chosen with great care. This means that creating, selecting and testing brand names should not be left to a minor meeting long after new product development has begun. It needs to be thought of at the start of the project or business, as it has the power to focus and shape the formation of the project and business structure. It can also inspire both internal staff and external trade and retail consumers.

Seven functions of a brand name

1. A brand name identifies the company or product/service as unique to the customer.
2. A brand name describes the company/product/service or core emotional brand benefit.
3. A brand name should be easy to pronounce and spell.
4. A brand name should be usable around the world, avoiding cultural mismatches.
5. A brand name should be protected and used to create a legal barrier to counterfeiting.
6. A brand name should be an equity that can be traded, regardless of tangible company assets.
7. A brand name must ultimately feel good in a subjective sense.

(See also Figure 6.3.)

It is sometimes easy to forget that the brand name should clearly identify the company or product. If this is not visible then it will be difficult for customers to ask for your product by name. This may be obvious, but simply putting your brand name on both sides of a pack can ensure that your brand name is always visible in a retail outlet. Similarly, in advertising, it is no good seducing the viewer with a mini-drama if they are not clear who you are. In certain

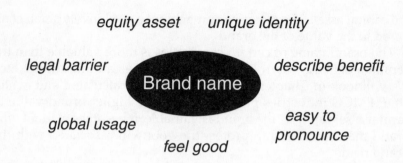

equity asset   *unique identity*

legal barrier   **Brand name**   *describe benefit*

global usage   *easy to pronounce*

feel good

Figure 6.3 Seven functions of a brand name

markets it is your name that makes you unique, and this is the best form of marketing. For example, the recent rise in quality of own-label goods in supermarkets means that more customers are leaving 'A brand' goods and trying own-label goods. In this scenario, convincing people to ask for Princes salmon rather than the generic brand or own brand is crucial for profitability.

The brand name should suggest the benefit or added value of the product you are selling. These can be denoted benefits like budget or rent-a-wreck car rentals, clearly expressing their different brand propositions, in the same way as Volkswagen ('people's car' in German) or the *Wall Street Journal* or CNN (Cable News Network). These brand names all denote the expected service or product that you are buying with clarity.

The benefit can also be expressed through the use of a connotative brand name such as Häagen-Dazs icecream or Jaguar cars. The Häagen-Dazs name has Nordic or Scandinavian connotations, with the benefit of ice expertise and technologies. The Jaguar car company name tries to connote the qualities of the big cat with nobility, power, agility and presence. In both these cases the brand name sets the tone of the expected benefit. This has high added value for customers who search for differentiators in a crowded market.

The brand name forms the basis of a legal barrier to protect company investment and profitability. It is the starting point of all trade mark protection along with any associated logo or device. The KFC (Kentucky Fried Chicken) name and Colonel Saunders icon are integrated to form a strong identity and protectable entity. It is important to use a name that is unique and can be registered properly. Companies will often develop a unique typeface for their brand name to further protect them from copying. The sunglasses company Ray Ban has developed its signature brand name into a brand mark, a combination name and logo.

Brand name strategy

1. Corporate strategic goals.
2. Brand architecture and sub-brands.
3. Legal protection.
4. Innovative product or me-too.
5. Does it feel right?

The brand name should try to fulfil the above criteria but it must also take into account the long-term objectives for the brand. These should be carefully considered before launching into naming sessions. Clarity of purpose at an early stage will help to focus the efforts of the team.

The brand manager needs to be clear about the strategic goals of the company and the role of the new brand within that strategy. For example, will the new brand simply be a support for the main brand or will it eventually take over from the current brand? Will the brand be used all over the world or will it be used in country-specific executions? What will be the structure of any sub-brand or diffusion brand executions and do these anticipate the expected growth of the company or product line? What kind of protection will be given to the new brand name (and what kind of budget has been provided), especially in countries where counterfeiting is likely? Is the product a new innovation that requires a completely new identity or is the company marketing a me-too product that may require alignment with other brands in the same market? Finally, the new brand name should *feel right*. This is not an objective test but requires a sense of understanding the brand personality and the perception of the new name.

Brand name creation

There are many proprietary name generation techniques based on brainstorming, computer software or pure inspiration. I would advocate any or all of these; it's simply not important how you get there, so long as the name is great and fits the above criteria. The first part of the process is to identify clearly the characteristics of the new brand, so that these can act as themes for the name generation. For a new soft drink this may emphasize the fresh fruitiness or the sparkling fizziness or the thirst quenching effect. It may be an international drink or have local connotations such as highland spring water.

Brainstorming sessions with a group or linguistically agile participants are often held. These people enjoy the mental manipulation of words and themes and can generate several hundred names in a few hours. They may include writers, poets, journalists, artists, salespeople, advertising creatives and designers (some larger agencies may have a separate department for this type of work). Their task is to generate streams of names around the identified core attributes of the new brand. They are not there to select and develop these names, so it is important to focus only on creation at this stage. Depending on the likely countries of distribution, it may be important to organize several sessions in specific countries.

Another route to name generation is to use a computer database, which searches based on the desirable attributes of the brand. These will list possibilities of names and phonetic and hyphenated word combinations. These should again be used for the generation of a list of preferred ideas and not final selection.

Brand name selection

Once a list of names has been generated, they need to be edited to produce a final list of 20–25 preferred names. These can then be analysed, developed and checked against existing copyright and trade mark lists. Computer databases are usually the easiest way to do this, although there are specific agencies that can help with this as well. It is best to use the original criteria (set out above) to edit what is likely to be a large list. So, for example, delete words that are already used as trade marks, are difficult to pronounce, cannot be registered, are not distinctive or do not describe the core benefit or company/product. This initial editing should reduce the list dramatically and enable an in-depth internal discussion and comparison of the remainder. The shortlist should also be tested in likely distribution countries to ensure that the connotations are transferable and that no negative associations are revealed. This can be done with small focus groups, possibly together with a conjoint analysis of the product offer/benefit/product and/or packaging mock-ups.

The feel of a great brand name

It is worth remembering that some of the best brand names break many or all of the above rules. This highlights the ultimate subjectivity of a name. It is important throughout the process to retain names on the list that just feel right or are interesting and unique. They may eventually prove successful or give added insight into another name. The range of opportunities is shown in Figure 6.4.

What is the sound of a great brand name? It's important that a name sounds right. Research has shown that the sound of a name has an important influence on the way that people perceive that name and that person. It is also true that some brand names just sound better than others do. In order to test this, imagine asking for the brand name in a store you would expect to stock the product. Does it sound right? This may include making the brand name sound likeable by avoiding harsh tones or sequences. According to Akio Morita, the founder of Sony, one of the reasons for choosing the Sony brand name was that it sounded like 'sunny' in many dialectics around the world. The cultural fit of a brand name may be irrational, but it clearly plays an important part in our perception and expectation of what a brand name should be. Figure 6.4 refines the one used by Hart and Murphy (1998) to include personal names and explain the boundaries of the chain of names.

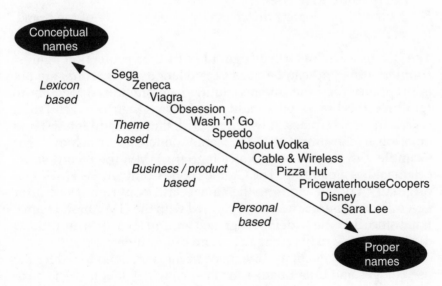

Figure 6.4 Range of brand name opportunities

Brand slogans and straplines

Brand slogans and straplines are equally part of the corporate identity and are usually adopted as a sub-text of the brand name. In Japanese corporations they are changed yearly, but other organizations may keep them for years and even decades. The current Philips slogan is 'Let's make things better', trying to suggest that Philips wants to work with the consumer as a team to improve things. The *Financial Times* slogan, 'No FT, no comment', suggests that it's the only opinion leader worth listening to. These slogans can act as the voice of the brand personality speaking directly to the consumer. It is crucial to market test these with pilot groups and regions before rolling them out across the company, to maximize appreciation and acceptance.

Brand logos and trade marks

Giles Lury (1998) has suggested that brand icons fall into three categories:

1. A brand icon depicts the brand's name, eg Jaguar, Penguin books.
2. A brand icon depicts an element of the product or what it does, eg Netscape, Mercedes.
3. A brand icon depicts the character or personality of the brand, eg Apple, Virgin.

The use of a trademarked logo adds further protection against counterfeiting and can be used where language or words are not appropriate. The brand name and logo are often used together to reinforce the brand personality and strengthen differentiation within the marketplace. If well designed, they can add interest and emotion to the brand that the name alone cannot achieve. For example, the His Master's Voice logo for HMV, the record store, originated as a painting. The Gramophone Company, as HMV was originally known, bought the image and copyright, and after several years of use it was incorporated with the HMV brand name. It has since become widely recognized around the world and adds a distinctive edge to the company brand proposition.

There is an inclination at the moment for companies to reduce the use of logos and brand names for their company identity. The business theory is that the use of two identities is confusing and reduces the overall impact by splitting attention between the two visual elements. I think this may be true in some cases, and as a rule it is always better to focus on one single visual element rather than two. Michael Abrahams suggests that a logo should be reserved for 'only the best items; it should never be on anything that gets destroyed or goes in the bin'. This means not over-branding items, especially internally, where companies have a tendency to put their brand logo on company teabags, biscuits, waste bins, carpets and even paper towels.

This trend has also led to more companies using their brand name as a kind of logo rather than duplicating brand name and a logo, though there is an increased emphasis on typographical style. For example, the original Philips shield logo has now been largely discarded in favour of an emphasized word mark, Philips. This can be achieved by incorporating the two, as BMW has with its roundel design; or Samsung with its dark, elliptical border reversing out the letters of the brand name.

Some confident companies have chosen to focus on the use of their logo in favour of their brand name, with the idea that it becomes a universal emblem for the brand personality. The Shell oil company dropped the word 'shell' from beneath its shell graphic element and has remained as recognizable as ever. In recent years Nike, the sports apparel manufacturer, dropped the word 'Nike' from below its trade mark 'Swoosh' emblem. The Swoosh logo can now be found all over its goods and even as tattoos or shaven head marks. It has been one of the first to attempt this, so it is still perceived as unique; if competitors such as Speedo or Adidas were to follow this lead it might create logo confusion.

Typeface identity

The choice of typeface can generate a series of brand associations in the mind of the customer. Typefaces are part of the complete corporate identity, and are often the most frequently seen element, on everything from letterheads to products and packaging. They can also help to consolidate the choice of brand personality of the product or company within the particular consumer field. They can help differentiate your brand from competitors in a crowded marketplace or they can confirm your brand as part of a group of companies within a particular sector.

There are two basic pairs of divisions within type: serif and sans serif, upper and lower case. Brand names with serif typefaces such as *The Times*, McKinsey & Co, IBM and Giorgio Armani suggest tradition, sophistication and ostentatious respect. Those brand names that are sans serif like Tefal, Microsoft, Nokia and Boeing suggest a modern and clean business approach to branding. Brands like Guinness, Snickers, Mattel and Levi's use upper case throughout to suggest strength and power. Other brands using only lower case often suggest unostentatious or relaxed approaches to their brand, such as lego, durex, adidas and benetton. It is worthwhile plotting your competitor brands, including brands that compete for consumer attention, even if from different sectors, on a matrix. This will help you to decide whether to include yourself within a sector, or define yourself as different from that sector.

Corporate identity

Corporate identity is the coordinated design and execution of the brand names, themes and logos across a whole range of applications. It is essentially a two-dimensional, one-way communication, whereas branding is a wider form of relationship marketing with two-way dialogue, including time-based brand experiences. Corporate identity and branding share the need to address both an internal company audience and the external consumer. Michael Abrahams believes that 'The role of the corporate identity designer is not to stop at any point, you have a responsibility to the business, you have to really care and be passionate.' This reflects an understanding that the business is a living thing and needs to be constantly refined both in its working model and in the identity that represents that model.

Once you have found a strong brand name that supports your brand proposition you may also wish to use a logo to reinforce the connection of the new brand with other brands from the same company (see Chapter 3). The rules for logo development mirror those for name generation and are best achieved with the help of a corporate identity specialist. They will be able to translate the meaning or essence of your brand into a series of executions that can cover everything, including the letterhead, packaging, architecture, signage and vehicles (see Figure 6.5).

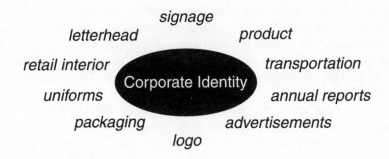

Figure 6.5 Functions of corporate identity

Company structure

A corporate identity should reflect the structure of the company and express this as a visual map. According to Olins (1989), 'Corporate identity programmes are emerging as major agents of change. Because of their high visibility and impact they mark out turning points in a corporation's life.' He goes on to suggest there are three elements to a corporate identity programme:

1. Coherence. Presentation of a coherent structure.
2. Symbolism. Symbolize its ethos and attitudes.
3. Positioning. Differentiate from the competition.

Companies that are visually cluttered with too many variants or individual executions of their corporate identity are probably suffering from a lack of coherence and direction. To address this, companies often have a corporate style guide or corporate identity manual that specifies the range of permitted variants. The recent changes in corporate identity of British Airways (BA) have led to consumer doubts about its brand. Traditionally, BA used red, white and blue in the form of part of the national flag on its tailwings. This was a clear statement about the strength of British power around the world, and typical of many national airlines. In the late 1990s BA unveiled a new concept that was based on multiculturalism, each tailfin being given a different design to reflect different nationalities and cultures. One had a Scottish tartan, another an African mask design, another a Polish flower pattern. The different identities were carried through to the back of tickets, business cards and other print material. The change from the accepted rigid ethos used by most airline corporate identities was both daring and bold. More recently, however, BA reversed its decision, returning to a constant format of red, white and blue, similar to its previous design. During the same period, BA's financial performance declined, although obviously, many factors contributed to this. Anecdotal evidence suggests that the lack of coherent identity has made the airline more difficult for consumers to be attracted towards. The symbolism and positioning elements of the corporate identity programme should be coherent with the brand personality, although they do not always have to be exactly the same thing.

Summary

⊛ Brand imagery and collateral can be developed from all parts of our cultural heritage, politics, pop culture, science, sports, etc.

⊛ The brand DNA is the core essence of what the brand means and should be present in all formats of the brand's expression.

⊛ The brand proposition should be a combination of the rational and emotional benefits that the target consumer desires. The brand personality is the visual identity used to best express those benefits.

⊛ Many processes can create brand names, but it is essential that the chosen name 'feels right' as well as being structurally correct.

⊛ Corporate identities should express and reflect the company structure.

CHAPTER SEVEN

COGNITIVE BRAND DIMENSIONS

Defining the rational benefits of a brand

Chapter 7 explains the generation and definition of the cognitive dimensions of the core brand proposition. This is achieved through an examination of the nature of cognitive needs in target consumer groups and their relative importance for the brand business. First, there is an explanation of the continual need to concentrate on core cognitive brand propositions and how they are communicated to the consumer through the brand personality. This draws on a number of frameworks to illustrate the differences in cognitive needs for consumers and against competitors' brands.

The cognitive filters that consumers use to make brand choices will be examined using case examples to illustrate the effect of the different filters. This chapter provides an insight into the opportunities for brands to be the master of a specific cognitive brand proposition, and advocates the mastery of one rather than attempting to master them all.

Objectives

- Define the use of cognitive dimensions for a brand.
- Illustrate the strategic cognitive dimensions for a brand.
- Express the tactical cognitive tools for a brand.
- Explain Maslow's hierarchy of needs.

Cognitive brand definition

All successful brands have a strong underlying cognitive value that creates and retains satisfied consumers. It is the ability of brand managers to be able to spot what that cognitive added value is and leverage the brand personality to express it that creates successful brands. This is not easy: secondary issues of brand extensions can pollute the purity of the cognitive value, the shifting marketing environment and competitive brand personalities can dilute the core brand value. Equally, as the brand matures, the original core qualities may fade and be replaced by other secondary values that do not entirely fit with the core needs of the consumer.

The cognitive dimension is the clearly stated pure need of the consumer, without being deflected by marketing speak or market driven solutions. To quote Philippe Starck, the French avant garde designer, 'The world wants water not taps, the world wants warmth not a heater.' It is this clarity of purpose that will define successful cognitive brand dimensions and avoid those that are spurious or irrelevant. Too many brands have missed their core cognitive value by expressing assumptions about the consumer or the market rather than being driven by real consumers' needs and desires. As Joanne Wallace of McVities suggests, 'Successful new product development always stems from an unmet need.' To categorize these needs, they must be analysed to separate the first-order needs from higher emotional needs that we shall look at in the following chapter. This can be achieved by gaining an insight into the consumer's mind or by studying human life to observe latent needs that the consumer was unaware of. Ethnographic and video observation techniques can often provide these kinds of insights to problems that consumers have adapted to or learned to cope with. There may be an excellent new brand opportunity that the consumer has been waiting for. The Dove brand of soap introduced the cognitive benefit of moisturizing plus soap cleaning as a new product brand. The company understood that consumers wanted clean skin, but that they didn't want the dry skin that resulted from soap. Had it not understood this it might have simply created a new soap brand with a different fragrance or pH value.

Brand managers need to recognize exactly what business they are in; to do this they should try to list the possible needs the consumer might have surrounding the product category. Taking airlines as an example, the obvious answer is that they are in the transport business; but the consumer may understand what they provide as:

* the vacation business;
* the meeting business (for businesses);
* the taxi business;
* the once-in-a-lifetime-experience business;
* the time-extending business (Concorde, London to New York);
* the glamour business.

Most of these are true for many consumers and it is important to identify which are the most salient to be used in building the brand proposition. Once you understand what business you are in, it is easier to express that added value through the brand personality.

Until that cognitive added value has been clearly stated, it will be difficult to build a successful brand personality to express the brand proposition. From that primary value statement, a series of possible secondary cognitive dimensions radiate out. Again, it is important to develop a clear understanding of which of the possible secondary values are relevant for the development of the brand proposition and brand personality. The following sections describe a series of tools that help to define the strategic (long-term) and tactical (mid-term) cognitive brand dimensions. They also help brand managers to distinguish between primary and secondary cognitive values. It cannot be stressed enough that critical thought must be applied to determining these and reducing the brand proposition to a strong, single clear statement. Without this the brand personality will be blurred, confusing and indistinct for the consumer, the overload of text and imagery generating more distraction than confirmation.

Strategic cognitive dimensions

There are four cognitive dimensions that develop brands along different routes to success:

1. *Brand weight*, the dominance of a brand in a market, eg Microsoft.
2. *Brand length*, the ability of a brand to diversify across business categories, eg Disney.
3. *Brand power*, the loyalty of the consumer group, eg Apple.

4. *Brand breadth*, the appeal of the brand across consumer groups, eg Coca-Cola.

Brand managers need to understand the differences between these in order to focus their activities to achieve their goal. Some of the best-known brands like Coca-Cola and McDonald's have been successful in several of these categories, but it is better to start by mastering one of them at a time. This is especially true for a new brand, or young brand development, where they have yet to reach a critical mass in the consumer's mind. By focusing on just one of the four goals, budget and strategic decisions can be made more easily.

Brand weight

This type of brand goal relates to the dominance of a brand within its chosen market; it is often referred to as simply the market share, but it is more than this. It can also be the total dominance that a brand exerts over the mind of the consumer, trade and the media. Dominance in a market can be developed through maintaining a rigorous innovation programme that keeps the brand at the forefront of the consumer's mind. Kellogg's is continually developing new technologies to enhance the taste of its products in order to deliver improvements to the core cognitive need of a great-tasting cereal. This may be a new toasting process to add crispness to its rice, or a new type of paper for the cereal bag to retain freshness. Everything it does is focused on enhancing the taste experience of eating Kellogg's Cornflakes, Rice Krispies, Coco Pops, etc. It never forgets that it is in the taste business, not the rice business, or the packaging business or the breakfast business. Of course all of these things are important and add value to the brand in a crowded competitive market; but they cannot be used to build the brand.

Traditionally, high brand weight has always been a core goal for businesses, especially if market share exceeds 40 per cent. Many Japanese companies followed this route during the 1980s, managing their businesses as large-volume, low-margin operations. This often resulted in high brand weight, which could then be used to manage markets as well as their brand, exerting influence over smaller competitors. Once a high brand weight is achieved, it is possible to increase R&D spend and innovation, while slowly increasing prices and margins to accompany this growth. It can also cause complacency in a business, as the market looks secure. Often it is new entrants that quickly reduce the brand weight of a brand that does not continuously invest. Many marketing directors still specify a number one or two market share position as a critical measure of a brand's performance.

Brand length

Achieving brand length focuses on increasing the flexibility of a brand across market categories and segments. Brands achieve this by displaying a power of expertise, not in technology but in their understanding of the consumer's mind. The Disney brand expresses family entertainment in all its film productions, theme parks, T-shirts, books, games and toys. The central cognitive need is clearly upheld in all these items, even though they represent very different business categories that other suppliers would not dare to cross. Each item also has a series of added value brand dimensions, but they succeed because the core brand proposition remains clear and fulfils the basic need for a large proportion of the consumer population.

Brands that achieve significant brand length do so by marking out a specific territory in the mind of the consumer and retaining that position across all their activities. They operate a basic brand promise that can be applied to a variety of categories via a franchise with the consumer. They are the ultimate lifestyle brands that people are attracted to because they fit their needs and desires in one category, but, once satisfied, continue to purchase the brand in other categories, often unrelated in the traditional sense. The thing that relates them in the mind of the consumer is that they deliver the same cognitive brand promise in all their guises. Whether this is a Disney baseball cap, a Disney soft drink, a Disney holiday or a Disney movie, the core benefit is reinforced by the Disney brand promise and itself reinforces the Disney-ness of the product-brand expression.

In the UK, the traditional world of banking has seen supermarket entrants Tesco and department store Marks & Spencer vying for the consumer's financial capital. Large-scale free Internet service providers have also come from the unlikely sources of NTL, Dixons the high street retailer and the Virgin group.

Some of these have taken advantage of several consumer reports that highlight the fact that more people trust Sainsbury's and Tesco than the government, the police or the high street banks. This is a clear indication of the power of a brand identity to convey strong messages to consumers and retain their trust, perhaps as a result of a mass faith in liberal market economics. Alternatively, it could emphasize the continuing mediation of identities and the reliance of consumers on those mediated identities to make choices about their lives, family and finances. The message for governments and institutions is that they must at least match these high levels of seductive media if they are to re-establish their standing and authority with the consumer.

When a brand tries to encompass a wide range of business categories it may fail to achieve significant profitability because at one point the brand promise will not stretch far enough. As this occurs, the dilution effect on the core brand and product combinations will also reduce the validity of the brand offer. Each new brand extension, like any stretch, must be carefully planned and executed impeccably if it is to succeed.

The bond of trust with the consumer is the critical dimension to any brand proposition; once broken it is difficult or impossible to retrieve. If you only say one thing with a brand message, it must be to convey the trust that the consumer needs to have in a product or service to buy it in the first place. If there is insufficient trust projected by the brand, the consumer may never know just how good the product or service is.

Brand power

Brand power is the strength of an individual or business to influence others, in this case the consumer. These companies have attained a brand fortress for themselves where they can heavily influence a usually intensely loyal customer base. The old adage about football can be rephrased here for power brands: 'Branding is not a matter of life and death, it is much more important than that.' Typically, consumers of power brands are acolytes and can be relied on to generate a formidable word-of-mouth campaign for the power brand. Brand power is often described as customer loyalty, but it goes beyond that with a quasi-religious connection between the consumer and the brand. It forms a dialogue that reflects a strong commitment from both sides to developing an enduring relationship. Young start-up businesses often have this type of brand dimension, but many quickly lose it as they become out of touch with their core consumer benefit. Once the corporate regulation and processes take over in a business, it becomes more difficult to retain the human characteristics that first attracted a large number of consumers.

Brands like Apple, Nike and the BBC all retain the strong brand power that connects the business closely with the consumer in a symbiotic relationship. Obviously, fashion-oriented brands are more likely to receive this kind of attention, but successful companies from Ben & Jerry's icecream to The Body Shop cosmetics chain can all achieve strong brand power. One of the critical elements for strong brand power is the depth of emotional attachment that a brand creates with the consumer. This goes beyond the implicit cognitive benefits to provide an explicit emotional benefit that can be highly distinctive for particular brands.

Brand breadth

Another strategic dimension for a brand is to develop a consumer franchise that spans the widest possible range of consumer groups. This may seem ideal, since it maximizes the selling opportunity to as many people as possible, but it is difficult to achieve, especially when the age, sex, class and other socio-economic dimensions create a huge diversity of needs and expectations. There are not many brands that are clever enough to satisfy across these target groups without diluting their brand promise too far. The danger is that when a brand is perceived to be appropriate for one target group it naturally becomes exclusive for that group, rather than inclusive for other groups. The problem is that to try to attract as many people as possible the message must be inclusive and this often results in a bland message. The result is a brand that is inoffensive to most people, but fails actually to attract anyone. Clearly, large businesses in consumer electronics, retailing and service industries need huge consumer numbers to be viable, but in a competitive environment they also need to retain distinctiveness for their proposition.

A brand that has successfully generated powerful propositions as well as wide consumer franchise is Coca-Cola, the world's most recognized brand name, drunk by small children in developing countries and CEOs in the world's capitals. McDonald's, Kodak, Visa and Microsoft have also achieved this kind of brand breadth. Their success is due to retaining a distinctive proposition compared with their competitors, while offering an inclusive attitude towards all consumer groups.

Strategic cognitive filters

To help understand what kind of unmet core need the business fulfils, it is worth understanding some of the filters that brands express to consumers. These include financial, gender and age filters.

By examining the core unmet need through these cognitive filters, it is possible to clarify the brand proposition. There are many more filters that can be used, depending on the nature of the market, your brand and the consumer target group; these are simply examples.

The cognitive financial filter

In the westernized world it is not surprising that one of the most basic brand dimensions is a financial filter. Free market economies encourage and enable brands to be successful based on the price that the consumer is willing to pay for the brand (a price above any notional commodity price). This is the fundamental advantage of a strong brand: an ability to generate extra revenue above that of competitors and the production/distribution costs. The chosen price should therefore best represent that enhanced proposition, or risk being undervalued in the marketplace. For consumers, the financial filter is not fixed over time but only at a single moment in time, the point of purchase; when economic capital (cash) is exchanged for brand capital (identity).

The market can always be sub-divided into many financial segments, whether coverage is across the whole market or simply a small niche. The brand may be a bargain own label, or a mid-priced value pack, or a premium top of the line product or service. This structuring of the market helps consumers to filter out the choices that are unavailable or undesirable for them. They use price as a key guide to which part of the market they fit into, and it acts as a starting point for a brand manager who is trying to reposition the brand. This structuring usually takes place as bands of prices that follow each other up the financial scale, sometimes overlapping. Brands at the bottom of the band may be considered to offer similar benefits but at a slightly lower price and therefore better value. Brands at the top of the band may be considered to offer better quality but at an inflated price. The brand manager needs to know which competitors fall above and below them in order to make tactical use of the brand proposition.

Most brands use sub-brands or brand extensions to increase the bandwidth of their business revenues. The Giorgio Armani brand occupies the luxury end of the clothing market and it carefully uses a financial filter to define its target consumers. There is also the Emporio Armani brand, which tailors itself to a lower financial target. Still lower on the financial scale are the Armani Exchange and Armani Jeans brands that cater to the mass market. Brand managers can use the financial filter to decrease or increase the bandwidth of potential consumers, because that bandwidth increases as the price decreases, and vice versa.

The cognitive gender filter

What is the core gender proposition for the brand? Is it masculine, feminine, universal, gay or straight? The fundamental choice of one of these will dictate a large proportion of the attracted consumer group. It can also be used to reflect a known majority market, or reposition a brand into a new market. The gender filter of a brand is often associated with the gender-related nature of the goods or services, but many brands can have a brand gender unrelated to these. The car company Renault and the coffee brand Nescafé have a feminine bias that can be used to filter target consumers. The gender filter helps consumers to structure their choices when they come to purchase these goods, creating typically dualistic options. The use of trans-gender branding has been evident in perfumes for the past 10 years, where CK One led the field of fashion brands to propose dual-use fragrances.

The cognitive age filter

Many brands will wish to target specific age groups and this will require appropriate brand personalities. It is important to be wary of ageist stereotyping of consumers; no target groups, young or old, like being patronized or explicitly denied opportunities. The 'grey' market is currently increasing as the baby boomers of the 1960s retire, making it one of the most financially fruitful. There are many examples of brands that have deliberately tried to filter consumers on the basis of age, only to find that their true consumer is typically from a different age band. The Renault Twingo was targeted at the young, first-car market, but was taken up by buyers in the 'grey' market, who have enjoyed its quirky styling.

Whisky brands like Glenmorangie and Glenfiddich have an inherent age filter in their brand proposition and personality that dissuades younger drinkers. This can be repositioned through a better focus on urban drinking, rather than the reflective and thoughtful, after a hard day on the hills approach. In Asian countries it is drunk heavily in urban bars and night clubs as well as at home.

My First Sony, the sub-brand of Sony consumer electronics, is the quintessential baby brand and it has encouraged many baby brands for clothing, such as Gap Kids. The My First Sony proposition uses sophisticated images to sell to the young themselves and, crucially, to their parents. The products have a youthful design, but the quality is identical to the adult products, unlike goods from most other manufacturers, who had assumed children had lower expectations. There is a fantastic advantage for a brand in capturing the consumer early, promising a lifetime of loyal purchases. By using a high threshold of quality, it also creates a strong barrier to inferior brands because the young user treats the Sony quality as the first standard by which all other products are judged. Conversely, of course, if the brand lets consumers down, they may never try it again. Any brand proposition to the young must be perfect in execution; they are no fools.

Tactical brand mapping

Radial brand mapping

The task of radial mapping can be undertaken in several ways, either with consumer groups, the marketing team, external experts or individually. When using consumer groups it is better to use words or phrases that they themselves generate to express the brand, or confirm the relevance of those chosen. The marketing team can also complete the radial brand map, and like the consumer group they must develop a consensus about the relative strengths of each dimension. If this is unlikely or there are too many strong-minded team members, then the maps can be completed individually, then cross-correlated afterwards. The resulting map is a footprint of the different values and their relevance to the core brand proposition; see Figure 7.1 for an example.

Radial maps help to determine which is the primary cognitive dimension for the brand proposition, and which secondary cognitive dimension(s) are also important.

What is the primary cognitive dimension for branding the internet brand Yahoo!?

* Transport business?
* Content business?
* Entertainment business?
* Knowledge business?
* Technology business?
* Communication business?

Nominal Value Ranking

Brand managers are often faced with a large number of similar brand attributes that need prioritizing. In order to avoid a personal bias or a biased group decision, consensus can be achieved through using a Nominal Value Ranking (NVR) chart (see Table 7.1 for an example). It delivers a quick and simple method of prioritizing the importance of brand values and expresses the level of consensus across the marketing team. This in turn makes visible the fit (or lack of it) of brand dimensions to the brand objective and any disparity can be openly discussed and resolved.

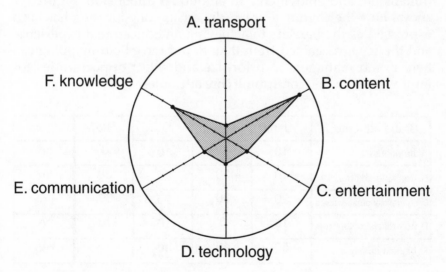

Figure 7.1 Radial map, Yahoo.com

Start by creating a list of possible brand dimensions and alternatives. Try to minimize duplication and ensure that the group has an agreed definition for each dimension. These are listed down the left-hand side of the chart and each member of the marketing team individually ranks the dimensions. This is usually done on a scale of 1–10 (for 10 attributes), where 10 is the most important; or they can be ranked as percentages, dividing the percentages among the number of dimensions available to make up 100 per cent. Each individual score is collated and the totals express the group's consensus on the relative value of each brand dimension. Table 7.1 shows a possible nominal value ranking chart for Heinz baked beans.

Brand force field mapping

Force field mapping helps to establish and visualize the critical barriers and rewards for a brand dimension. They separate the negative restraining forces from the driving reward forces that consumers appreciate and desire from their chosen brands. The negative force barriers are the most interesting as they show areas of weakness in your brand proposition. Force field mapping on competitors' brand values can highlight their weaknesses but also the unique rewards they may be delivering to their customers. The Lego toy brand has two brand dimensions: education, a cognitive dimension, and enjoyment, an emotional dimension. Figure 7.2 shows how the cognitive brand dimension of education has been expressed as the barriers to achieving an educational experience and the rewards gained from that. Brand force field mapping can help brand managers to prioritize and select opportunities for improvement while confirming core attributes.

Brand attribute	Jane	Simon	Lucy	Steve	Total
A. nutritious	10	0	10	0	20
B. fresh ingredients	10	30	20	20	80
C. no artificial preservatives	20	30	30	30	110
D. no artificial colourings	10	0	10	10	30
E. highest quality	50	40	30	40	160

Table 7.1 Nominal Value Ranking (NVR), Heinz baked beans

educational toy

REWARDS	BARRIERS

stimulating ⟶	⟵ little mental effort required
encourages creativity ⟶	⟵ monotonous
releases imagination ⟶	⟵ fixed opportunities
generates experimentation ⟶	⟵ incompatible elements
hand–eye coordination ⟶	⟵ boring
easily renewable ⟶	⟵ single level of end game
complexity matches user pace ⟶	

Figure 7.2 Brand force field, Lego brand, educational toy

Quality Function Deployment

Quality Function Deployment (QFD) is a Japanese system originally designed to check the match between customer needs and product attributes, but it is also effective in defining both primary and secondary cognitive brand values that fulfil consumer needs (see Figure 7.3 for an example). The aim is to articulate consumer needs (both current and latent) and then assess their likely fit with the brand proposition. The QFD session usually takes a couple of hours' preparation, two to three hours with the marketing team and then another couple of hours to analyse the results.

By starting with the consumer, it encourages intense and critical understanding of the cognitive consumer needs and the marketing team can quickly get beyond the current brand slogan and positioning statement. This results in a list of descriptions of consumer needs from a consumer perspective, preferably using the consumers' own language. They can be clustered together to create groups of related needs, and given a weighting depending on their relative importance; this is usually a percentage figure based on market research or experience and consensus. Using a matrix, the list of consumer needs is arranged in a vertical list down the left-hand side.

Once these groupings have been identified, a list of possible brand attributes that might fulfil those needs is generated. Again, clustering these attributes will help to distinguish primary from

Primary brand attribute

Primary consumer need	Secondary consumer need	Secondary brand attribute	stylish	fashionable	sexy	youth	charisma	
				Glamour				
increase status	increase status at work		3	10	10	3	5	
	increase status driving		3	0	0	0	3	

Figure 7.3 Quality Function Deployment (QFD) matrix

secondary brand attributes. These should be succinct but descriptive enough to be precise rather than generic. The word 'glamour' may be strong enough for a primary brand dimension, but it is insufficient for a secondary dimension. The value 'glamour' is sometimes not precise enough; it could be stylish, fashionable, sexy, charismatic or youthful. The more consensus in the team about the exact meaning of a brand attribute, the higher the value of the end result.

The extent of the relevance and strength of the effect of each brand attribute on the consumer need is determined by the team. This can be achieved using a points scale of:

10 points for a strong influence.
5 points for a medium influence.
3 points for a low influence.
0 points for no influence.

The group should try to come to an objective consensus about each consumer need/brand attribute interaction. The completed matrix should clearly highlight the most valued consumer needs and the most likely successful cognitive brand dimensions that will fulfil those needs. It will also express the comparison of the brand with the competition and its relevance and strength to the consumer needs.

Maslow's hierarchy of needs

Abraham Maslow, the behaviourist, developed a useful framework for understanding our needs in terms of cognitive and emotional requirements (see Figure 7.4). Despite the fact that his hierarchy of needs was developed in the 1950s, it is still widely used and recommended by many leading corporations. Its simplicity generates an immediate understanding of the needs of consumers, from the core physiological needs to higher self-actualization needs. It also provides a language with which to discuss those needs and the subtlety of the differences between them.

* The lowest layer contains physiological needs: the need for shelter, sex, food, water, sensory pleasures, etc.
* The second layer contains the safety needs: the need for financial security, family stability, trust and predictability.
* The third layer contains group needs: the need for love, group belonging, family relationships, etc.
* The fourth layer contains esteem needs: the need for achievement, status, respect, etc.
* The final and highest layer contains the self-actualization needs, as Maslow describes them, the need to be who we can be, the need to be as good as we can be.

The first two are generally ascribed as cognitive needs, while the remaining three are largely emotional needs and will be dealt with

Figure 7.4 Maslow's hierarchy of needs

in the next chapter. Maslow has suggested that people tend to fulfil their needs systematically, starting with the basic physiological needs and then progressing up the hierarchy towards self-actualization. This means that brand managers need to be aware of the different stages of development of distinct markets and consumer groups within those markets. They should not treat disparate consumer groups, especially socio-economic groups, as being at the same starting point on the hierarchy or with the same balance of rational and emotional brand dimensions.

Summary

- Cognitive dimensions are the clearly stated rational need of the consumer, and should be used as one of the starting points for the brand.
- Strategic cognitive dimensions in brand management are brand weight, brand breadth, brand length, brand power.
- Tactical cognitive tools are radial brand mapping, nominal value ranking, brand force field mapping, Quality Function Deployment.
- Maslow's hierarchy of needs is a model of human needs, starting with the basic physiological needs, rising up through the need for safety, group belonging and esteem to the final goal of self-actualization.

CHAPTER EIGHT

EMOTIONAL BRAND DIMENSIONS

Defining the emotional benefits of a brand

This chapter examines the possible emotional dimensions of a brand. One can analyse all brands using a matrix of four critical dimensions. The characteristics of these four dimensions are emotion based and therefore difficult to analyse quantitatively. They can, however, be revealed through qualitative research approaches. Also, since they rely on emotional rather than cognitive thinking, they are suitable for new brand development where existing knowledge of identities is naturally limited. This is vital in today's consumer-focused business environment. The four emotional dimensions are ideological pleasure, psychological pleasure, sociological pleasure and cultural pleasure.

Objectives

- ※ Describe the use of pleasure as an index of brand satisfaction for consumers.
- ※ Characterize the emotional dimensions of brand management.
- ※ Illustrate the four emotional dimensions of ideological pleasure, psychological pleasure, sociological pleasure and cultural pleasure.

The pleasure dimension

This pleasure-based approach to emotive satisfiers focuses directly on consumer needs in a way that goes beyond the traditional dimensions of a brand. It also considers the need of consumers to hold different values at different times and in different contexts. The post-modern arguments that consumers are now demanding new forms of self-expression and flexible, fragmented identities can be analysed through an understanding of emotional desires. Pleasure with brands can be defined as 'the emotional, hedonistic and practical benefits associated with brands' (Jordan, 1996; Tiger, 1987). A pleasure-based approach to brand management seeks to maximize these benefits and is an expression of consumer satisfaction with a brand. This is an important and tactical element to consumer loyalty. Because these satisfiers are based on emotional characteristics it is often difficult to define a rational campaign to meet them. It can be a strong defensive position for a brand, if the brand manager understands why it retains that position.

It is important to recognize that brands can also be a potential displeasure or source of dissatisfaction to consumers. Displeasure with brands can be described as 'the emotional, hedonic and practical penalties associated with brands' (Jordan, 1996; Tiger, 1987). Active brand management of these pleasures should avoid generating or communicating displeasure with target audiences. For example, if a brand disappoints consumers (post-purchase dissonance) or they have been outraged by a brand's actions, the emotional underpinning characteristics for such dissonance must be addressed if consumer loyalty is to be retained. Identification of potential brand displeasure characteristics is a useful weapon in the round of competitor analysis of brands. They can be used to successfully differentiate a brand that may be identical in rational performance to a competitor brand.

The four pleasures

The four pleasures or four satisfiers of branding, shown in Figure 8.1, are:

1. Ideological pleasure, belief systems, eg green consumer.
2. Psychological pleasure, task achievement, eg usability.

Figure 8.1 The four pleasures matrix

3. Sociological pleasure, group meanings, eg teams and status.
4. Cultural pleasure, iconic satisfaction, hi–low cultures.

These four pleasures form a framework to understand the characteristics of emotional attraction for consumers. Brand management needs to define the focus of a brand's personality; there may be more than one, but it would be unusual if all four were equally balanced. Like most good marketing practice, it is difficult to sell too many messages to the consumer at any single time.

1. Ideological brand pleasure

Brand ideology works on the highest level of consumers' values. These are the deep-seated beliefs that they may have held for a long time and often relate to their specific context of education, class or race. Subsequently, these are often the most difficult to change, since they require a complete shift in a consumer's position. This can be an advantage to a business and help to build a brand fortress of loyal customers. In the context of brands, ideological pleasure relates to the meaning that a brand, service or product embodies.

Potential ideological pleasures and displeasures:

* Pleasures
  - religion;
  - patriotism;

- morality;
- aesthetics;
- ecology.
* Displeasures
  - immorality;
  - ugliness;
  - racism;
  - fears;
  - negative self-esteem.

Idea in practice, including examples from the car and cosmetics industries

Patriotism

The country of origin of a brand may have deep connotations for the consumer. These can be ideological brand satisfiers when they align with the consumer's ideology. German automobile companies such as Mercedes-Benz, BMW and Volkswagen-Audi have all used their national heritage in their company brand identities. Audi has continued to use its *'Vorsprung durch Technik'* tag line in its television advertising in the United Kingdom. Consumers can recognize supposedly German national characteristics such as precision, quality and reliability, and are then able to transfer these to the car companies' products. This overt connection of national identity characteristics and company identity has often proved successful. National identity characteristics are common, widely held concepts that require little additional marketing explanation. Our impression of a nationality is often gained through our exposure to that country's products and services. This is then reflected in our expectation of other products and people arriving from that country.

The strategy of using national characteristics can support a defensive brand position against competitors from other countries. A country such as Germany that has a reputation for engineering precision, reliability and quality has a much stronger position than a country such as Russia. Automobile manufacturers in Italy enjoy the connotations that their cars will be full of style, energy and flair (common Italian national traits). However, they must also accept that their Italian heritage has a connotation of being temperamental or unreliable. Consumers will decide which of these brand dimensions are more appropriate to their needs and expectations. This means that decisions will often be made based on an impression of a nationality rather than any specific facts about the product or the nationality. National stereotypes are difficult to avoid and are long lasting in the consumer's mind. This reflects the deep-seated nature of ideological pleasures such as patriotism.

Brands need not always come from a specific country to benefit from a connotation associated with that country. The brand name and its visual promotion materials can suggest a particular origin. Häagen-Dazs is a prime example of the use of borrowed heritage. It is a company set up by two American marketers to make luxury ice cream. They chose to use a name and spelling specifically to suggest a Scandinavian or Nordic atmosphere. A common understanding of this type of normative association is that the company would have a great deal of experience and knowledge about freezing processes. This is an implicit characteristic of the brand and therefore needs no further marketing effort.

Ecology
The environment and ecology are contemporary ideological issues that can be used as a significant brand personality trait in certain sectors. Companies can be divided between those with a good environmental policy and those without. Using environmental issues as a core of a brand's personality can attract consumers who have similar beliefs – a large and growing group of consumers. The Body Shop is an excellent example of a brand that has differentiated itself by its environmental stance; it uses a range of specific techniques to express this brand personality. It promotes recycling of containers and it does not test its products on animals. The Body Shop also claims to work with smaller farmers in developing countries to promote a sustainable future. Branding executions are often in natural materials and colours. The perception of the use of simple shaped jars emphasizes utility over hedonism.

Environmental concern can equally be a brand dissatisfier for the target group that wishes to luxuriate. These consumers wish to pamper themselves without a guilty conscience. They can satisfy themselves on a personal basis without the need to balance their desires with conformity. Companies that have a strong environmental stance may be seen as too boring or politically correct for some consumers.

Consumers can negatively associate environmental brands with alternative lifestyle groups that are undesirable. There is resistance to eco brands because they often seem aggressively righteous about their cause in a way that alienates certain consumers. Consumers rarely wish to be lectured to in a moral or ethical tone by companies to which they have paid money.

2. Psychological brand pleasure

Psychological brand pleasure refers to the sense of personal achievement gained from a brand personality. This could relate to the performance image of a brand. It satisfies due to its sense of triumph or victory. Brands that offer a total sense of enjoyment are also psychological brand satisfiers. Certain brands can also offer a sense of mental stimulation through the sophistication of their positioning. Psychological brand displeasure can involve a sense of boredom, failure or defeat. Brands that maximize the use of psychological benefits are more often found in private domains such as personal care or the home environment. Psychological brand pleasure is essentially personal as it fulfils the needs for individualization. Psychological brand pleasure can be changed more easily than ideological beliefs and often changes as the consumer develops knowledge of the category.

Potential psychological pleasures and displeasures:

* Pleasures
    - personal satisfaction;
    - achievement;
    - performance;
    - triumph;
    - mental stimulation.
* Displeasures
    - boredom;
    - failure;
    - lack of enjoyment;
    - low interest;
    - low success.

Idea in practice, including examples from the male grooming and aircleaner industries
Gillette's advertising campaign has always associated itself with ultimate performance. Its headline, 'The best a man can get', is difficult to ignore as it addresses customers on a level of psychological brand pleasure. It calls on customers to decide whether they need or desire the best for themselves and suggests that the only way to

achieve this is with a Gillette. Branding on performance has been a key weapon in many categories, especially when targeting male customers. The use of power, technology and performance all engages with the male psychological need for aggression and competition. Gillette's use of ultimate performance challenges other manufacturers to generate a larger superlative for their own product, although it is possible that consumers will feel 'superlative fatigue' when the performance has been so overstated that they no longer believe or accept the extravagant claims of the brand.

Endorsements

Brands often use forms of endorsement to confirm the authority or performance claims of their brand. This can be extremely effective so long as there is not an 'endorsement war', which will only confuse the consumer. Authority can be claimed through accreditation by a professional, institutional or medical organization. These suggest independent evaluation that can be separated from the manufacturer's own claims of performance. Consumers appreciate this kind of independent advice as a method of distinguishing between brands. These are often graphically presented as approval stamps or signatures of accreditation on the packaging or in promotional material. They may also be presented in advertisements with actual professionals such as a famous lawyer or scientist, or they may simply use connotations of professionality such as actors wearing a white laboratory coat to connote scientific or research knowledge.

In the case of air-cleaner brands in the United States, these forms of endorsement have been a key element for customer approval. Since the category is relatively new, consumers require psychological confirmation of the claims that manufacturers are making. The brand Enviracaire uses an endorsement by the American Heart and Lung Association. The psychological benefit transferred to the product brand by this external and independent assurance has had a strong impact on the success of the brand. Other brands simply offer domestic or appliance knowledge in the air-cleaner category. These organizations require rigorous testing of products that costs time and money before they will take part in any endorsement scheme.

A different route to endorsements is using a tie-in with two companies recognized as experts in their fields. This often occurs between hardware and software manufacturers, as both gain the benefit from cross-exposure and cost saving on marketing. They do not, however, have to worry about cannibalizing each other's market share or dominance in the field. For example, soap powder companies often collaborate with a particular washing machine manufacturer to cross-endorse their products. The psychological benefit gained by the customer that a particular powder was made for a particular machine is more convincing than one that is not. The added suggestion that this has been achieved under scientific conditions is effective.

Total enjoyment and the five senses
Psychological brand pleasure can also be gained by offering the consumer a feeling of total enjoyment. This kind of consumer delight can be achieved by stimulating all of the five senses, and is particularly important in service branding. It is extremely effective in creating a living brand experience that will be remembered by the consumer long after mono-dimensional brands are forgotten.

People have a strong and sensitive fragrance recognition and recall ability that should be maximized in campaigns. Engineers working on Honda cars have invested in a leather smell that reinforces consumer perceptions of quality and a specific 'Honda-ness'. Consumer electronic companies have also started adding subtle fragrances to their plastic mouldings, trying to develop a company-specific brand fragrance that the consumer will recognize and appreciate.

Sound has always been associated with the perception of performance in the car industry. It has been reported that the Mazda MX-5 engineers listened to classic English sports cars before tuning their new engine. Sound, which is created and defined, must be distinguished from noise, which is an unwanted by-product. Schweppes has built its brand personality around the refreshing fizz of opening a bottle of its carbonated drink. It has literally defined itself as the fizz company; all other drinks companies are then usually defined against this in consumer perceptions. A Japanese noodle company ran two advertisements in Osaka to test the impact of sound on the perception of their brand, one of them with the traditional slurping noises associated with eating noodles and one without. The overwhelming consumer response was that the version with sound was more delicious than the silent one.

Visual images are usually the starting point for branding: colour in particular can have an enormous impact on consumer perceptions and gratification. Colour psychology can be effectively used to reinforce brand personality traits; when these match with consumer expectations post-purchase resonance is highest.

Language and text can also play an important role in developing and fulfilling consumer expectations. The tone of the language is as crucial as the message, or, as Marshall McLuhan had it, 'the medium is the message'.

Taste is naturally used mainly in food and drink branding. Developing a distinctive McDonald's essence to all its food and drinks is a priority in markets that have strong competition of virtually identical products. The inconclusiveness of blind taste tests in the cola wars suggests that it is difficult for companies to brand tastes. This may be due to the fact that they are extremely subjective and therefore irrational. There is also very little consumer awareness of a definitive and usable scale to classify different tastes. However, once a consumer finds a brand taste that he or she enjoys, there is a strong likelihood of consumer loyalty.

The physical evidence of a brand can also help define its personality. The weight and thickness of a corporate brochure often suggest quality. Manufacturers often use the sturdiness of a car door as an example of quality and safety. The physical design of a branded product can have a significant impact on consumer perceptions of the contents, performance and reliability of a product and the brand.

3. Sociological brand pleasure

Sociological brand pleasure is derived from the satisfaction that customers get from group association and recognition, as it is part of human nature to form groups and sub-groups. The use of brands has particularly helped groups to define membership and their social territory. Branded clothes are clearly used to include yourself in a specific social group, or they can exclude you from a group. What your clothes say about you has largely been translated into a 'you are what you wear' philosophy; your fellow group members recognize and interact with you on the basis that you have something in common. Wearing visibly branded clothes offers an easily recognizable statement of values that can be read by others. However, sociological brand pleasure often changes, since it is particularly prone to fashion or trends. This type of brand pleasure relies on the recognition and understanding of a group identity, to satisfy the needs for socialization. It is glib to suggest that a simple badge can define our character, but research has suggested that most people do relate in part to such symbolism.

Sociological brand pleasure is particularly important for consumers as an expression of status. The external recognition by our peers that we have attained a certain social position can be easily expressed through sociological benefits. Consumers can communicate real or aspirational identities towards their peer group.

Sociological brand displeasure relates to the exclusion of people from a specific group because of the brand they use or do not use. Brands should therefore be careful to avoid turning customers off their brand. Niche marketing is particularly effective through the use of sociological branding.

Potential sociological pleasures and displeasures:

* Pleasure
  - friendship;
  - group identity forming;
  - aspirational feelings;
  - gregariousness;
  - belonging;
  - love.
* Displeasure
  - loneliness;
  - isolation;
  - distrust;
  - hatred;
  - fear;
  - anonymity.

Idea in practice, including examples from the fashion and car industries

Fashion brands generally rely on group identity characteristics and therefore offer sociological brand pleasure. The Ralph Lauren Polo brand has been particularly successful in defining a specific niche group of customers, offering a brand experience that is casual yet classic. It has developed a total brand experience encompassing product, display, retail, customer service and advertising materials.

The Polo brand draws on themes that have been described as 'country house clout, cottages and castles and *Brideshead Revisited*'. These all suggest a form of brand personality that is retrospective and nostalgic. They also suggest a form of upper-class lifestyle intended to be aspirational. The Polo name and logo suggest a leisure activity of the upper classes, yet it has been presented as available to a wider audience. It is seen as more approachable than the typical Savile Row tailor yet purports to offer similar brand values.

Use of such explicit branding as a logo on the outside of a polo shirt indicates its strong social function in forming brand personality. The brand logo is there to be recognized by fellow consumers or friends. It is a badge of membership to Ralph Lauren's aristocratic club. This form of membership has increasingly been used in the fashion industry to capture and retain target groups. Consumers wearing heavily branded clothes are publicly affirming their commitment to that brand.

Members can easily recognize each other on the street and accept that they are more likely to have similar values than those not wearing the same brand. The sociological value gained from belonging to a chosen group is strong, so branded clothes have become a distinctive device for consumer groups. Equally, the sociological discomfort from being visibly excluded from a group is strong. For example, not having the correct brand of training shoe can be embarrassing for teenagers and adults alike. While this is not necessarily a good thing, evidently it generates a huge aspirational market for such brands.

The danger for sociological pleasure brands is that they may become untrendy. When they are strong, they can enjoy huge sales and success; when they have become old or established, they can easily be overtaken by newer, trendier brands. Many companies in the fashion industry try to avoid this by developing diffusion ranges. This allows the same company to sell almost the same clothes under a different brand that is fresher than the previous one. For example, you can buy blue jeans from Ralph Lauren Polo brand, Chaps brand, Double RL brand and the Polo Jeans co brand. All are parts of the Ralph Lauren company, but offer small distinctive differences in the consumer's perceptions.

The car industry also uses forms of sociological branding to develop distinctive brand personalities. Owning a Mercedes or Porsche, for example, says more about who you are than how you drive. They are classic status symbols that gain most of their value in the public context. The development of the sociological brand pleasure that owners gain is crucial to their success. The car brand Lexus has similar performance, features and qualities to the Mercedes. But it cannot achieve the public or sociological status the Mercedes enjoys. Lexus still positions the brand personality based on the psychological gratification of actual driving and value. This underestimates the need for exclusivity and status as a visible and tangible benefit, as derived by Mercedes owners.

The Skoda brand of car suffered from the sociological brand displeasure associated with its car brand, at least in the United Kingdom. Customers were reluctant to buy and be seen in a car with such a negative social brand personality. However, in a recent J D Power car survey the Skoda has performed brilliantly in cognitive tests. It is a well-built, well-featured and good-value car. But the biggest task for the brand was to develop its sociological personality, not its psychological personality. Only then would customer acceptance be high enough for new customers to try out the Skoda experience and be proud to be seen in its cars.

4. Cultural brand pleasure

Cultural brand pleasure works on the holistic ambience and position of a brand. Brands that maximize the use of cultural value are often the spiritual leaders in a business category; their brand name has become the category name. Examples of these are the Hoover, the Post-it note and Aspirin. These brands have become a verb or a noun in common usage, ie 'to hoover the room', or 'I need an aspirin.' Consumers talk about these brands in place of a specific brand that they actually own or desire. Brands that can achieve this kind of cult status enjoy the rewards of a formidable word-of-mouth marketing campaign.

Potential cultural pleasures and displeasures:

* Pleasure
  - icons;
  - intellectual category leaders;
  - spiritual category leaders;
  - cult identity status.
* Displeasure
  - lack of charisma;
  - followers;
  - spectators;
  - ambiguity.

Idea in practice, including examples from the television and airline industries

Cultural brand pleasure is often highest among the founders of a product or service category. They have often invented the technology or have been crucial in implementing it in a new form in the marketplace. The 3M company, for example, invented and developed the Post-it note. Competitors have since introduced similar versions but everyone still asks for and refers to simply Post-it notes, as a generic term.

Cultural pleasure brands are often the spiritual or intellectual category leaders. For example, Rolex did not invent the wristwatch, but it has become an icon for the ultimate watch. Its use of higher cultural values such as associations with the 007 James Bond identity and the use of space age technology help establish the brand personality.

The Barbour jacket has achieved a high form of cultural brand pleasure in its brand identity. Customers ask for a Barbour weatherproof jacket, even though they may actually buy an alternative brand. In this sense Barbour has become the icon for the category. When consumers do buy the cultural pleasure brand, the depth of loyalty for the brand is likely to be highest.

Brands can also become the intellectual leader of a category by developing the cultural pleasure of their brand identity. To gain cultural leadership brands need to define their position as the most innovative in developing the category as a whole. This requires more than any single product improvement, and can best be achieved over time. The chain of continuous improvement helps establish the brand as the one that has all the ideas. The consumer translates this as a brand interested in the long-term future of him or her as consumer and the category itself.

Tesco has continuously shown the lead in developing the highly competitive supermarket business. It was the early provider of loyalty cards for customers, at a time when most retailers thought they would be just a passing fad. Tesco has built up a strong loyalty system that gathers information and reorganizes product ranges based on that information. It has also introduced clothing ranges to its stores and is in the process of developing in-store takeaway convenience food outlets for pizzas and curries. It is the combination of high-quality service and process of continuous innovation that leads consumers to respect Tesco as the category leader, rather than any specific price or food offers.

The UK football team Manchester United has successfully become a cultural brand personality. The team's football performance is excellent, but it is Manchester United's ability to develop as a brand business that is particularly significant. It was one of the first football clubs to float on the stock market, and has been the most financially successful while many others have failed. Manchester United has a strong merchandising approach that covers a large range of goods. It has decided to take its broadcasting future into its own hands by launching its own TV channel, MUTV, which coincides with the pay-per-view digital era. The TV channel helps build up a total brand experience by matching the games with merchandising interviews and in-depth analysis. It is also the first club to be bought by a media conglomerate. All these firsts help to build the brand personality of Manchester united as one of *the* cultural brands of the past 10 years. Brands that develop the category as Manchester United has will always be seen as strong because they offer cultural pleasure to the consumer through their leadership.

Brands may express cultural displeasure and are more open to risks of customer change than those with a strong cultural dimension. These brands can be seen as followers, as they usually lack ideas or innovation. These brands must concentrate on offering superior prices or service to overcome the glow of the culturally appealing brands. For example, Pepsi Cola has always struggled to compete with Coca-Cola in the soft drinks market, even though in taste tests Pepsi Cola is at least as popular as Coca-Cola. This is because Pepsi Cola lacks the essential cultural pleasure that drinkers perceive when they buy and drink 'the real thing, Coca-Cola'.

This form of intelligent leadership requires an organization to be agile and confident. Brands that are slow or uncertain of their own future are unlikely to offer customers strong cultural value. In today's increasingly competitive global markets that agility is being tested to the limits. Brands that can offer the customer a strong leadership value are more likely to remain competitive.

Emotional brand pleasures and competitive analysis

As we have seen, the four emotional dimensions of a brand can play a significant role in the definition and development of a brand's personality. These offer a method that categorizes a brand based on consumer perceptions, rather than organizational perceptions.

In categories that offer very similar service levels it is often the emotional dimension that clearly differentiates competitors. The airline industry offers the same product but often at different price levels. Virgin Atlantic and United Airlines both offer similarly priced flights to Boston in the United States. On the rational brand dimensions they may score equally well. It is only when we start to analyse their emotional brand dimensions that we begin to clearly understand the differences in brand personalities. Virgin offers a high level of cultural brand pleasure, as it has high levels of continuous innovation in its in-flight service. It offers all economy passengers a seat-back LCD TV with six channels (usually only found in business class), and is the first airline to offer in-flight casinos and gambling. Virgin offers business class passengers a free high-speed motorbike shuttle service into and out of central London. It even serves you icecreams halfway through the movie on long-haul flights to Tokyo. The Virgin brand clearly shows that it can develop what was an identical service into something much more valuable to consumers.

United Airlines relies more on the psychological brand pleasure dimension. Its core values are safety and reliability, and is therefore the airline to fly if you are nervous about flying. In contrast to Virgin Atlantic's rather more entertainment-led approach, United Airlines provides the big-company security that comes from being largely employee owned. It offers a sense of psychological stability that is attractive to certain target groups.

We have seen how each of the four emotional brand pleasures has been used as a core for a brand's personality. They can also be used as a combination of values and dimensions that have different emphases for different target groups and locations. It is rare to find brands that can be successfully strong in all four, but it is not unusual for one or two to be combined.

We have also seen how these four emotional brand dimensions can work as displeasure for a brand. It is important that active brand management minimizes the unattractive dimensions and maximizes the desirable ones. Careful post-launch customer satisfaction testing or continuous qualitative analysis should keep the brand manager informed of shifting customer perceptions (see Chapter 12).

Summary

* Brand pleasure is a core expression of how much people enjoy and are satisfied by a specific brand. Displeasure is their expression of how much dissonance or little enjoyment they have with a specific brand.
* Emotional brand pleasures are intangible and irrational but nevertheless very powerful decision makers in the mind of the consumer.
* Ideological pleasure relates to belief systems like nationalism and the ecology; psychological pleasure relates to the sense of personal task achievement; sociological pleasure relates to group belonging and status; cultural pleasure relates to the iconic satisfaction of consumers.

BRAND EQUITY

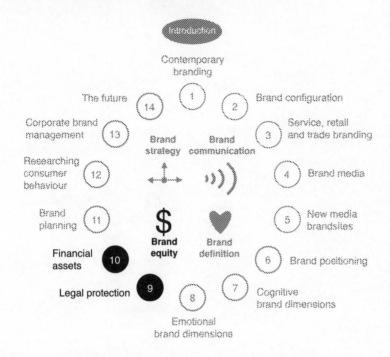

Figure 9.0 Brand equity

The third part of this book introduces the legal definition of a brand. This illustrates the frameworks for the protection of intellectual property and trade marking procedures. The definition supports the financial evaluation of intangible brand value and goodwill from the customer. It includes:

* legal definitions;
* trade marks;
* copyright protection;
* registration process;
* financial evaluation;
* multiple criteria;
* licensing;
* royalty agreements.

CHAPTER NINE

LEGAL PROTECTION

Protecting the brand and its expression

The next two chapters are linked, because they address the need to transform and quantify what is essentially the intangible quality of a brand into a tangible form. This chapter looks at the need to represent the brand as a distinguishable entity that can be protected under the law. Chapter 10 examines the need to represent the brand in the form of a specific financial asset that can be accountable and traded if required. The two are also linked because the qualities used to define the brand as a legal entity can be used to help establish the financial value of the brand.

There is an initial description that looks at the history of trade marks and their transformation from a maker's mark to a brand. This is reflected in the change in the economy from the purchase of a signal to the increasing purchase of a symbol of identity and the creation of goodwill. The methods of creating a distinctive and therefore protectable brand identity will include the trade dress.

The key part of this chapter will explain the legal definitions and basis of inclusions and exclusions from protection by law for trade marks in particular, but also copyright and patents. This will introduce the specific laws that affect the United Kingdom, the European Union and the United States. Since most other countries have a legal system based on similar laws, the information is valuable, and for any specific case I would advise seeking legal representation anyway. This will be followed by an analysis of the act of passing off or creating confusion in the mind of the consumer, and its relevance to own label branding. The issues of copying, counterfeiting and piracy will be explained, particularly with reference to luxury goods and software.

Finally, there is an overview of the application procedure for registering a trade mark in the United States and the United Kingdom.

Objectives

* Describe the key legal definitions relating to brand management (United Kingdom, Europe and United States).
* Characterize the differences between a trade mark, copyright and design patent.
* Illustrate the 'act of passing off' or copying.
* Show how to use the design elements of a brand to increase protection.
* Describe the trade mark application process.

History of the trade mark

To understand the current position of the trade mark and its value to a brand identity we can trace its growing importance in commerce. From the earliest Roman times, makers have marked their goods with a signature mark or brand to distinguish accurately the maker of the goods. This became particularly important when the goods were traded over large distances throughout Europe and the Middle East. It served as a guarantee of ownership in the event of piracy, confirmed that the goods were genuine, and ensured that they were easily identifiable by the largely illiterate population.

During medieval times, another form of brand emerged that reflected the nature of commerce at that time; these were the guild marks. Guilds were associations of craftsmen for a specific type of manufacture, like carpentry, pottery, brass work and silversmithing. Only members of a guild were allowed to practise, and the guild set the standards of quality, price and protocols for the workmanship. This created a monopoly on skills for each type of goods and often in each region, through the easily identifiable guild mark or logo. Although there was a provincial connection between producer and consumer, unlike the Roman example, the guild mark did allow the manipulation of local markets in favour of local goods and against external competition. In both cases the primary task of the brand mark was to maintain and confirm the quality of the goods to the consumer, by directly linking it with a specific, named producer.

It was during the Industrial Revolution that the trade mark became an effective asset of a company. With economic expansion, and the increase in availability of goods, a link between producer and consumer was needed to help consumers to identify products. The reliance on local stores to package and distribute goods was reduced as companies began to make and distribute their products nationally. The need to package individual portions of produce emerged, and its corollary of product identification. The trade mark was a guarantee between the producer and consumer that the goods were genuine and of a specific quality. This invested the brand mark with the quality of goodwill between the then distant producer and consumer.

During this period the value of the trade mark shifted from what Pickering (1998) has described as a signal to a symbol – from a simple message to the consumer from the producer, to a powerful symbol capable of multiple meanings to the consumer. This is important because it marks a change from the expression of the brand residing with the producer, to one where the power of the brand image resides with the consumer. Consumers are the ones that build the brand identity from the mass of communication materials, products, packaging and advertising messages into a single coherent brand personality.

The creation of goodwill

This concept of goodwill emphasizes the pre-purchase value of a trade mark in the mind of consumers, allowing them to ask for a specific product by name. This has now become the basis of brand equity, or the identification of a separate asset value of a trade mark. The character of this goodwill was often embodied in the producer's name, like Kellogg's cornflakes or Waterman's fountain pen. Other trade marks have abstract names, but they have embodied a set of values that the consumer can recognize and use to help choose between a variety of goods. The maintenance of this goodwill is crucial to the long-term goals of a business. This clearly indicates that brand building is a strategic tool for profitability, and investment decisions need to reflect that.

It also highlights the role of brand management in relation to the function of trade marks and other intellectual property rights. The formal trade mark is the protected sign of a brand, and as such the core of an identity or personality. The elements surrounding the trade mark that make visible the expression of that personality are the task of brand management. These often include visual metaphors, advertising campaigns, slogans and other communication devices used to stimulate consumer demand. The brand is therefore the accumulation of all these activities, the product, the packaging and the trade mark.

This change in emphasis from the generic product – often loose, dry goods, for example – to the name or brand of a specific producer's goods created the role of advertising and marketing communications. Not only did the brand mark become a symbol of goodwill, but also it changed what were universal commodities into identifiable products and brands. This is clearly the case today where the proliferation of goods is so great that there are hundreds of functionally identical types, separated only by their brand marks and associated personalities. The computer chip manufacturer Intel has achieved this spectacularly, considering the chips it produces are never seen, look identical to other chips and are not generally understood by consumers. It has changed what was a commodity into a very identifiable brand that consumers will demand is inside their computer. There is rarely a rational basis for this demand, except the power of advertising to identify and persuade consumers that this commodity is important. This in turn forces computer makers to ask for Intel chips in place of other manufacturers' chips, creating for Intel an ideal type of commercial monopoly. It is an excellent example of a company that has maximized its trade mark potential through using advertising and protection. Intel insists on displaying its trade mark on the outside of computers for consumers to see. It has also been careful to protect its trade mark against counterfeiting.

Two functions of a trade mark

There are two clear functions that a trade mark can help achieve: a guarantee of consistency to the consumer, and advertising and informing the consumer of a specific product (Figure 9.1).

The guarantee function is vital as it links the consumer with the producer and acts as a 'brand promise' that the quality of the goods is consistent. This in turn enables the consumer to buy the goods without risk, as the quality is a known quantity. It also encourages

Figure 9.1 Two functions of a trade mark

new customers to try the product, as the quality of the trade mark similarly reduces the risk of the first purchase. Obviously, this is vital in all branding to enable brand switching to take place, and brand owners should maximize this benefit in the eyes of the customer.

The advertising function, in its broadest sense, simply tells customers what the product is and what they can expect in terms of brand experience and quality. The use of a brand personality to express these qualities is crucial to differentiate one brand from a competitor. The informing nature of the trade mark increases consumer awareness of a specific brand, and this evidence helps to protect the brand during any legal proceedings.

Trade dress

A trade mark is expressed through the trade dress elements that build up the total protected trade mark. As we have seen, these can consist of aesthetic elements to represent the name, logos, sounds and even smells; and even the packaging shape. The critical factor in all these elements is that they must be distinctive if they are to be registrable for protection. There is a great synergy of effort here for the brand manager, since the most important expression of the brand is its unique selling proposition. The more distinctive the trade dress, the more successful the brand will be in terms of consumer identification and protection afforded in law.

The key element of trade dress is usually the packaging design, which often incorporates distinctive design elements that have been protected. This brand component is the essential element of differentiation in FMCG branding, so it pays to develop a distinctive pack. The provision in both UK and US law is still that the pack shape cannot be based solely on the function of the goods, which would limit other manufacturers. However, Pickering (1998) suggests that the Toilet Duck pack for disinfectant probably would receive protection, since it is highly distinctive and yet not simply material to the carriage of liquid. Other examples include Coca-Cola's distinctive bottle shape, since it is clearly part of the total trade dress of the brand. Advertising can play an important role in generating consumer awareness and recognition of the trade dress of a brand. Consistency of the brand and trade dress will also help to build recognition and increase the chances of successful protection.

The trade dress of a retailer's brand, like The Gap clothing store, may be the combination of several elements that build up its distinctive identity: the use of steel sheeting in the stores, the typeface and logo of The Gap, the graphic elements of the ticketing and displays and the style of the advertising. The Gap's coherency and distinctiveness are successful elements in identifying its brand proposition and have led to a strong, protected brand.

The distinguishing factor is whether the original brand has secured, through brand building and advertising, associations with a secondary meaning. The *Financial Times* newspaper might be said to have secured the association of a specific pink colour in the public's mind. The Dulux paint dog, an Old English sheepdog, has been used in its advertising for the past 39 years, so this type of dog has a secondary meaning associated only with Dulux paint. The distinctive copper and black stripes around Duracell batteries have been applied consistently, creating a secondary meaning associated only with Duracell. The Direct Line insurance company consistently uses a red telephone on wheels with a jingle tune to advertise its brand, and this would represent its trade dress in the mind of the consumer. The brand manager needs to formulate and maintain the trade dress, if it is to be distinctive in the market and enjoy strong legal protection.

Own-label brands

The trade dress protection issue is a recurrent theme for many leading brands, as new entrants try to emulate their success by following their trade dress as closely as possible. This is a specific issue for own-label goods, where a retailer might introduce a brand to cover a category of a lead brand. In attempting to emulate the success of the lead brand, the retailer might choose a strategy that replicates their brand trade dress, hoping to gain some of the goodwill achieved by the 'A' brand.

Legal definitions

Intellectual property has many rights of protection under the law, and this chapter examines the one most relevant to brand managers, the trade mark laws, although later there will also be a brief look at patents and copyright where these affect brand identity. Historically there has been little clear protection for the trade mark, and it is still the case the onus is on the plaintiff (in this the legal owner) to provide evidence against the defendant (the counterfeiter). CDG Pickering (1998), Paul Carratu (1996) and Schmitt and Simonson (1997) have examined in detail the UK and US trade mark laws; it is worth reading them in more detail. In both countries, it is not actually necessary to register trade marks to be protected under civil or common law. However, this protection is limited, and if the trade mark is registered it can be protected under criminal law, using the police as agents. Furthermore, the clarity that trade mark registration brings to a case makes it far easier to prosecute in either civil or criminal law. Trade marks can refer to products as well as services, and offer equal protection to both. The expression of trade mark registration is also a powerful deterrent for would-be counterfeiters and those attempting passing off actions. Trade mark ownership should be clearly claimed and expressed to competitors by the use of one of the following symbols:

™ Indicates that the work is a trade mark but that it is unregistered.

® Indicates that the work is a trade mark and has been registered.

© 2002 Indicates that the work is copyrighted, and should always be suffixed by the date.

Patented works should be marked either 'patent pending (2002)' or 'patent registered (2002)' depending on the point of product introduction.

Despite recent attempts at harmonization with the Treaty of Madrid, and the Trade Mark Treaty, there is little cross-border protection; it is therefore vital to register trade marks in every country of distribution. This needs to be done by a trade mark professional

who can efficiently search and check databases and advise on any specific legal issues.

Features of European directive and UK trade mark law

In the United Kingdom the Trade Marks Act 1938 provided some protection, but the nature of modern commerce has changed significantly since then. The introduction of the Trade Marks Act 1994 has done much to improve the clarity of the afforded protection, and included several features that recognize the wider notion of what constitutes a brand. It also harmonizes with the first EC Trade Mark Directive (89/104/EEC, OJ [1989] L40/1), bringing UK law further in line with that of the rest of the European Union. The Act applies to 'any sign which is capable of being represented graphically which is capable of distinguishing goods or services of one undertaking from those of another undertaking'. In this case a sign is defined as 'anything which can convey information'. The primary rule of registration is that the sign must be distinctive (this can be tested using consumer awareness research).

Types of registrable marks (Figure 9.2) now include:

* words;
* designs;
* letters;
* numerals;
* shape of goods (3D);
* packaging shapes (3D);
* sounds;
* smells;
* colours (only some colours in specific contexts).

Community trade marks (CTM)

The introduction of the CTM has made it easier to gain protection across the whole of the European Union (EU) through a single application and registration process. This covers the United Kingdom, Austria, Belgium, Denmark, Finland, France, Germany, Greece, the Republic of Ireland, Italy, Luxembourg, the Netherlands, Portugal, Spain and Sweden. The scope of registrable marks is the same as in the

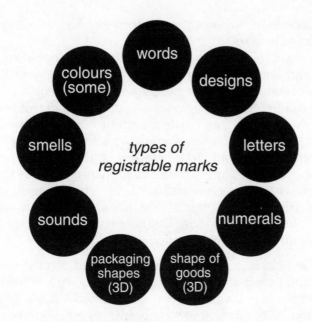

Figure 9.2 Types of registrable marks

previous national registrations covered above. Therefore any current national registrations can be allowed to lapse once a CTM is granted. A CTM protects a mark for a period of 10 years from the date of filing and can be extended every 10 years indefinitely. The grounds for challenging a CTM are the same as for a national registration, generally the lack of distinctive visual elements or its closeness to existing trade marks. Because the CTM covers all countries of the EU it is more likely to be opposed or attacked because of the increased difficulty of creating conflict-free, distinctive marks that do not already exist.

Prohibition of a trade mark registration

The parameters for prohibition include the following:

* The trade mark must not be representative of the relevant trade, process, kind of good or service, geographical or other origin.
* The trade mark shape cannot be that which is based on the nature of the goods or used to achieve the technical production of a product.
* The trade mark may not run contrary to public decency and morality.

* The trade mark must not be deceptive or an infringement of an earlier trade mark.
* Trade mark registration must be for currently commercial activities, and not for future opportunities (this prevents the stockpiling of trade marks as a purely preventive tactic).
* Some colours have been deemed as unacceptable for trade mark registration since they create an unfair monopoly owing to the limited numbers of colours available, although the 1994 Act has allowed some colours to be registered: the green colour of the BP oil company, for example. In the United States the case is similar, where some colours have been refused registration, and a few distinctive colours that have acquired a secondary meaning have obtained registration.
* Time limit of trade mark registration.

Once the application has been completed and accepted, the trade mark is valid indefinitely, provided the necessary fees are paid and it does not become invalid for any other reason. A trade mark can become invalid because of any of the points covered above and in two other important cases. The first is if the trade mark becomes the generic title of a process or category through the actions of the owner rather than simply general usage. The second case for loss of registration is if the product falls into commercial disuse.

Features of US trade mark law

The intent of the US trade mark law, the Lanham Act (1946, revised in 1988) is similar to the laws of other countries, and in 1994 the United States signed the Trade Mark Treaty that is intended to harmonize global trade mark legislation. The following extract from the Lanham Act section 43(a) is from Schmitt and Simonson (1997):

Any person who, or in connection with any goods or services, or any container for goods, uses in commerce any word, term, name, symbol, or device, or any combination thereof, or any false designation of origin, false or misleading description of fact, or false misleading representation of fact, which is likely to cause confusion, cause mistake, or to deceive as to the affiliation, connection, or association of such person with another person, or as to the origin, sponsorship, or approval of his or her goods, services, or commercial activities by another person, or in commercial advertising or promotion, misrepresents the nature, characteristics, qualities, or geographic origin of his or her or another person's goods, services, or commercial activities, shall be liable in civil action by any person who believes that he or she is or is likely to be damaged by such act.

As is the case with UK law, the trade mark remains valid and protected while it is in commercial use. Its basis for protection is the likelihood of confusion in the consumer's mind between one company brand and another company brand. The first element (A) of the sub-section covers protection of the core identity against misleading counter-brand activities. The second element (B) refers to protection against misleading advertising or promotional activities that a second brand might undertake. In the United Kingdom this action is known as 'passing off', and will be examined later in this chapter.

Likelihood of confusion

The principle of the likelihood of confusion in the mind of the consumer is the basis of most court judgements in trade mark cases. This is different from counterfeiting, sometimes called piracy, where there is a deliberate attempt to copy goods as though they were official. Counterfeiting will be dealt with later in this chapter.

Kohli and Thakor (1997) have indicated that the likelihood of confusion can be broken down into the following seven categories:

* the degree of similarity between the marks in appearance and suggestion;
* the similarity of the products;
* the area and manner of use;
* the degree of care likely to be exercised;
* the strength of the plaintiff's remark;
* actual confusion;
* intent of the alleged infringer.

These are guidelines, as each case must be assessed on its own merit in its commercial context. They do suggest several ways in which trade marks can be improved to increase the protection available; the distinctiveness of the trade mark is crucial, especially the name or logo. A trade mark for Sun dishwasher powder is less distinctive than it might be because it might be confused with Sun computers, although in this case the difference of product category is sufficient. In contrast, the washing powder Persil is unlikely to be confused with another product because its trade mark is unique. The choice of brand name is therefore crucial to its ability to be protected in the marketplace, and should not be left as a minor activity.

Monopoly versus free market

The use of a protected trade mark might be seen as a total monopoly in the marketplace. The reality is that it does not give this total monopoly, and courts are aware of the attempts of businesses to use trade marks in such a way. 'The essence of the right deriving from a trade mark registration is that it allows the proprietor to object to certain uses of marks identical or similar to the registered mark; it bears repeating that it does not confer a monopoly in the particular word, device, shape, colour or whatever' (Pickering, 1998). Trade marks do, however, create a monopoly in effect, and constitute a powerful monopoly in the mind of the consumer, which is often equally valuable. They provide sufficient rights for the original business to be able to exploit its investment, without infringing the free market economy ethics of western capitalism. The exception to this case is that both copyright and the patent protection do create a monopoly in trade and law.

Parallel or grey imports

This kind of business activity is increasing as global supply chains become more effective, but it can damage and dilute the brand identity. It refers to the practice of a supplier buying a product more cheaply in another country by exploiting differences in pricing policy, then importing it and reselling it through a discount chain. The Tesco supermarket chain has bought quantities of Calvin Klein jeans and Nike trainers in other, cheaper European countries, imported them into the United Kingdom and sold them in its supermarkets – a 'grey' area of the law. The image of the Calvin Klein brand can be severely damaged if it becomes associated with cutprice outlets. This is the argument used by Calvin Klein and similar companies as the reason they will not supply such supermarkets in the first place: that the whole image of their brand is exclusive and requires exclusive merchandising to maintain its value. A recent court victory for premium brand owners like Calvin Klein and Nike has enforced this view against the supermarkets. This 'grey' import trade highlights the fact that elements of a brand identity are not always owned by the manufacturer, but can be seen to be in the mind of the consumer. This is highly frustrating for exclusive brands that devote their entire marketing effort towards portraying a high-quality image. This situation may change and improve for the brand owners as European prices and currencies harmonize.

Copyright protection

Copyright registration is used to protect works of originality that are embodied in a tangible medium, from unauthorized copying or use. It is typically used for the protection of written work, audio and video works, melodies and arrangements or other compositions. The amount of originality is the determining factor for copyright registration, although in many cases this does not have to be significant. Copyright is best used to protect compositions, which are naturally lengthy pieces, rather than short words or phrases, which are best protected with trade mark registration. As with trade mark protection, the copyright work cannot be a functional item; it must be aesthetic or decorative in nature. In the United Kingdom, copyright protection only lasts for the lifetime of the originator and a subsequent term of 70 years for the originator's estate.

Design patent protection

Patents are another class of intellectual property rights that brand owners may need to protect their ideas or inventions. Brand managers typically use them for the protection of products and sometimes packaging designs. Drawings of the design are referred to as the ornamental design or style of a product, again highlighting the non-functional nature of the aesthetic expression. Like copyright, the patented design must be original and not similar to other designs already on the market. In the United Kingdom the act of registering the design under the 1997 Patents Act creates protection for a period of 20 years only.

The act of passing off

An 'act of passing off' is where brand X tries to confuse the customer into thinking it has similar brand values to, or is made by the same manufacturer as, brand Z; by assuming an almost identical trade dress, as is often the case for own-label goods. Obviously for leading brands this is problematic and they should attempt to enforce trade mark protection vigorously to deal with any infringements. They need to assert that the consumer has been confused, or that the own label or look-alike brand has misrepresented itself as the lead brand. This is usually checked with consumer perception research, to assess the ability of consumers to differentiate between the two brand packs. There have been several cases where the plaintiff has won, but more often than not, since the own label has the retailer's brand mark on the pack, it has been decided that the consumer does not actually believe it to be the same as the lead brand.

A further problem for the lead brand is that the consumer may recognize the two packs as different but assume that the goods inside have been made by the same manufacturer. Consumers may therefore think they are purchasing the same quality for a lower price. This is why some brands like Kellogg's often say in their advertisements, 'We don't make cornflakes for anyone else.'

The core question of passing off is whether another brand is benefiting from the goodwill and associated symbolism of the lead brand. Consumers might assume that brands that show similar aesthetic elements stand for similar brand values, and so undermine the distinctive proposition of a leading brand. Passing off suggests that the two may have similar performance, taste or quality standards to each other.

This is continually irritating for the brand leaders since they may find their own distinctive trade dresses diluted by their becoming the generic typology for their categories of goods. As we have discussed earlier, this is especially prevalent in the use of colours in packaging design, where certain categories have a colour setting. For example, the red colour used by Coca-Cola on its cans has often been replicated by supermarket own-brand label colas. Retailers have suggested that the use of similar trade dress does in fact help consumers to distinguish a specific category among the 20,000 items in the store, while using their own brand mark on the pack ensures that the goods are not mistaken for the leading brand.

The connotations that a specific colour brings to a brand can be used as protection once that connection has been made in the mind of the consumer. Ralph Lauren has attempted to secure the legal right to use images of polo players as part of its trade dress, and prevent the American Polo Club from doing so. The company's argument was that the connotative images in its advertising were more associated in the mind of the consumer with the clothing company than the original American Polo Club. While it is true that the company had invested heavily in connecting its brand to these images, the ruling went against Lauren. Other cases have been won on the basis of this argument. Heinz baked beans relies in part on the turquoise colour of the can, for example, and the colour is so unusual that it is strongly linked to the individual Heinz brand.

Dilution

This type of infringement of trade marks results when a company attempts to draw value from the original brand associations. For example, Pickering (1998) notes the case of McSleep, a new entrant in the hotel market, which could be thought to draw benefit from the McDonald's restaurant chain, thereby diluting over time the distinctiveness of the original brand. However, in a recent case in the United Kingdom, a sandwich bar that used the name McDonald successfully asserted that it was based on the original Scottish name, which is part of general usage and therefore unprotectable.

The strategic value of a brand is based on the maintenance of a strong and distinctive brand personality. This means that any dilution in the trade dress or other elements of the brand personality may not appear significant at the time, but in the long term could reduce a brand to a generic proposition. Any attempt by competitors to dilute the distinctiveness of the brand should be challenged immediately. The power of the monopoly of the mind of the consumer should not be confused or weakened by new entrants into the market.

Counterfeiting

Counterfeiting is the deliberate sale of inferior copies of products and brand marks based on the reputation of the original brand mark owners. This type of activity is clearly criminal, as well as a violation of civil law, and should be prosecuted at once. According to Carratu (1996), the value of worldwide counterfeiting exceeds US $ 50 billion a year: this includes everything from pharmaceuticals to luxury goods, aircraft parts, perfumes, video games and computer software. While counterfeiting has been going on since Roman times, the modern counterfeit operation is highly sophisticated and an efficient business.

The damage caused by counterfeiting is to the reputation or goodwill of the original brand, goodwill that may have been built up over decades with a huge financial investment. The most precious thing that a company owns, the brand, can easily be tarnished by the sale of poor-quality counterfeit goods. In Hong Kong, street traders sell Calvin Klein T-shirts for a fraction of their usual price, and perfume-sellers on Oxford Street in London and watch-sellers on Times Square in New York pursue the same trade. The problem is a global one, and the speed of these operations is the main problem for legitimate brand owners trying to apprehend them. They may have moved on before enough evidence has been collected, or the source of the fakes may not be found, only the street traders.

Typically, brand owners rely on protection through the legal system of trade marks, copyright and patents, but for most counterfeiters the two years it often takes to bring proceedings allows them enough time to make a substantial profit. One of the best ways to use this registered protection is to gain an import ban from Customs and Excise, to stop the goods entering your markets.

In order to benefit from official help, all the trade marks must be up to date and clearly presented to the authorities. This means that brand managers should assign this task to someone specific in the organization; it is not worth leaving to chance, especially as even slight modifications to the trade mark need to be registered to be valid.

Trade mark application procedure

The procedure for registration is different for each country, but the list below provides an outline of the usual process required.

* Selection and definition of the precise trade mark.
* Search of trade mark databases to ensure that the mark is unique and not likely to be rejected. As this may take a long

time, since often many countries are involved, some of which may not have computer databases; it is best left to a specialist agency to complete.

◈ Application for registration.

◈ The application is examined and a report given to the applicant detailing whether the trade mark is sufficiently distinctive or it infringes any earlier trade marks.

◈ The trade mark is published in a journal: the *Trade Marks Journal* (for the United Kingdom) or the *Trade Mark Reporter* (in the United States).

◈ There is a period of three months during which anyone can file an objection.

◈ A registration certificate is issued.

The process may take from between a year and 18 months, depending on the complexity of the case and the clarity of the trade mark.

Summary

◈ The core legal definitions for trade marks focus on the likelihood of confusion between one supplier's goods and another. Therefore in order to be registrable they must be distinctive and original.

◈ A trade mark is an unregistered but defined element or design. Copyright is a dated mark that asserts the individual originality of a work. A design patent is a registered drawing of the visual or technical elements that are original.

◈ The act of passing off is when a supplier tries to sell goods that look remarkably similar to an earlier mark or element.

◈ Trade dress is the total description of the design elements that make up a distinctive mark. These may be words, designs, letters, numerals, the shape of goods (3D), the packaging of goods (3D), sounds, smells and certain colours.

◈ A trade mark can be registered by the following method: the mark is selected and defined, a search is made for current trade marks, application for registration is made, the application is examined by the authority, the trade mark is published, a period of three months must pass in case of objections, and finally a certificate of registration is issued.

CHAPTER TEN

FINANCIAL ASSETS

Valuing the brand as a business asset

The most important value of a brand to a business is the equity it adds to the balance sheet. Businesses like Coca-Cola and Disney rely on the 'brand valuation' factored into their business model to generate increased business performance. Strategic brand management must therefore incorporate financial investment and benefit within the budgeting process. As I have previously demonstrated, the return on investment in branding programmes is convincing.

This chapter examines the need for a financial evaluation of a brand in relation to other company assets. This is an extremely new concept for brand and financial managers and therefore there is little research and good practice on which to draw. There are several concepts and proprietary methods and tools for brand evaluation, but no agreed standard operating procedures. The situation across the globe is even less defined, with different countries attempting to follow local financial practices. However, it is clear that it is increasingly important to be able to separate the financial benefit of a brand from other assets. This has been encouraged by the increase in mergers and acquisitions that accompany the globalization of business activities.

One of the reasons for a lack of accepted rules to generate financial brand equity is that the valuation of intangibles is highly complex. First, the concept of the value of a brand to the company and the customer needs to be clarified. Underlying the value of a brand is a series of core attributes that help to distinguish and protect it from competitors' brands. These concepts ground the various methods used to define a quantitative analysis of brand equities. These fall into several categories that cover accounting practices and economic forecasting, through to complex weighting and structured attribute evaluations. The advantages and disadvantages of each method are analysed to help crystallize best practices. This chapter will also look at the benefits of having a highly valued brand in the marketplace, in terms of brand fortress and merger costs.

Tangible and intangible assets

All companies have a combination of tangible and intangible assets that help to create the brand proposition. Companies in different categories will have a different ratio of value between the value of the intangible and tangible assets that they own. Manufacturing companies like Panasonic, British Steel and Boeing are more likely to have a larger proportion of tangible assets such as factories, machinery, stock of components and finished goods, while FMCG or software companies like Disney, Intel and Gillette are more likely to have a higher proportion of intangible assets such as patents, knowledge and their brand name. However, the way that companies express the value of these two types of assets is different. The tangibles are clearly assessed, depreciated and taxed on the balance sheet. Intangible assets, by their very nature, are difficult or almost impossible to quantify because they represent the potential for earnings in the future. They have often been represented as 'goodwill' on the balance sheet, but there is a growing need to be more accurate, specific and lucid about the value of intangibles, especially brands and brand names.

The need to assess the financial value of brand assets

It is relatively easy to analyse company value by calculating the financial value of the fixed assets that make up most of the constitution of the company, especially manufacturing organizations that until recently dominated western economies. Automobile companies own large factory buildings and the machinery that fills them, and the value of the stock of finished cars is also straightforward to calculate. The price to earnings (p/e) ratio gives an expected range of profit size within a fixed time period. Intangible assets are primarily accounted for in 'goodwill' figures on the corporate balance sheet.

However, in contemporary businesses the balance of tangible and intangible assets owned by a company has altered dramatically. This may be for several reasons including the proliferation of brands and products available to the market, the increased interest in symbolic identities of consumers, the increase in service and virtual businesses, and the increase in wider public shareholder interest in company management.

Proliferation of brands and products

As communication across the world gets easier, the opportunity for export increases and the volume of goods available to the consumer explodes. This means that the total product environment becomes more competitive so companies have to find new ways to differentiate their product offer. Branding has become the critical tool to express that differentiation to the consumer in a convenient and seductive way. The role of brand as navigator helps consumers to find their way through the multiplying propositions. In this case the brand reduces customer time and effort needed to search for goods on the shelf, or it reinforces the choice the customer makes through guaranteeing the quality level.

Increased interest in symbolic identities of consumers

Consumers have become more self-possessed, in the sense that they feel that they have greater control over the management and presentation of their identity. Whether this is actually true is debatable, but the perception for the consumer is great enough that they make purchase decisions based on these feelings. They have come to rely more on visible brand personalities to make choices than underlying physical attributes. For example, consumers can buy good-quality jeans from The Gap or Levi's at a reasonable price. But some of them will pay two to three times that price to buy Armani jeans, which are physically indistinguishable except for the brand mark.

Increase in service and virtual businesses

Virtual businesses or services naturally rely more on the symbolic elements of their branding to convey personality than any physical elements. The only way people can get a sense of the value of the company is on the balance sheet, which must counteract the sense of immateriality.

Increase of wider public shareholder interest in company management

Wider public shareholding has encouraged businesses to account for the value of their business in ways that express their earning potential. For a company like Nestlé Rowntree, the value of its brand portfolio is far in excess of the tangible assets; if these were not expressed, the company would be undervalued.

Acquisition costs

Many companies are going through cycles of merger and/or acquisition to build up strong, globally competitive businesses. They need to know the correct price of another company, especially if their assets are principally intangible. The selling business needs to avoid undervaluing the brand and the buying business needs to avoid overvaluing the price. The total price must therefore include the tangible and intangible values calculated by an ascertainable method.

For all the above reasons, it has become imperative that businesses clearly express the financial value of the ownership of their brands. The relationship of brand asset values to tangible asset values is an important criterion for purchasing or selling brands, or for making investment decisions. For example, Tomkins (2000) estimates that the value of the Coca-Cola brand, as calculated by Interbrand, was 60 per cent of the market value of the whole company. This means that the brand and brand name were worth more than the manufacturing operation, the bottling plants, offices and the distribution networks together. The brand is the key asset for this company and as such should be managed from this perspective.

What is the value of a brand?

The value of a brand can be different depending on whether a company is buying or selling, and whether its value is included on a company balance sheet or used as a decision-making tool for future investment. If we start with the assumption that a brand is an asset, something that will generate future profits, then we must look at the context of the business and the market. A company that has excellent distribution resources may be better able to maximize this profit than one without. The value of that brand to the first company is therefore higher, and this would be reflected in the price that it might pay to buy that brand.

Accountancy methods

Currently, all accounting methods suffer from a lack of global coherence in practice and in law, with wide variations on taxation and exemption clauses. Specifically, attempts to treat brand-building activities as an investment instead of an expense would forfeit tax relief in most countries. The wide differences of approach are unlikely to be remedied in the near future.

In accountancy terms the value of an intangible asset is referred to as 'goodwill' on a company or consolidated balance sheet. Millichamp (1997) points out that in the United Kingdom, 'SSAP-22 – accounting for goodwill' outlines the premise of this financial accounting protocol. The core element of this is: goodwill explicitly bought (in this case in the form of a brand) cannot be a permanent article on a balance sheet. Usually, goodwill should be written off from the balance sheet immediately on acquisition. This is problematic for companies, because immediately after an acquisition there is a net reduction in assets due to the written off intangible brand asset.

Cost-based brand valuation

A cost-based analysis could try to determine what the cost of creating and developing a successful brand has been. This is problematic for several reasons and highlights the separation quandary that accompanies all intangible property issues. It is virtually impossible to separate a specific amount of capital from integrated business processes, especially from other intangibles like quality of personnel, patents and other internal knowledge or experience. For example, a computer software brand like Microsoft cannot easily place a value on the creativity of a programmer or value of a patent, or the cleverness of the marketing director or the experience of the logistics manager. The very intangible nature of these skills makes them difficult to quantify; the same is true of the value of a brand to a customer, a trade partner or the bank.

It is likely that any analysis will centre on explicit costs, rather than those that are integral to business development. These would include external marketing costs like advertising, direct marketing and promotional materials such as packaging or service provision. But this would place a higher value on those brands that uniformly use these types of marketing, especially those with heavy TV advertising budgets. Since there is no correlation between the value of a brand and the amount it has spent on advertising, this would be an unreliable result. After all, many brands have spent millions on promotional activities and yet their brands remain low in terms of value or, even worse, have failed completely. The case of the introduction of New Coca-Cola showed that even top brands can get it wrong. Despite its expensive R&D programme, television campaigns and in-store promotions, the value to the customer, and so ultimately to the company, remained so low that it had to reintroduce Coke-Classic.

Cost-based analysis is, as its name suggests, focused on costs, rather than value; it looks backwards rather than forwards. Another problem with cost-based analysis is that for older brands this approach would be impossible, as many of our favourite brands have been built up over decades. What period of investment would be appropriate? How would we determine the weighting of different investments in marketing, R&D and production?

An analogy with insurance policies is that goods will be replaced on a new for old basis, suggesting a replacement cost for a brand. But brands are unique assets by their very nature, with a unique relationship with the consumer. If it were easy to formularize the success of Kellogg's, Nokia and Amazon.com then we would all be doing it by now. The reality is that their success is unique, achieved under a unique set of contexts and influences, with a unique group of employees at a specific time in history. The high risk associated with new product development – only one in 25 launches is a success – means that many companies would still prefer to purchase a brand with a known value. We may be able to learn from their success, but we cannot ever hope to truly repeat it. These points all leave the concept of cost-based analysis as too historic, too subjective and lacking any reliability to be a useful tool.

Market-based brand valuation

Following the logic of capitalism, an alternative would be to let the market decide what the value of a brand is. As Kapferer (1998) points out, the housing market works on this basis because there are sufficient reference houses available for sale to ensure a fair assessment of a specific property. As this is not yet the case with brands, then any form of comparison is unavailable. I would argue that while this is true now, there might be a time when there are sufficient examples available to start a comparison. The map of market-led brand valuations is being drawn as each brand merger or acquisition takes place. The past 10 years has seen the beginning of brand-based financial assessment; the next 10 will see those tools used more frequently as globalization continues. The use of typologies and groupings will form the signposts to more detailed market-based value assessments. However, for the present there is still a paucity of reference points to act as guidance.

Market-based analysis does not take into account the different value placed by different buyers on a brand. When Nick Leeson bankrupted London's oldest bank, Barings, the ING bank of the Netherlands bought it for just £1. Of course it bought the associated debt as well, but the market price of a single pound does not seem to reflect the brand value to the customers of the Barings brand. Alternatively, the purchase of the Automobile Association (AA) for £1.1 billion in 1999 reflects not just any value of the brand, but the value specifically to Centrica, which also owns British Gas and Goldfish. The expected synergy between two national service operations that run fleets of vans and large call centres is likely to be high. Centrica clearly wishes to diversify in the UK market through the acquisition of strong brands rather than creating new ones.

Income-based brand valuation

The question of separation still needs to be addressed in these cases, especially when a company like Unilever has many significant brand names, patents and expertise. The price premium placed on buying brand names is one of the core defining financial attributes, even though the brand name is still not the total picture of what makes a brand successful. What would our lives be without brand names to help us navigate? Buying a Mercedes car means very little without the Mercedes name and badge; using a FedEx service that is not FedEx has a different risk level. As we have seen, the cost of replacing the position in our hearts and minds is impossible to calculate and is anyway almost certainly impossible to achieve.

The price that the customer is willing to pay above the generic product price in the market can be seen as the premium associated with the brand. This can often be ascertained through standard market research techniques or through the mechanism of the market itself. They both give a bandwidth of likely price points, usually in a comparative sense rather than an absolute price.

Many market research firms use blind (without visible brand names) hall testing of products and ask what kind of price customers would expect to pay for similarly specified products that have different appearances. The answers often reveal a hierarchy of opinions on which are the most valuable and which are the least valuable. However, when the brand names for different models are revealed, respondents often change their minds, placing a higher value on some models because of the association of the brand name. These kinds of results can also be revealed in conjoint research that is more appropriate for services and intangible products such as mortgages and pensions. Customers make preferential choices based on the combination of factors that include the brand name, clearly suggesting the potential and numerical value of the brand name. All of these research techniques are discussed in Chapter 13.

As Aaker (1991) points out, the value of a brand name is also a measure of loyalty or preference for a specific product over the generic rival. This can be obtained by the blind testing or conjoint analysis method, with the brand value represented by the difference between preference ratings for the unnamed and the revealed brand scores. For example, the approval rating for Pepsi Cola in blind taste tests is higher than for Coca-Cola. However, when the two brands are revealed, the approval for Coca-Cola is higher than that of Pepsi; the change expresses the value of the brand Coca-Cola. If this loyalty dimension is researched regularly over time it can form the basis of a measure of market share distribution. Although this is a current valuation, rather than a prediction of future income, it does nevertheless provide a structured method that is repeatable and the results are reasonably valid. This method can be augmented with probing into an intention to buy, although the results become less reliable.

Licensing and franchising

Companies may wish to sub-contract the manufacture of their goods to another company in the form of a licence agreement or franchise. This may be to develop products that they have little expertise in, or to allow them to enter new markets with less investment costs. The licensee usually pays a fee for the privilege of using an intellectual property right, in this case usually a brand name or trade mark. Many of the fashion houses like Calvin Klein and Giorgio Armani operate licences for the production of sunglasses and bags, items for which they have little in-house expertise. A franchisee makes a similar payment, but is clearly contracted to operate the franchise along rules set out by the franchiser; McDonald's is a famous franchise operation.

The financial benefit to the brand name owner is created through a system of payments not dissimilar to royalties. Anecdotal evidence suggests there is no such thing as a standard royalty agreement. They range from a large initial payment, like those used to sell TV rights, through a balance of initial payment and regular instalments like a Benetton franchise, to serial payments throughout a specific period like the manufacture of many Disney goods. In each case it is important to be able to place a specific financial value on the brand equity that can be paid to the holding company. The recent purchase of CNA by Allstate Insurance in the United States included part payment for the brand equity in this kind of structure. As reported by Joliffe (1999) in the *Financial Times,* 'Allstate will pay CNA $140m in cash and use $950m of its capital to support the premium.' In addition, 'Allstate will pay a marketing royalty worth $109m to CNA for the use of its brand name for the coming six years.' Partial selling of a brand name through licensing is a double-edged sword: it is a benefit because it adds visible profit to the balance sheet but it also involves brand extensions from an external company which need to be carefully monitored.

For the brand name holder, the ability to market a successful brand proposition across a wider range of goods is seductive. The Disney brand has achieved an extremely high brand length, an ability to reach across business categories with the same basic proposition. In Disney's case this is usually achieved by character merchandising, a type of sub-branding based on invented characters (usually cartoon). Disney sells movies (*Pocahontas, Beauty and the Beast*), holidays at theme parks (Disney world), a huge range of clothes, toys, food, books, CDs, jewellery and watches of all their characters. Every one of those licensed products makes a payment to the Disney Corporation for the use of its brand name equity.

For a technology licensor it may be more worthwhile to sell a licence for a brand rather than a patent. The patent will have a fixed lifespan and then it may be superseded by a newer technology. The brand has the potential for a much longer life in the mind of the consumer, and the underlying product can be updated and innovated successfully. The artificial sweetener Nutrasweet has managed to achieve this type of brand licence. It has converted what was a patented technical solution to the problem of fake sugar into a brand name that consumers demand. Its use of co-branding beside the manufacturer's brand, for example with Canderel, has stimulated a market pull for the licence and made Nutrasweet a more valuable brand asset.

Royalty rates

In order for a licence system to work, there must be some method for the separable value of the licensed brand to be established and paid. This is generally a royalty payment scheme that considers the property value of the brand as a leased item for a defined term. The actual amounts paid in royalties are closely guarded secrets, although Murphy (1991) suggests these fall between 5 and 16 per cent. The method used to assess the value of the brand is habitually derived from a free market pitch approach rather than a series of standardized agreements. This suits both the buyer and the seller, since they are free to negotiate the price, on the basis of the value to them, at that specific time. If there are a large number of bidders, then sealed bids may be taken and the licence awarded at the discretion of the seller. The opportunity for under- or over-valuing a brand licence is significantly increased through this method.

Multiple criteria methods

As an asset, a brand is a symbol of the expected future profits of a company; the problem is how to determine the earning power of a brand. For the stock market the p/e ratio is a multiple of expected earnings; it reflects the relationship between the capitalization of the business (price) and the profit (earnings). The higher the p/e value, the more profit is predicted by institutions and investors; although some would argue that this suggests the share price is expensive (*Guardian*, 17 July 1999). Different categories and industries have their own bandwidth of expected p/e ratios; UK banks' current p/e values range between 20 and 25 and UK water utilities' range between 8 and 12.

To develop a multiple of a brand's strength, there needs to be an assessment of a range of factors that are averaged over time to avoid any remarkable events in a previous year. The question is, which of the many possible factors and over what length of time should the brand be assessed? Interbrand has led the way in defining an appropriate method for brand strength assessment and publishes a yearly chart of the top performers. While this is one of the most reliable approaches, there are still large gaps in knowledge and assessment. As Tomkins (2000) reports, private company brands like Lego and Levi's do not publish financial data and so are absent; many media conglomerates are missing because of the inseparability problem, and most of those present are US brands, which slants the results table considerably. Despite all these problems, the Interbrand method is becoming a reliable and respected tool for the financial evaluation of brands and has been used to assess over 2000 brands around the world.

Kapferer (1998) outlines the Interbrand method in four key stages, based on the assumption that the brand is an intangible asset but generates a separable set of earnings year on year:

1. It establishes the net profit earnings for the brand:
   - Interbrand uses only publicly available data to establish the likely profit margin from the last three years;

- it uses a notional 2% growth rate per year;
- it deducts a capital charge at 8% return on the employed capital;
- it uses a notional 35% tax charge on the brand profit.
2. It establishes the added value of the brand on those calculated earnings by:
   - analysing the brand strength across seven criteria;
   - the criteria are weighted to give a maximum score of 100:

   leadership   25
   stability   15
   market   10
   internationality   25
   trend   10
   support   10
   protection   5
   brand strength   100
   (source: Penrose quoted in Kapferer, 1998)
3. It produces a multiple that closely matches the multiple used in previous merger and acquisitions of similar companies in the sector. The multiple relates to its S curve model of brand behaviour and indicates the amount of risk associated with a brand (see Figure 10.1).
4. Calculates the brand value. This is achieved by multiplying the net brand profit and the multiple together.

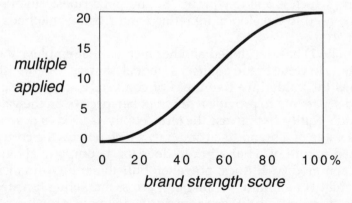

Figure 10.1 S-curve model of brand strength vs multiple applied (Source: de Chernatony and McDonald, 1998)

This system produced the following table of results for the top ten valued brands in 1999:

Brand	Value (£ bn)
Coca-Cola	47.99
Marlboro	47.64
IBM	23.70
McDonald's	19.94
Disney	17.07
Sony	14.46
Kodak	14.44
Intel	13.27
Gillette	11.99
Budweiser	11.99

(source: *Financial Times*, 1999)

The veracity of the input of any calculation is always reflected in the reliability of the output. While Interbrand's methods are good, they still depend on a large number of subjective choices and viewpoints. This means that any internal attempts at defining these values are likely to prove too biased with a high degree of error. The use of an independent source will provide reasonable objectivity and, perhaps more importantly, the perception of objectivity among third parties.

There have been critics of the Interbrand method. One criticism highlights the lack of specificity with which it treats different types of brands. For example, it treats Gillette as a single entity, even though it has many sub-brands and extensions, and treats Marlboro, which is a single brand, by the same rules. This reinforces the need to develop more refined and rigorous methods of brand analysis.

Aaker (1991) has developed another method that employs multiple criteria to value brand equity. His model, shown in Figure 10.2, structures the value into five areas of concern. Each of these is analysed separately to provide a different perspective on the value of a brand's equity. In this case the term 'equity' is used to describe the total value of a brand to a company, which reflects the correct, integrated nature of what a brand does for a company above a generic commodity. It does, however, blur the annual financial accountability of a brand, by linking it across marketing functions and long-term growth. It also remains as the present value of a brand, rather than projecting the future revenue potential of a brand, information that would be necessary in an acquisition.

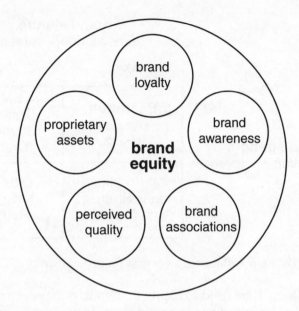

Figure 10.2 Aaker's (1991) model of brand equity

Young & Rubicam have also developed a multiple-criteria method to assess brand equity growth. This involves analysing four criteria:

1. brand differentiation;
2. brand relevancy;
3. brand esteem;
4. brand familiarity.

Differentiation + Relevance = Vitality (potential for growth)

Esteem + Familiarity = Strength (present size)

An example of their use is shown in Figure 10.3. They are all suitable criteria for evaluating brands, although unsurprising in their range and still generally subjective. Brand differentiation is the power of a brand to express its uniqueness and reach top-of-the-mind status with the customer. This is the core of a successful brand proposition with a distinctive position in the marketplace that will promote long-term growth. Once customers are aware of the brand, it needs to be relevant to their needs, satisfying and exceeding their expectations. The way that the brand manager is able to express that relevancy in a language that the customer appreciates will determine its success. Once customers understand what the brand

brand stature
(knowledge + esteem)

		low	high
	high	Budweiser The Gap Heinz	BMW Guinness Starbucks Orange
brand strength (differentiation + relevance)	low	Kodak Levi-Strauss Xerox	Hewlett-Packard Kellogg's Reuters

Figure 10.3 Young & Rubicam power grid (Source: Murphy, 1991)

can do for them, they need to aspire to own it, or have esteem for it. Finally, when the brand has communicated its unique, relevant and aspirational message, it will be able to achieve familiarity through repurchase and re-use. The assessment by Young & Rubicam suggests that the scores relating to brand differentiation and brand relevance indicate the potential for growth, while those relating to brand esteem and brand familiarity indicate its present strength. This is a good attempt to overcome the issue of brand equity because it looks at the present and potential earning power of a brand. It does, however, still rely on subjective analysis of those four criteria in relation to the market, the customer and the company; although again there are market research techniques that can help to overcome some of these. Clearly, the accuracy of the final valuation, whatever the method used, is paramount, but it should always be accepted with a tolerance margin.

The financial assessment of a brand's value is best used as a tool to help maximize the long-term potential of a business. It should not be used to achieve short-term goals that are often detrimental to the long-term health of the brand. Licensing too many poor-quality products that do not reinforce the brand, like Pierre Cardin did in the 1980s, is a clear example of what happens when brands try to milk their brand equity. Any brand extension, brand merger or brand acquisition needs to build the aura of the personality, adding to its richness if it is to be successful in the long term. With this goal in mind, many people inside and outside the organization can use a financial brand valuation:

- CEOs can use it to make strategic purchase and selling decisions for long-term growth.
- Financial directors can use it to make effective licensing and franchising agreements and represent the true value of a business on the balance sheet.
- Marketing directors can use it to make strategic investment choices regarding brand and sub-brand introductions.
- Financial analysts can use it to assess the likely performance of a business and advise institutions.
- Stakeholders and shareholders can use it to make investment portfolio decisions.

The variety of methods explained clearly emphasizes that there is a long way to go before we see a single approach to the problem of quantifying a brand's value. There are some that are more successful than others and some will be more appropriate for a particular business category. There is room for adaptation and refinement of several of these tools, which together with an increasing database of valuation examples to draw on should provide a sound basis for calculations. But the critical characteristic remains: to match the needs of the buyer with that of the seller under the context of the sale, whatever the appropriate financial tool may be.

Summary

- As the economy becomes increasingly driven by the circulation of intangible brands and services, there is a need to express these as a tangible financial amount.
- The main methods of assessment are cost-based, market-based and income-based, although all three have their weaknesses as a methodology.
- Licensing income can provide a method of evaluating the performance of a brand.
- Multiple criteria methods currently offer the most accurate method for brand valuation.
- The stronger performance of heavily branded businesses compared with competitors' businesses reinforces the need to invest in strategic branding. The return on this investment is striking.

BRAND STRATEGY

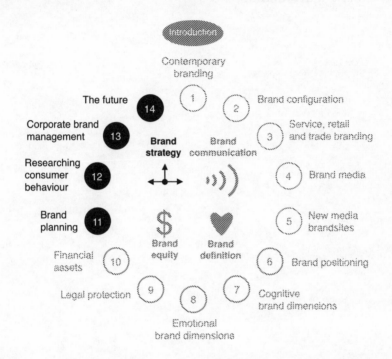

Figure 11.0 Brand strategy

The final part of this book demonstrates how to assess, manage and develop the value of a brand. It takes a strategic view of brand management and illustrates the techniques necessary to motivate the entire business to deliver the brand message. It includes:

* brand planning;
* brand strategy;
* brand management;
* brand portfolio management;
* brand extension management;
* consumer segmentation research;
* strategic and tactical research methods;
* the CEO as brand manager;
* internal employee brand motivation;

* internal communication programmes;
* new rules of branding for the new economy;
* clicks-to-bricks new business model;
* experiential branding.

CHAPTER ELEVEN

BRAND PLANNING

Strategies for brand revitalization, brand extension and new brand creation

Brand planning is a strategic role in a business, responsible for the holistic creation and development of the brand. It is also a methodology for brand creation and development, generating strategic concepts and choices that enable brands to grow and become profitable. This chapter looks at several different successful branding strategies, exposing their strengths and weaknesses. They confirm that brand management is a long-term strategic tool for profitability, business strength and power in the market. The range of strategies is not exhaustive, but should be sufficient for most brand categories and situations, from new start-ups to large corporations, from service led to product led businesses.

Portfolio management is one of the most critical elements of any strategic review of a business and this chapter deals with all variations of portfolio management. It also explains an approach to developing a new brand, and the brand planning that needs to be done to ensure success in the market. The redefinition of a brand requires tools of change management, helping to restructure a proposition and identity. This process is also effective during merger and acquisition activities where two brand identities need to be resolved into one strong future brand that maximizes the equity in both.

Strategy and tactics

There is a significant difference between a brand strategy and the tactics developed to deliver that strategy, but marketing depart-

---

Objectives

- Explain the differences between a strategy and the tactics to realize that strategy.
- Demonstrate how to assess all elements of the marketing environment.
- Compare many diverse strategies and their appropriateness, including those for portfolio management and brand extensions.
- Describe the steps for new brand creation.

---

ments often confuse them. A strategy is a long-term approach to the development of a brand and requires strength of leadership and insight to recognize small competitive issues and not be deflected by them. The Nike brand has a strong DNA and yet is losing sales; it has become too successful and is no longer unique enough for some consumers. Celia Lury, who has researched the Nike brand, confirms this strategic issue: 'It's no longer exclusive, Nike is everywhere. The question it needs to confront is: what can it do to differentiate its brand?' Nike's strategy has been so successful in the past five years that it has lost its place as the urban avant-garde brand and is perceived as a multinational corporation. The strategy for the brand has been successful, but it has created an unsustainable business model that needs to be rethought. It needs a different strategy and tactics for the next five years to recapture its core territory. The brand that is constantly ruled by these minor squalls of the business world will not retain the integrity that customers expect. This is not to say that the brand should not evolve over time, but these shifts should be expressed through changing personalities rather than altering the successful underlying proposition. If the underlying proposition has not been successful, then clearly a substantial and sustained change of direction is necessary.

A tactic is a short-term tool to create an effect on the competition, the market or other stakeholders. The strategy should always be proactive and never reactive. It's a bit like accepting loss of a battle in order to win the war, or in a game of chess where sacrificing a knight brings the reward of checkmate. This tactical approach is not always necessary but brand managers should not shy away from it either. Jane Merriman, New Brand Development Manager, William Grant & Sons, suggests, 'Baileys was always drunk on its own, then a tactical advertising campaign and the sponsorship of a big ice dancing event launched Baileys over ice, which encouraged people to extend the usage; and the drinking moment.'

Brand planning

Building and sustaining a brand requires a strong understanding of what differentiates it from other brands in the mind of the consumer. Jane Merriman explains:

Branding is important because it is more and more difficult to build a business; the successful key to this is differentiation. If you are not going to be a tertiary brand then you need to build some values into your brand that make it a premium profitable brand.

Brand planning is the process of defining what the core differentiators are for a brand and the competitive environment. The following broad approach to brand planning has been developed by David Cox, co-founder of Cobalt. This has been complemented by a range of brand strategies that cover both strategic business and marketing needs. It uses the analogy of a journey to cover four distinct elements of a brand-planning programme. These are: the research and analysis of the map, the definition of the DNA, the choice of tools from the toolbox, and the verification and the sustainability of the ecology of the brand.

The map

This phase is concerned with assimilating and understanding the context of the current brand proposition and describing the location or target for the desired brand proposition. It should also describe the terrain that needs to be covered in order to move from the present position to the target position. This involves an analysis of the current context of the brand based on the four elements shown in Figure 11.1. This activity may involve the use of external focus groups, management interviews, desk research, and a review of the current published market research data; all of these are covered in Chapter 12.

The results of this analysis can be mapped out along a matrix to define a footprint of the current status of the opportunities and

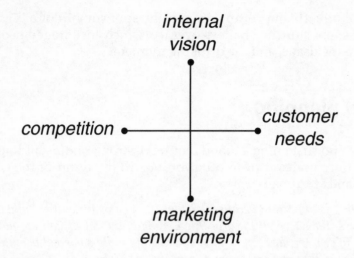

internal
vision

competition • — customer
needs

marketing
environment

Figure 11.1 Four core contextual elements for brand planning

hazards for a brand. This type of exercise is best completed within a marketing group rather than individually. A consensus of the strength of each element is reached and marked out on the chart. These are then joined to create a distinctive footprint. This type of mapping should be repeated at regular intervals (quarterly or yearly, depending on the category), building up a pattern of the shifting strengths of individual elements. This provides the brand manager with a powerful tool to anticipate what the next phase of those movements will be and he or she can therefore prepare for and pre-empt them.

The key words that characterize the issues pertinent to that brand should be added next to each axis of the footprint. These should focus only on the few critical factors that differentiate the brand from the competition. A footprint map can also be developed for each competitor's brand and again, tracked over time, this will provide a unique insight into their strategies. It should tell the brand manager which of the brands are fading and which are strengthening, allowing an efficient distribution of resources. A footprint can be developed to express the desired target positioning, along with the incremental steps necessary to reach this. This helps to identify which dimensions need to be addressed in what order and gives some indication of the obstacles that need to be overcome in order to reach the desired positioning. This should in turn identify the level of resources required to overcome those obstacles and achieve this goal.

Customer needs

Customers' needs should be analysed to ascertain whether the current brand proposition is still fulfilling the target customers' articulated and latent needs. If this is not the case, then this may suggest that either the proposition is no longer viable to that target group, or the target group needs to be changed. The Mitsubishi car company has spent several years in the 1990s repositioning its brand to appeal to a younger audience. In 1996 the average age of Mitsubishi owners was around 50; the current average age is around 35. This has been a strategic move for the company and requires a strong vision and investment over a sustained period. Customer needs should be mapped out along a matrix of customers' understanding and knowledge of what they require or desire and the power or ability they have to achieve this through purchasing (see Figure 11.2). Clearly, the area for most opportunities in the future lies in the experiential brand dimension, which engages the customer in a multisensorial immersive experience. The rational dimension offers implicit fulfilment, while the emotional dimension satisfies through explicit fulfilment. The ethical dimension is important as a niche trend, but is unlikely to develop into a mass-market dimension.

Rational brands

Rational brands fulfil consumers' need to organize their lives through a reasoned approach, and include brands such as Pizza

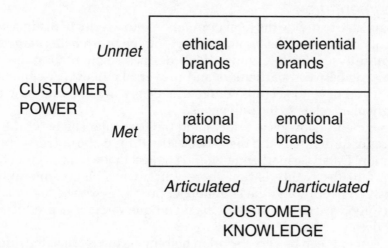

Figure 11.2 Brand power knowledge matrix

Express (fast service is paramount), Wal-Mart (value proposition) and Nissan (feature driven proposition). Chapter 7 describes these in more detail.

Ethical brands
Ethical brands are some of the newest brands, which attempt to address the growing concern over the environment, or child labour sweat shop conditions; they include The Body Shop; the Co-op, with its ethical investor policy; and Planet Organic, which caters to health food customers.

Emotional brands
Emotional brands are a broad range of brands that satisfy the psychological and sociological needs of customers for self-identity or status and group membership identities. Mercedes cars deliver on both these dimensions, as do Häagen-Dazs and Nike. Chapter 8 describes these in more detail.

Experiential brands
Experiential brands are the future power brands, delivering immersive brand experiences that engage and delight the customer. They will deliver a combination of entertainment, education and fantasy in a choreographed environment, product or service. The few businesses that have begun to deliver experiential branding in their retail sites are the Disney Store, Watch 2 Watch and Nike Town.

Segmentation
Being able to divide the total population into a series of distinct segments means that the brand message can be much better targeted. Woudhuysen (in interview; 1999) defines segmentation as 'the dialectic between particulars and universals. In every segmentation, you have to keep the universals firmly in mind and how the particulars relate to the universals.'

Segments allow us to understand the particular shades of differences of individuals and their social structures in the universal population. Database marketing would suggest that we can segment by one, but the reality is that there will always be commonalities between people, and the commercial processes we use are not yet very good at creating individual and unique versions of products or services.

Segments can be very useful in helping us to visualize the differences between customers and match them with different products, which should try to use the language of the segment rather than be universal and complete. It should represent a small cameo of the type of segment, but recognize that it is an average, and that customers are not exactly like that.

Segments are also useful in determining which customers are better prospects, which are laggards, and which are likely to provide the most growth. They can be used to segment internal employee populations on the basis of their understanding and commitment to the brand. This may have four segments: the ambassadors, the catalysts, the spectators and the inert group. These groups can then be tracked over time to see which are growing and declining.

Segmentation studies are, however, only as good as the structure itself. If there are not enough segments, or they are wrongly defined, then their usefulness decreases rapidly. Peter York, founder of SRU Ltd, also suggests, 'One-size-fits-all segmentations are nonsense because people are volatile.' This means that it is not wise to try to use a standard segmentation for every problem. The segmentation should derive from the data and not be used to force a fit with the data.

Marketing environment

The marketing environment should be continually monitored for changes in socio-cultural, technology and market trends. Often the biggest threat to a brand is not from the immediate peer group but a brand that moves in from another field, unexpectedly. For example, the competitive environment in the European airline industry has changed dramatically in recent years. The previously state-owned airlines used to charge premium prices in a virtual monopoly. Deregulation has allowed new start-up brands like easyJet, buzz and Ryanair to steal much of the tourist business. The older airlines had simply relied on watching their immediate competitors and matching their propositions, ignoring the small start-ups until it was too late. The speed of this change was dramatic, over only two or three years, which proved too fast for the large corporations like British Airways, which were slow to react.

Book stores have also found themselves in competition with unexpected new brands. Barnes & Noble, Borders, Waterstones and Blackwells have all been forced to innovate to keep pace with the new online brands Amazon.com and BOL.com. The point is that brand managers must take a wide view when it comes to assessing the competitive environment. Jane Merriman of William

Grant considers that in the drinks world, 'the more mature the market the more categories polarize'.

Competitors

However, brand managers must also keep a sharp eye on their direct competitors and the detail of their brand proposition. This means assessing any shift between the above the line and below the line spend, or when competitors refocus to target different consumers or regions. This type of analysis should be a continuous process, tracking the brand footprints of the competition, so that their movements can be anticipated. Simple matrices can be used to achieve this, either with internal marketing teams or with consumer focus groups. The axes of the matrix can be changed depending on the breadth of viewpoint that is needed to assess the competition. For example, a narrow viewpoint of expensive watch brands would deliver a concentrated picture of direct watch brand competitors. However, a wider viewpoint of the luxury goods would deliver a broader understanding that customers may decide between leather goods, fashion or watches as a graduation gift. Similarly, the UK drinks market has been changing rapidly with the introduction of the Red Bull high-performance drink. The previous brand leader, Lucozade Original, needed to reposition itself to maintain a competitive proposition (see Figure 11.3). This involves careful portfolio management decisions to maximize revenue and minimize cannibalization.

Depending on the category, competitor analysis should be repeated every three, six or 12 months and across as many regions as necessary. The resulting snapshots of the market build into a tracking map of competitors' brand propositions in relation to your own.

Internal brand vision

The internal vision needs to be regularly re-examined in the light of these changing contexts. This is sometimes difficult to be objective about, but an open mind and willingness to change will result in a flexible and proactive business. Often businesses will use external consultants to help with this process: they are ideal because they have a clear, objective viewpoint and are in touch with developments of other brands in the market place. The assessment should crystallize the two issues of market attractiveness and the current competitive position, which can be used as a brand portfolio management tool, changing the emphasis across the line up of brands.

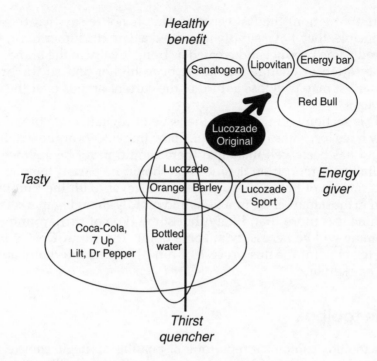

Figure 11.3 UK energy drinks market competitors matrix

Brand DNA

The development of the brand DNA needs to be driven by the direction of the map produced earlier. The definition of the brand DNA is detailed in Chapter 6 but the following summary outlines its components:

- rational benefits;
- emotional benefits;
- brand proposition;
- brand personality.

These are defined from the business culture, the consumer culture, and the self-image and social image of the consumer. The list of successful brands throughout the last century reveals that many have sustained their leadership through retaining a consistent brand DNA. The formulation and expression of those values have been updated and kept pace with social change, but the underlying fundamentals remained strong and well defined. Brands like Coca-Cola, Colgate, Gillette and Heinz are current brand leaders and were throughout the last century. That is not to say that they are invincible: they have simply identified a core consumer need, produced a fine product and created a strong loyalty to the brand. The expectation of change has never been higher and so the brand leader list may well lose a third of the current brands over the next 10 years.

This section will deal with the issue of revitalizing a brand that may have lost some of its appeal. Some marketeers argue that if the brand has been well managed there should never be any need to revitalize or reposition it, since this should be part of the ongoing programme of brand management. However, with the fluidity of staff in most marketing functions and rapidly changing market conditions it is more than likely that some type of turnaround programme will be necessary at some point. The brand DNA will be the focus point for this process of repositioning, internally and in the marketplace.

The toolbox

The toolbox contains a repertoire of possible strategic choices and some of the tactical tools to achieve profitable success. The choice of which strategy to choose will depend on a number of factors:

* category characteristics;
* ability to implement change;
* investment and resources;
* long-term business vision.

One of the core choices of any business strategy needs to be whether the business will offer a range of extensions to a brand, or adopt a policy of a portfolio of product-brands. Jane Merriman suggests, 'you have to manage the portfolio according to the opportunities in the market and consumer needs to maximize profitability.'

Portfolio brand management

Brand extension strategy
This is a core strategy of many clothing brands like Calvin Klein, where the original suit brand has now been extended to include related items like underwear, T-shirts, jeans and even fragrances. Anheuser Busch has a range of extensions to its Budweiser beer brand: Budweiser, Bud-Lite and Bud-Ice. The same umbrella brand proposition is created and used, but with variations that

allow consumers to choose something that more closely matches their desires.

This strategy is an excellent way to sell complementary product offers to consumers who have already bought into the brand. These consumers are warm rather than new and cold. The Gillette Series shaving foam is a standard product that has now been extended to include pre-shave, aftershave and several fragrance versions such as Cool wave and Pacific cool. Similarly, the Nivea Visage brand started with a face wash offer, and now includes moisturizers, facial scrubs and creams. These use the generic brand names of Gillette Series and Nivea Visage to sell a range of related products.

Once a brand has been successfully introduced and is generating high margins and market share, a brand extension programme is often a likely strategy. This is because it requires lower risk and lower investment costs to launch an extension than a new brand. However, the more a brand is extended, particularly outside the relevant category, the more the sum of the brand equity is eroded. The challenge is to maintain profitability for the long term and increase turnover with brand extensions. It is easy to suggest a brand extension, but much more difficult to regain some of the lost equity from a diluted brand.

Product brand extensions
An alternative strategy is to create new sub-brands with a different product range from the original brand name. Nivea has its original brand and identity, Nivea Intensive Care with its own identity, and the Nivea Visage range with its own identity. The coherence of the three Nivea identities is critical to its ability to leverage the brand capital accumulated in the original brand. It has successfully incorporated the dark blue and white that is its traditional identity into the new sub-brands. However, it has also introduced a light blue colour element and transparency to create a contemporary feel to the packaging and differentiate it from the original and its competitors. The advantage of this strategy is that it maximizes the consumer goodwill towards the original brand of Nivea, while encouraging new consumers to try it for the first time. It also helps to differentiate and target separate consumer segments: those who need intensive care, those who can live with the generic original, and those who appreciate pampering with Visage.

Each element of this type of strategy needs to be created to add value at each stage of the purchase moment. For example, the Nivea umbrella name gives confidence to consumers because it is a well-established and trusted name. It fulfils the rational need of consumers for trust and security. The next level, Visage, creates an emotional fulfilment for consumers by making them feel psychologically better because of their inherent desire to look beautiful.

When assessing the levels of a brand structure it is important to ensure that a brand hierarchy creates a distinctive proposition rather than reducing the total value. Clarity of message and the association of images with the brand name(s) will help to crystallize this issue. These should not compete with each other either for prominence or in character. The potential maximum number of brand/sub-brand levels should not go beyond three and in most cases this is already confusing for consumers. Many of the most successful brands have focused on one or two levels, which concentrates the message and makes awareness campaigns easier and more cost-effective.

The types of associations that are chosen to express the brand hierarchy can have a huge impact on the total brand message. The specific choice of words and connotations can add value across the whole range. Gillette's Mach 3 shaving system is a clever sub-brand for several reasons (Figure 11.4):

* The number three clearly supports the physical design, which has three blades instead of only two.
* The number three is used to suggest something that is better than the current competition, which usually have only two blades, suggesting higher performance.
* The Gillette brand already provides the security and trust values for the sub-brand; so the Mach 3 can provide the emotional benefits of excitement and thrills.
* Mach 3 is faster than Concorde, the sole supersonic passenger airline, which only travels at Mach 2 across the Atlantic.

Other examples of selective associations are frequent flyer clubs. The Dutch airline KLM uses Royal Wing, Silver Wing and Blue Wing. In BP's Premiere Club, drivers collect points in the form of credit that can be spent at various stores. These often indicate the hierarchy of benefits available to members and encourage them to progress up the scale. Typically they use a similar prefix/suffix or family word to express their connection to the same umbrella brand.

The Intel Corporation uses the speed of its processors to indicate different ranges of products – 1.4 GHz, 1.8 GHz or 2.0 GHz. Most consumers do not understand the true function of that figure, but

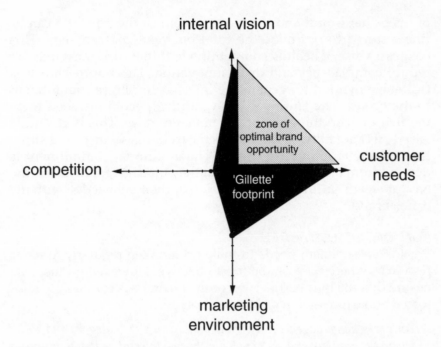

Figure 11.4 Gillette brand map

they can easily grasp the order of the hierarchy of their performance. It is usually preferable for brands to adopt a hierarchy in
which they know they can perform better than their competitors,
although often number inflation takes place, devaluing the whole
scale. Sainsbury's supermarket recently doubled the value of its
loyalty reward card scheme: a voucher that was previously worth
250 points is now worth 500 points, although the redemption value
remains identical. Escalation of this type of sub-branding can get
out of control and benefit neither brand in the end.

Brand portfolios

The use of brand portfolios is based on the classic Procter &
Gamble model and is also used by Unilever and Nestlé. Each
product has its own brand, which is distinctive in the marketplace, and the company brand is subverted by that product brand.
For example, clothes washing powders are often presented in
three or four different formats to consumers under different brand
names. This strategy allows a business to target several niche segments while maintaining a strong R&D, sales and management
structure. Each brand manager is responsible for the profitability

of his or her brand and the management of the portfolio can be finely tuned to optimize the total business performance. This creates a sense of healthy competition within the business that can reduce complacency and drive innovation. This approach uses a two-stage method for generating internal employee commitment to the brand. The Unilever values and expectations need to be implicit in everything the brand manager does. This is generally based on rationality, so it provides the training, security and structure for the employee to thrive. The emotional commitment is derived from the specific brand that they manage; for instance, the Nescafé team culture is an expression of their connection with the coffee brand.

Portfolio assessment

Portfolio assessment needs to to be undertaken regularly to focus resources where they can be most effective. However, it must also ensure that the long-term vision of the business is continually reinforced and expressed. Jane Merriman suggests:

> For portfolio management we try to map the whisky category and see where the gaps are and see which are the most useful, is it a premium market, is it an emerging, developing or mature market. Because the brand is at different stages of its lifecycle and we need to know when it is appropriate to build market size.

One of the most effective methods is to use the matrix shown in Figure 11.5 to assess the market attractiveness and competitive position of each brand individually and then determine a course of action. It is not a tool simply to reduce brands, but it will enable you to clarify the role of each brand in the portfolio and therefore shape a strong and competitive business.

The competitive position of a brand can be the strength of its customer loyalty like the Apple brand, or it could be the uniqueness of the brand differentiators like the Harley Davidson brand. A competitive edge can be gained through the longevity of a brand's position in the market, such as the Aunt Jemima maple syrup brand or the Heinz ketchup brand: they have become the family standard for these items. Having a large market share usually consolidates a position of strength for a brand, eg Kellogg's in the cereals market. The quality and motivation of the staff create a competitive edge in near identical service industries such as airlines, eg United Airlines and Swiss Airlines, or bookshops like Borders and Waterstones. Owning an ideological brand like Manchester United football club

COMPETITIVE POSITION

		Strong	Medium	Weak
MARKET ATTRACTIVENESS	Strong	Maximize dominance	Challenge leader by building on strengths	Find a niche, acquire, flank or exit
	Medium	Challenge leader by building on strengths	Manage for cash flow, flank	Milk and specialize
	Weak	Cash Generator	Milk or consider exit	Divest

Figure 11.5 Brand portfolio assessment matrix

creates a deep competitive strength that is almost impossible to change, even over a long period of time.

The market attractiveness will also determine which brands in a portfolio receive more attention and which are either milked or sold. The first dimension to consider is the status of the category: whether it is adolescent and growing, median and steady or mature and shrinking. The competition also needs to be considered, and whether competitors are gaining strength or weakening over time. The barriers to entry in the category need to be assessed: the Internet, for example, has relatively low thresholds for new brands to cross, while the car industry has high thresholds that would take a long time for new entrants to surmount. Of course, the potential for high margins and profits needs to be defined in any decision-making process. The final choice should also take into account the appropriateness of the category to the rest of the portfolio or internal brand vision; the energy wasted on diversification will not create long-term profits and stability.

Each of the brands in a portfolio needs to be there for a specific reason. By using the matrix it becomes possible to see which brands fit with the overall strategic direction of the business and which don't. Try to separate each brand/family brand/sub-brand/line brand or product brand into the following categories:

- *Core brand*: strong fit with core business proposition, profitable, with a high competitive position and market attractiveness, eg Kellogg's cornflakes offers consumers a top-quality product that is continually innovated, well supported and well managed.

❋ *Flanking brand*: a supporting role to protect the core brand from competitors stealing market share. Should have reasonable competitiveness and market attractiveness, eg the Dr Pepper carbonated drink acts as a flanking brand for its parent Coca-Cola, which cannot change its drinks formula to try different flavours. The Dr Pepper brand competes against Tango, Fanta, Seven-up and other fizzy flavoured drinks, while protecting the Coca-Cola brand.

❋ *Cash cow brand*: requires little investment and provides healthy returns with adequate fit to core strategy, eg Heinz soups require little investment and trade on the back of the core Heinz ketchup and beans ranges.

❋ *Entry brand*: one that allows customers to try a brand for the first time without a high purchase barrier, eg the Armani jeans brand allows a lower cost entry in the exclusive world of Armani clothing. Value propositions also provide volume and with seductive retailing, consumers can be encouraged to trade up to the core brand. Another example is the My First Sony range of children's consumer electronics, which creates an initial point of entry to the core Sony brand.

❋ *Niche brand*: provides a specific proposition to a segment of the target audience, eg Levi's 501 jeans.

❋ *High-end brand*: often the best brand to start a new business with. It uses narrowcast, exclusive codes to generate a high-profile, aspirational position, which can later be complemented with a core brand proposition for the mass market. For example, BMW Z-series sports cars (as driven by James Bond) create prestige for the standard car ranges.

❋ *Weak brand*: one that should be divested or combined with another brand to provide collateral, usually where the brand has become a commodity or the market is shrinking rapidly, eg Somerfield supermarkets.

New brand creation strategies

Most new brands gain entry into current markets with either a premium or a value driven strategy. They can create a high end, premium proposition, which sets an aspirational tone for the brand and delivers the following benefits:

❋ the brand has high margins and low volumes when production is starting;

❋ the brand creates an aspirational tone, which is highly seductive for the mass market;

* the range of products or services can be high quality;
* a premium brand naturally attracts early adopters and opinion leaders who develop a strong word of mouth campaign for the brand;
* rarity of a brand helps to create positive PR because it is available in limited numbers or as a limited edition;
* premium brands can use narrowcast codes rather than diluted broadcast codes to consumers, providing the richest, most seductive imagery and experiences.

Value-driven propositions gain market entry by a different route; they undercut current competition through:

* low price points that encourage purchase;
* accessibility to the brand through channel distribution;
* broadcast media codes that affect a large proportion of the population;
* large initial volumes that create positive PR through news headlines such as, 'the quickest/largest selling brand this year.'

A preference for the premium route is based on the long-term needs of a brand to build a strong position in the mind of the consumer. Consumers naturally respect premium associations more than they do value-driven ones, whatever they may say publicly. The best policy for growth is to start with a premium brand, build the exclusivity associations and consumer desire, then selectively fulfil that desire with sub-brands and diffusion ranges. Figure 11.6 suggests a possible brand development programme to maximize investment in the core premium brand and generate mass-market sales volumes. The important issue is that the premium brand is the core of the business, continually generating an aspirational image that consumers will desire. Without this premium core brand proposition in the portfolio, the mass-market appeal will quickly fade and sales will dry up.

It is almost impossible to try to turn a mass-market brand into one that has a premium positioning. The Ford car company bought Jaguar to add a premium brand positioning to its portfolio that could not be achieved through internal organic brand management. Similarly, the Nissan car company created the Lexus brand as a premium proposition, because the Nissan brand would not stretch all the way from super micro cars to premium luxury cars in the mind of the consumer.

One way to try to elevate a brand is to introduce a more powerful version of the original brand and develop this into the core brand

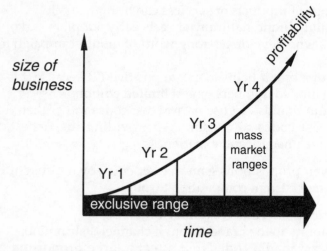

Figure 11.6 New brand roll-out plan

proposition, slowly replacing the original. This has been achieved with washing powder brands by adding the suffix 'Ultra' to create Bold Ultra, and with the headache remedy changing from Panadol to Panadol Extra. These moves do not fundamentally change the brand proposition but can help in a competitive situation. The best way to elevate a brand is to take a long-term view and invest constantly in redefining the brand image upwards, step by step.

Porter's strategy

Porter's (1986) matrix concentrates on the strategic choice of differentiation, cost leadership or focus as the core approach for a brand. The Porter matrix can be used to map out key competitors in an industry or category and identify which dimensions are most threatening and where their weaknesses lie. The car market can be segmented along Porter's matrix to reveal the different strategies that individual brands have taken; see Figure 11.7.

The differentiation brands include Rover, BMW, Audi and Alfa Romeo. They have all attempted to offer mass-market ranges of cars while maintaining a distinctive position in the mind of the consumer. Rover uses its Englishness to achieve this with elements like subtle wooden panels on the dashboard and a slightly retrograde feel to the styling. The cost leadership group includes the Ford, Nissan, General Motors and Fiat car brands that use a value proposition. These all have mass-market propositions and seek to reduce costs while increasing features as a proposition. The focus

STRATEGIC ADVANTAGE

		Distinctive proposition	Cost-reduction focus
STRATEGIC TARGET	Wide	Differentiation Rover Audi BMW	Cost Leadership Ford General Motors Nissan
	Narrow	Focus Jeep Jaguar Mazda	

Figure 11.7 The car industry analysed with Porter's matrix

group of brands includes Jeep, Jaguar and Mazda, which all use a selective product range and selective image proposition to build their brand presence. They do not seek to cover all segments of consumers or price points but aim to be the best for a narrower group of customers.

Cost leadership

Every brand needs to ensure that its cost base is as low as possible to generate the highest margins of profit. The accent on cost leadership suggests an emphasis on the reduction of cost (efficiency), which is important, but should not risk the reduction of the market differentiation or effectiveness of a brand, which Drucker (1989) defines as *efficiency* – doing things right, instead of *effectiveness* – doing the right things. Coca-Cola has been extremely successful at reducing costs while maintaining high margins and strong brand differentiation. This is often a technology- or production-based strategy that was successful in the last century, but most businesses have now recognized that a consumer- or marketing-driven strategy is more effective in western societies.

Differentiation

Differentiation is the key strategy for most brands: it is the added value that the intangible brand means to the customer that justifies the premium price they paid over and above the commodity version of the product. The strength of differentiation will determine the level of any price premium. Differentiation will also create barriers against competition and help to increase customer loyalty. The use of patented technologies and formulae can create strong differentiators that can be used as part of the brand proposition. Intel uses its branded Celeron and Pentium microprocessors as a unique proposition in the market. Starbucks has developed its own names for coffee types to differentiate itself in the crowded café category. Customers ask for a skinny latte rather than skimmed milk café au lait. This allows Starbucks to own that type of coffee and make it more difficult for competitors to copy it.

Focus

The focus strategy is different from the previous two in that it cannot be implemented as an industry-wide strategy; it is by its nature a category- or segment-specific strategy. This means that a business should dominate and lead a smaller part of the generic market for products. This could mean a shift from branded clothes to branded suits like Suits & Co, or The Gap, which primarily concentrates on jeans, khakis and T-shirts, and not suits.

SWOT analysis

Part of any strategic review needs to include a Strengths, Weaknesses, Opportunities and Threats (SWOT) analysis of the current brand proposition, personality and positioning statement. This should cover:

* market penetration;
* market growth;
* brand extension; and
* new brand development.

A SWOT analysis should also be completed for all major competitors, including other competitors in the broad marketing field. The ability to define who the real competitors are will enable brand managers to compete more effectively against them.

The ecology

Once the choice of brand strategy has been made and the tactical tools are delivering an invigorated brand proposition, there needs to be a constant check to ensure that any gains made are sustained. This means that there needs to be a programme of reviews and audits put in place as an integrated part of the chosen brand strategy. It is only through these that real progress will be made in changing the position of the brand in the mind of the consumer. Several leading business management experts believe that incremental change will not be sufficient to sustain a new business model, and that it will inevitably return to the previous state. They argue that revolutionary change is a necessity, not an option, in order to create sustainable progress.

There are many tools that can be used to ensure that a brand becomes part of a learning organization that constantly questions what kind of business it is and who its customers are. It is always easier to keep pushing a ball once it has started to move, and the same is true of a business that has already started to change. Opportunities for continuing these changes include:

* post-change review meetings;
* identifying examples of improved brand behaviour and rewarding this;
* undertaking an external audit at regular intervals;
* post-change interviews and training to consolidate the improvements.

All these elements need to assess the overall performance of a brand strategy, including how well has it been digested and ingested in the culture and people of the business. There needs to be a check to find out which parts of the strategy were more successful, and what can be improved for the following year. The internal and external conditions need to be monitored to create a sustainable improvement to the brand's performance. The change programme will have raised some new issues with internal and external customers; these need to be addressed. Internal customers need to receive continuous training to embed new processes and missions into their regular work.

The ultimate performance check of the new strategy will be by the customer in the marketplace. The criteria for success will have been decided during the initial mapping phase, but they need to be assessed to check how well they have been met. These may have included raised awareness levels for the brand across customers and/or potential customers. The stock price may also have been an indicator of the consolidation of the brand mission; interviews with analysts will reveal just how close the strategy is to their concept of the brand's performance targets.

Brand strategies for merger and acquisition

One of the greatest needs for brand planning arises during the synthesis of two brands during a merger or acquisition (M&A). Essentially, the approach of building a map, assessing the brand DNA, developing the tools and strategies and checking the ecology remains the same. Because there are two interested parties, there is probably more need for external, impartial advice to help construct the best possible future brand. One of the key reasons for M&A is that the boards and shareholders feel there are significant savings to be made by combining rather than remaining separate. This inevitably creates an atmosphere of tension and imperial attitudes towards what the future brand might represent.

There must be a good cultural fit between the two brands if they are to merge successfully and emerge as a stronger, larger brand. This is not always the case, and results have sometimes been disastrous. The techniques described in Chapter 13 should help to manage many of the issues that a brand manager faces in shaping an internal audience into strong brand ambassadors.

One of the key questions to consider is what banner brand name the new brand will use. Will it be some form of combination of the two previous brand names, or will it be an entirely new name in the market? Both approaches can work well, although the former is usually less costly in terms of raising awareness about the new brand. The latter can be advantageous when the merged brand wishes to reposition or realign itself with a different category. The recent merger of accountancy firms Price Waterhouse and Coopers & Lybrand has resulted in the new brand PricewaterhouseCoopers. This approach benefits from retaining the previous goodwill associated with the two brands and the new brand equity may be enhanced as the new business is able to convey the stance of a powerful global brand. The merger of the UK banks Lloyds and TSB has also proved workable, although in this case the internal cultures of the two businesses were clearly more diverse, requiring more effort to synergize them into a strong single business. The new business, Lloyds TSB, once again retains much of the goodwill of the previous separate brands while maximizing the benefits to the customer of reduced costs and increased presence on the high street. The identity for the new bank uses a combination of the colours from the previous banks, green from Lloyds and blue from TSB, which creates a modern, family image.

Consolidating brand names

When a brand is bought and needs to be incorporated into a larger brand, careful management of the process should ensure little loss of custom and awareness. One of the most effective methods is to visibly transfer the name from one to another over time. For example, a sweet bar used to be called Marathon in the United Kingdom and Snickers in the United States; the management decided they wanted to consolidate the brand into a single global product brand. The strategic choice had been made for Snickers to be the global brand name and the problem was how best to achieve this changeover. The chosen tactic was to start by adding a 'known as Snickers in the US' label in small text on the rear of the Marathon bar wrapper. Sales of this bar were continued for two or three months before the Snickers name was printed on the front in small text below the large Marathon brand name. Finally the Snickers name took the place of the Marathon brand name and was relaunched using a high-profile above the line advertising campaign. The loss of goodwill and awareness had been minimized and the brand continues to be a market leader all over the world.

The value of a portfolio of international brand names continues to grow. Unilever has recently announced it is reducing the breadth of its portfolio by 35 per cent over the next three years to concentrate more energy on developing a stable of 10–15 world class brands. The initial financial burden of these actions is huge in terms of the cost of change over, reduced interim revenues, re-branding programmes and divestment actions. But this is further evidence that brand management is a strategic tool and needs to use that power to shape the businesses of the future rather than remaining in the past. It also highlights the need for top management involvement in branding issues: to make these kinds of decisions requires a strong CEO and board who can manage change in a complex environment.

•

Summary

* A strategy is the long-term approach to brand management; the tactics are the operational tools that are used to express that strategy. The strategy should rarely change, but the tactics will need constant adjustment and refinement.
* Brand planning needs to assess all elements of a business including the marketing environment, the competition, the consumer's needs and the internal business vision.
* Portfolio management techniques need to assess individual brands on their competitive position against the attractiveness of the market. Businesses need to categorize which of their brands are core brands, flanking brands, cash cows, entry brands, niche brands, high end brands or weak brands.
* New brands need to start with a distinctive proposition and preferably an above average positioning; it is always easier to move down into the mass market than to try to take a brand upmarket.

CHAPTER TWELVE

RESEARCHING CONSUMER BEHAVIOUR

Evaluating the research process and methodologies

This chapter examines the uses of research to help in the decision-making process for brand strategy. The objectivity and accuracy of research results are paramount to decision making and the tools to use to help ensure the delivery of high-quality, relevant information are discussed.

The methods of collecting and analysing consumer behaviour data will be explained, along with a comparison of the strengths and weaknesses of some of the major techniques. The field of research is split into primary and secondary research, and may be further split into qualitative and quantitative approaches, using exploratory, descriptive or causal methodologies. This chapter explains the different values of each to the brand manager.

This chapter will also show the direct use of research on testing brand names, brand slogans, corporate identity designs, packaging concepts or advertising campaigns. The typical processes used to design, collect, analyse and report research results will be explained in order to give the brand manager access to the important characteristics of consumer research.

Brand management decision-making processes

The successful brand manager is one who is able to understand the mind of the consumer and make timely decisions about the health of the brand proposition. This means taking a proactive approach to research in order to have sufficient information when it is required. It does not mean continually researching for the sake of supporting weak brand management, as often too much information is the cause of procrastination. Research should only be undertaken with clear objectives in mind, fixed within a defined time and budget framework. Of course, there may always be one more piece of information that will help clarify the consumer needs, but often this may be at the expense of missing a market opportunity, while competitors move more quickly.

Consumer research can be used to enhance the decision-making process; it cannot be used to replace it. The practice of relying too heavily on research data is witnessed in the inexperienced or the timid. The best brand managers are able to draw out the value of the research, while taking an inclusive view of all the issues before making a decision. In fact some of the best brand managers are those who look one step ahead of the consumer, using the research simply as one of the weathervanes of trends.

The tradition of quantitative research has lost much of its importance as brand managers need to go beyond 'How many are buying my brand?' to 'Why are they buying my brand?' There is still a strong western culture of relying on hard numbers on the page, as translations of consumer desire; these are often good to know, but far more crucial is knowing the underlying subjective feelings and attitudes of consumers.

Information pollution

Researching consumer behaviour is not difficult, but researching the relevant part of behaviour is very difficult. It is all about asking the right questions and interpreting the information in a way that adds value. Given enough time and money, one could research every aspect of consumer behaviour, but it is important to balance the need for information with that of business efficiency. The introduction of networked computers, the Internet and retail databases has logarithmically expanded the available information, much of which will be irrelevant to a precisely posed brand management question. In order to avoid wasting large amounts of time, it is critical to invest some time making sure the question is properly defined.

Representing the world through research

Research condenses human and market behaviour into a recognizable and digestible picture of the patterns of consumer action. There are many types of research and they offer three fundamentally different views of the market, the consumer and brand personalities. These views are based on the techniques that are used to investigate the problem elements and this should always be taken into account when using the results to make decisions. They can be categorized as being based on past, present and future performance (see Figure 12.1).

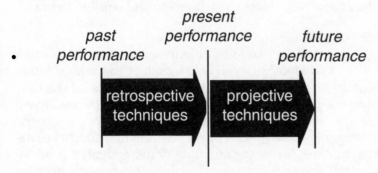

Figure 12.1 Research perspectives

Past performance

This type of research gives the brand manager a view of the past performance of a market or brand. If used regularly it can build into a library of performance that allows for some decisions to be made on the evidence of cycles of performance or trends. For example, the slow but constant increase in fish-eating in the United Kingdom should be seen as an opportunity for the Bird's Eye or John West brands. It is unlikely that these kinds of trends will be dramatically different from one year to the next. However, sometimes past performance figures can mislead the market. Past performance of Apple computers in 1997 would have suggested that there was very little competition from the Apple brand. With the iMac becoming the best-selling computer in the United States in August 1999, and newly launched iBook, the Apple brand represents a stronger threat to other computer brands.

Present performance

Present performance research provides a snapshot of markets, brand performance and attitudes. It signals what was happening at that time, and every day after that the information becomes less valuable and reliable. It can be used typically as a tactical tool to counteract competitors' promotional activities and successes, or it can be used as part of the continuous brand development programme to make sure that the brand personality keeps up to date with consumer opinion. This could be in the form of advertisement testing or new packaging design testing where the product will be introduced soon afterwards. The strength of present performance testing is that consumers rarely change their attitudes swiftly or drastically, so reliability is high. The weakness of present performance research is that following minute market movements often obscures the vision of the long-term direction and equity of a brand.

Future performance

Obviously, we would all like to be able to see the future; research cannot allow us to do this but it can help to reduce the risks of future changes in markets, brands and attitudes. Depending on the time distance from the present, the future performance can be researched in many ways. For the short-term future (depending on the industry), consumer focus groups provide excellent insights. For the medium to long-term future (again industry dependent) it is advisable to research through management interviews with opinion leaders and experts in the field. This is because consumers have little experience in imagining the hypothetical concepts and naturally tend to prefer the recognizable and the familiar. Also, as the forecast distance from the present increases, then the likelihood of transformation of markets and technologies increases, adding to the complexity of the problem. It is therefore necessary to include experts from a wider selection of fields to ensure that there are no large threats from disparate disciplines. For example, the former US Ambassador in London, Philip Lauder, recently told the story of the American Horse Post Company, which spent all its efforts building stage posts across the country and ensuring it had the best riders and fittest horses. But by the time they had linked across the vast country, the telegraph wire had been commercialized and in a short time completely destroyed its business. Future forecasting demands a wider picture to reduce risks and maximize opportunities.

The research process

While the complexity of research programmes may vary, there is a simple underlying process that defines and ensures high-quality results (see Figure 12.2). These can be applied to everything from a quick headcount to an extensive global focus group research programme. In all cases it provides the basis for understanding and clarifying what piece of information is needed for the decision-making process and what is the best way to collect and analyse the data to produce results.

Problem definition

The importance of this first step is to ensure that the research is asking the right questions of the right people and that the results can be used to aid decision making. To achieve this, the problem needs to be defined as accurately and succinctly as possible, before any choices about research methods are made. A clear set of objectives should be written down to make sure that the results can be judged against these objectives and that they will fulfil the brand manager's need for information. In larger companies, which are constantly researching, there is a tendency to frame questions in the same style as previous questions. While the problem may be similar, it is not the same and will always benefit from revisiting the exact definition of

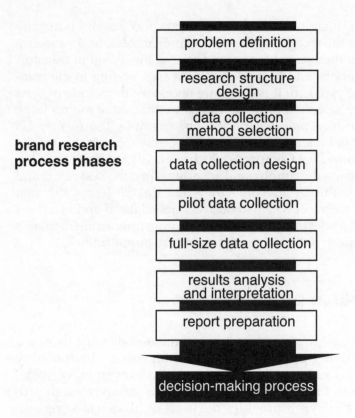

brand research process phases

Figure 12.2 Brand research process

the current brand management problem. Brand research costs time and money so the expected benefits of the research results should clearly outweigh the lengthening of the brand development process and delayed introduction to the marketplace.

Research structure design

If the problem cannot be accurately defined, a programme of exploratory research needs to be undertaken to help define the problem boundaries and parameters. This will provide an initial view of the scope and depth of the market, brands and consumer attitudes. If there is a lucid problem definition, then a series of descriptive or causal research programmes can be undertaken (see Figure 12.3). The research design can target a precise and specific set of questions, target audiences and conditions, and the results

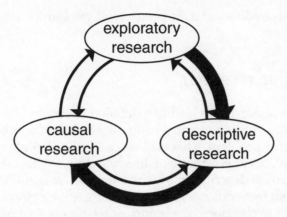

Figure 12.3 Relationship between research structure designs (after Churchill, 1988)

should provide incisive insight to the problem and enable rapid action to be taken.

Exploratory research

Exploratory research is used when the brand problem definition is not sufficiently clear or where not enough is known about the general market area. This may be because the brand concept is new, or it may be needed when entering a new category or new market. For example, if a brand is successful in a home market, a decision to expand abroad into new markets may be taken. While the business has strong experience of the local market, it does not know enough about the parameters affecting the new market. Exploratory research would elicit detailed information about consumer expectations and motivations, about competitor brand propositions and likely opportunities for a new brand. It leads to a helicopter view of the market and suggests the most fruitful places for a brand to position itself. It may also confirm ideas that are likely to be unsuccessful for a brand proposition, especially as many brand names or personalities do not travel well.

Exploratory research cannot give answers to tactical brand questions, but it is excellent at providing insight for strategic brand choices to be made. Because little is known about the problem, the research structure should be open and flexible in order to accommodate new ideas. It may also require the research to be continuously redirected as it progresses, evolving with the nature of the problem.

Descriptive research

Descriptive research can lead to a detailed portrait of the characteristics of a consumer segment, a competitor's brand proposition, or a type of brand problem. This will often be divided along age, sex, geo-political, socio-economic or lifestyle dimensions. They help to give an accurate description of who a consumer is and what differentiates them from other segments. Or it can give a clear description of consumer perceptions of a brand, or a new piece of packaging or their associations with new brand names.

Descriptive research can also cross-reference any of the above dimensions and the percentages of a target segment and their brand preferences. They can show where most of your purchasers live or what age they are or how often they buy more than one brand. All these can be used to retain profitable consumers or to predict and target future consumers or prospects on the basis of previous successful targeting.

Causal research

Causal research illustrates the existence of a relationship between two variables of a brand or in the market. It may be trying to establish a causal link (ie that one thing causes an effect on another) between the new colour of a corporate identity and increased sales in a market. Or it may be trying to show that a change in brand slogan has encouraged a change in the demographic profile of purchasers. These types of causal research help to show the strength of connection between variables and whether they should be enhanced or reduced. It can also show whether there is no connection between the two variables; some phenomena may be related but not causal. For example, a hypothesis might be tested to see if there is a causal relationship between watching World Cup football and an increase in pizza eating. These two things may occur together, but the reason may be different, for instance a promotional offer by the big supermarkets. This highlights how difficult it is to define exactly which single cause has generated which buying effect. It is therefore advisable to be cautious about generalizing cause and effect relationships; an understanding of the bigger picture always needs to be brought to bear on the detailed evidence. For brand managers it is vital to know whether consumers connect one set of emotional attitudes with purchase behaviour.

Data collection method selection

The appropriate method for data collection should be selected: the two main categories are primary and secondary data collection. Primary data are information that has been expressly commissioned for the current research question. Secondary data are general data that have not been specifically commissioned for that particular research question. Secondary data are usually the starting point for most research, as they provide a cost-effective and quick coverage of the problem. They may also provide sufficient information and analysis for decision making that a primary study is unnecessary. When secondary sources cannot provide either the accuracy or suitability for the problem, then a primary research programme must be commissioned.

In addition to choosing the source of data, the type of research data should be chosen – either quantitative or qualitative. Quantitative data present a numeric expression of brand and market phenomena; they show the status quo of brands, markets and consumers. Qualitative data attempt to explain why these phenomena have occurred and the motivations behind consumer buying behaviour.

Primary research data collection

Primary research involves collecting original data for a specifically defined problem within a context and consumer group. This obviously means that the relevance and accuracy of this type of data are high, but the problem definition needs to be clearly delineated from other general marketing needs. Because it is a bespoke service, it usually costs more than other types of research, but for a large organization it is vital to have this kind of precise data. Primary research should generally be used only after initial secondary sources have been explored, which help to provide the broader picture. It is not always necessary to use primary research in all cases, especially if this would excessively delay the decision-making process. Types of primary research include questionnaires, focus groups and hall testing, conjoint analysis and management interviews. Primary research is also unique and confidential, giving the brand manager a knowledge and insight advantage over competitors.

Secondary research data collection

Secondary sources of information can provide enough data for certain situations, and especially at a relatively low time/financial cost. The data are more generic than primary data, but they may include data on the variables that are important to the brand problem. Since they are paid for and used by many groups, the cost is correspondingly lower than primary data. The accuracy of these data may also be lower, as they comprise research into a group similar to your target group but not the exact target group. Also, the source of secondary data may be less reliable than primary sources, since the conditions and accuracy are difficult to check. Secondary data help to generate a hypothesis about the brand, which can then be tested using primary research. In some cases, secondary research will deliver enough to make a brand management decision; it should not be regarded as lower-grade research. Types of secondary data sources include desk research, Mintel reports, A C Nielsen reports, business and trade journals, and newspaper surveys.

However, it is often the insight and imagination that individual brand managers bring to bear on the data that generates the best market advantages. This topic is covered in more detail below under literature and Internet searching.

Quantitative data

Quantitative data is information presented as facts and figures in a report, usually dealing with the numeric dimensions of a brand problem. Simonson and Schmidt (1999) have sub-divided quantitative consumer research into brand awareness, brand attitudes and beliefs and measurement of brand behaviour:

* Brand awareness – the extent to which consumers are aware of a brand, its logo, its proposition and brand personality. This can also include awareness of advertising campaigns and competitors' brands.
* Brand attitudes and beliefs – these assess consumers' understanding of the brand's meaning and its connoted imagery, or their attitudes towards certain identity elements.
* Measurement of brand behaviour – this type of research can be used to research the reaction of consumers to a brand experi-

ence through the use of a brand retail site, new brand packaging or brand product and the comparison of that brand experience as a reflection of the core brand values.

Quantitative research data could include the size of markets, brand awareness levels, and market share percentages and sales figures. The data show the state of a brand's position or strength in relation to the market or competitors. Because of this numeric objectivity, quantitative research can easily be used to set specific measurable targets for performance increases or targeting consumer segments. It can be used to track cycles of brand performance across seasons or districts. It can also be used to compare the success of different sales teams or promotional offers with the investments made in them. However, crucially, it does not tell brand managers why their brand is successful or otherwise, although some insights can be inferred from the data. Jane Merriman of William Grant & Sons uses both forms for different reasons: 'If there is a question of pricing we would use quantitative research, but for a new packaging concept we would use qualitative research.'

Qualitative data

Qualitative data comprise information that gives the brand manager an understanding of why consumers buy a specific brand over another or how they perceive their needs and desires. They can also help explain which elements of the brand expression are adding value to the brand and which are detracting from it. Qualitative data can reveal the language that consumers use to discuss their needs and their underlying motivations and desires, which gives the brand manager a chance to understand how the consumer thinks about brands. All of these help the brand manager to get closer to the consumer, which should help to refine the brand to fit better with consumer expectations. The weakness of qualitative data, like most research techniques, is that the consumer can have difficulty in relating to future concepts or brand ideas. In this case it would be advisable to use a Delphi technique, by individually interviewing trend makers, opinion leaders and industry decision takers. Following this, a new brand hypothesis can be formulated which can be re-evaluated by those experts to confirm or deny its strength of probability.

Data collection and sample design

The specifics of the data collection need to be carefully considered in order to maximize the pertinence of the results and avoid biased or irrelevant data. This means using unbiased language, phrasing and non-leading questions. The use of a scale of preference or a scale for personal details should be balanced and relevant. The choice of technique such as telephone interview, focus group, questionnaire and the openness of the purpose of the research need to be designed to maximize success.

The sample to be researched needs to be carefully chosen in order to avoid unintended bias and generate an accurate picture of consumer behaviour. The sample needs to be either large enough to be statistically significant during analysis so that the sample opinion can be extrapolated to fit the whole population, or small enough to show evidence of a trend or opinion, or that is indicative of a behavioural characteristic. The sample may be defined along many variables such as age, gender, geographic location, political persuasion, educational achievement, attitude, previous buying behaviour, familial status or others.

Pilot data collection

In order to avoid spending large amounts of money asking the wrong questions, it is always advisable to test-pilot the research on a small group of the target audience. This can sometimes seem time-consuming but since it involves the general public (typically), it usually reveals some flaws in even the best-structured research. It inevitably improves the accuracy of the results and helps to reduce time and therefore costs.

Full-size data collection

Once the pilot study has been completed, the research programme can be adjusted and refined to incorporate any necessary improvements. The full sample can then be interviewed/observed and detailed notes taken to ensure total data capture. It is surprising how much information is generated from even a simple research study; the more precise the original problem definition, the fewer data may be needed. It is often the case that the researcher and brand manager receive too much information from the consumer/market, resulting in information pollution. This can cause the brand manager to see the problem as highly complex and start on a cycle of always requiring more and more information in order to proceed.

Results analysis and interpretation

Depending on the nature of the problem and the research design, the analysis may be in the form of quantitative, statistical correlations, or it may be based on analysing qualitative impressions and comments. Accurate and unbiased analysis is crucial if the results are to be trusted and used effectively. While it is tempting to use data to reinforce currently held opinions, it will lead the brand manager astray into an unreal world. The use of external research agencies generally ensures a sufficient degree of independence and reliability. As with all analysis and interpretation, it is based on how people see the events and is therefore ultimately subjective, although researchers are thoroughly trained to be objective.

The research report

The reporting of research data should include three broad elements: a background to the methodology, the results, and recommendations based on those results. The methodological overview helps the brand manager to trust the results and ensure that the problem and people studied were the intended target. The results should clearly indicate the direction and the valency of consumer opinion, preferably in a visual format. It should also acknowledge the areas of strength and weakness in the research study, including dimensions of accuracy. Finally, the report should recommend further action on the basis of the results; for example it may recommend one of two commercials to be broadcast. It could also recommend that production should not go ahead, or should go ahead in a modified format, or that further research is necessary.

Sources of error in research

The accuracy of research data is crucial to the quality of the decision-making process, so it is vital that the tolerance of accuracy is expressed and understood by the brand manager. There are several likely areas where accuracy may be reduced in research; these are with the consumer, the research agency or the methodology:

* Consumers may give:
  - inaccurate responses owing to memory problems, etc;
  - they may not understand the question properly;
  - they may have little or no knowledge of the subject;
  - they may try to give the answer they think is required.

* The agency may:
  - rely on previous research knowledge without telling the brand manager;
  - not question the exact stated sample group of consumers;
  - distort (slightly) the findings to emphasize a point of view;
  - draw the wrong conclusions from the data collected.
* The methods used:
  - may be unethical;
  - may be inherently biased towards a certain segment;
  - may not deliver the most effective results;
  - may be statistically insignificant.

Of course, all research is done by people and on people, meaning that the degree of accuracy is as good as the people who do the research.

Research methods and media types

This section will cover a range of different techniques that are used to address specific brand management problems. They are arranged in the most likely combinations of use, ie hall testing for new packaging designs, but these combinations are not exclusive and many can be applied successfully to different brand problems. The examples should help to give an insight into the strengths and weaknesses of the different media, the choices of research method and the expected type of information it delivers:

* Strategic research tools
  - management interviews for market trends and business environment research;
  - observation for in-store buying behaviour;
  - A C Nielsen, GFK, Euromonitor for purchase statistics;
  - questionnaires for brand awareness;
  - focus group research for new brand personality development.
* Tactical research tools
  - hall testing for new product and packaging designs;
  - conjoint analysis for brand proposition testing;
  - databases for brand segmentation;
  - brand loyalty card and consumer preferences;
  - benchmarking for competitor analysis;
  - perceptual proximity mapping;

- advertising effectiveness (DAGMAR);
- literature and Internet searching.

Research companies

Several large companies like GFK, A C Nielsen, TGI (Target Group Index) and Euromonitor produce independent statistics about the sales for brands over a period of time. These may be based on the volume/value/customer profile/political or geographic segment of different brand sales across specific categories. For instance, they would highlight the number of people who bought Colgate toothpaste in comparison with Signal, Arm & Hammer or Oral B. They also can be cross-referenced against most socio-economic and lifestyle variables, like Colgate buyers who read the *Guardian* newspaper or are heavy lager drinkers, for example.

The figures can be viewed across different regions or stores to see if there is a trend emerging. This type of data is usually bought continually by larger companies on a subscription basis, with monthly reports. It forms part of the general marketing intelligence for a brand and helps to revise sales forecasts and warns of competitor advances and brand degradation cycles. Its strength is as a simple snapshot of the market at any one time and it can build into a broader biography of brand performance. Its weakness is that it tells you what has happened with the brand in the past but offers no insight into why the brand may be under- or over-performing in the sector or what future performance to expect.

Hall testing for new product and packaging designs

Hall testing can be used to assess the appropriateness of a piece of brand packaging with its expected brand personality. Several mock-ups of different packaging designs can be displayed and a group of consumers (typically a few hundred) are asked which one they like best and which one best expresses the desired brand personality. This can be done without the brand names present and later with brand names present to test for shifts in brand perception.

The strength of this approach is that it tests the packaging shape separately from other brand elements, and the results can be used to refine the packaging independently. A car oil brand like Shell may want to shift its personality to attract more female buyers; developing a softer, more feminine package design can help this. The hall test could then assess which of the new designs best reflects this femininity and if this is still a desirable characteristic. The weakness is obviously that in the mind of consumers all the brand elements build into one picture; they can rarely separate out elements individually. The choice of sample and conditions can be carefully controlled, but it does take a long time to organize and execute.

Questionnaires for brand awareness

Questionnaires are a simple and direct way to elicit brand awareness and preference information from the general public. It is important to decide whether to make it clear to the respondent the purpose of the survey, or to disguise it among other questions. Respondents often try to give the answer they think is expected, rather than the one they believe to be correct, or make different choices because it is a hypothetical situation. It is especially difficult to ask questions of a personal or financial nature to strangers on the street, so these should be avoided. Questions are often split into unaided or spontaneous responses and prompted responses to differentiate between knowledge of brand awareness and detailed brand attributes.

The weakness of this kind of research is that it is difficult to get beyond one-word or one-sentence answers, owing to the format. This may mean that the underlying reasons for brand preferences remain latent or untapped, revealing only the top-of-the-mind information. The strength of questionnaires is that they can provide a quick overview of attitudes and can be easily carried out in many locations at once. The data delivered can be both quantitative and qualitative.

Observation for in-store buying behaviour

This kind of research is being developed through the use of technologies like mini video cameras and head movement monitors. It provides feedback on two aspects of buying behaviour: the process of identifying and choosing brands, and the effectiveness of brand packaging and point of sale displays to facilitate this process.

Siamac Salari has worked extensively in the field of video ethnography (observation) of supermarkets for advertising agencies. He has suggested that there are four distinct stages in the buying process in a typical retail outlet:

1. Reference point: consumers find a reference point on the shelf, often by placing their hand on a product or visually marking a point on the shelf.
2. Survey: from this fixed mental point they survey the field of products to either side of it within the category.
3. Choose: consumers choose the brand they want.
4. Final check: they make a final quick survey of the shelf, possibly as they are walking away, to check that a better brand choice is not available.

This process may be almost immediate for low-interest or low-cost regular items, but can be extensive for high-interest and high-cost items. Siamac Salari also suggests that the point of most likely brand switching or trialling is in the last phase, when consumers make a final check of the shelves.

The effectiveness of a retail space and its layout of brands can be carefully analysed through the use of a head monitor. This is a wearable computer that tracks consumers' eye movements as they move down the aisles, scanning the shelves. It can show which part of the store or shelf is dead space and which types of brand packaging are eye-catching. The strength of this type of research is that it accurately reflects the purchase situation, with competitor brands alongside each other. The weakness is that it does not provide a mechanism for feedback as to why consumers have made specific brand choices. It is also relatively expensive and time-consuming, since large numbers of consumers must be viewed and analysed for the buying patterns to emerge.

•Focus group research for new brand personality development

Focus groups are the core of brand development research, because they provide predictive information about brand preferences and they allow a detailed exploration of the motivations for brand choices. An expert facilitator usually runs them in small groups, in a non-threatening environment (possibly a home). This atmosphere allows and encourages personal wishes and concerns to be voiced even on embarrassing subjects such as personal hygiene or financial matters. They provide a wealth of information about how consumers think about brands and the language they use to describe themselves and the brand personalities. These types of sessions can provide excellent pre-development material that can be used to brief advertising creatives and designers. They give qualitative insight into the emotional background to brand choices and which brand personality characteristics are favoured.

They usually begin with open questions and discussion about a subject area, say oral hygiene. This is followed by more detailed probing of specific issues and brands relating to the brand problem, say a mouthwash brand and its competitors. The strength of focus groups is that they allow the brand manager a ringside seat to the mind of the consumer. The weakness is that managers can become slaves to the results of the focus group; in the United Kingdom and the United States the political parties use focus groups extensively, which reduces their self-reliance and vision. There is a tendency therefore to treat focus group results as fact, rather than opinion, and once a brand manager has started using them, he or she can find it difficult to make a management choice without requiring another session.

Conjoint analysis for brand proposition testing

Conjoint analysis allows brand managers to test different combinations of the variables that go to build up the total brand personality. These may include the price, the brand slogan, a piece of brand imagery, the packaging and product design, and the point of sale material. Respondents are offered a series of combinations such as a price and a brand slogan at the same time; they must rate this against other combinations they are shown based on a future intention to buy. These combinations may contain contradictions, such as the slogan they most like with the brand imagery they least like. Respondents must balance their wishes and, through repetitive testing, a pattern emerges as to the most preferred combination of all of the elements researched. It also highlights combinations that are definitely appreciated by the consumer, although again it is based on hypothetical reasoning, and the results tend to be biased towards the rational elements of a test rather than the emotional.

This process has become cost-effective through the use of laptop computers that can display the information (including pictures and sounds), collect the responses through key hits, and analyse and display the results using an algorithm. Their inherent portability makes them ideal to take to several locations and they are easy to set up and use.

The weakness of this type of research is the artificial nature of the brand study, which can make some respondents feel disassociated from the proposition. It may initially also be problematic for non-computer users, although this is usually quickly overcome. The strength of this approach is that it can indicate which brand attributes work best in combination, building a larger gestalt brand personality than their constituent elements.

Databases for brand segmentation

Database marketing has become a sophisticated source of consumer marketing intelligence, relying heavily on the power of technology to cross-analyse massive amounts of detailed information about our personal shopping behaviour. Brand managers can now easily tap into a rich source of diverse parameters relating to the brand and the consumer. They can then use this to individually target other consumers who have the same profile of behaviour, narrowing the brand relationship to an ideal one-to-one.

The weakness of these systems is that there is often too much information available about the consumer, along too many parameters, leaving brand managers who cannot see the wood for the trees. Obviously, the strength of these database systems is the individual nature of the information and accuracy of the profile across large numbers of the population. Databases provide a snapshot of past behaviour on brand preference and must be carefully analysed to predict future behaviour.

•Brand loyalty cards and consumer preferences

Brand loyalty can be researched through a variety of techniques, but it is important to stress that repeat purchase behaviour is not necessarily an indication of brand loyalty. Brand loyalty cards from supermarkets or frequent flyer cards from airlines attempt to lock-in consumers to a particular brand while providing accurate information about their purchasing habits. Consumers using the loyalty card at the supermarket give the brand manager information about exactly how often they frequent a store, how long they typically spend there and, especially, what brands they buy regularly and in how many units. The correlation between frequency of purchase and number of units purchased gives a strong indication of loyalty, although low-interest purchases often may not signal loyalty – a consumer may simply need a bottle of bleach, and having made the purchase is unlikely to switch brands.

The cards show the past performance of brands and need to be carefully extrapolated forwards. For example, if your usual brand of pasta is out of stock several visits in a row, you will buy an alternative brand each time. The evidence on the loyalty card is that you have switched brands and the response may be to reduce further the stocks of the original brand, negatively reinforcing consumer preferences.

Benchmarking for competitor analysis

Being able to research and analyse a competitor's brand proposition is a vital tool to increasing the competitiveness of your own brand proposition. Any of the brand dimensions and brand personality characteristics discussed in the earlier chapters will provide an excellent basis for this type of analysis. This helps to understand the nuances of similar brand propositions, and when repeated over time can build into a map that shows the direction in which a brand is moving. Brand mapping sessions are held ideally with groups of target consumers who position brands along a crossed axis of attributes. These attributes can be predetermined, or generated by the consumer group's own perception of the market and the brands.

The value of this kind of benchmarking lies in its expression of the spread of brands across the total market and the clustering of various competitors. This type of map also helps to identify the white space in a market where there are few or no competitor brand • personalities. Small notes and quotes next to the brand marks can augment the consumer reasoning behind a brand's positioning. When a company has a portfolio of brands or a range of brand extensions, the brand map can show how spread apart or focused the brand footprint is. Although neither of these cases is necessarily better than the other, it is based on the strategic choice of the individual companies. The weakness of competitive benchmarking is that it remains an expression of the current brand choices and personalities.

Perceptual proximity mapping

This type of research is similar to benchmarking, but instead of plotting all the competitive brands, the associations of one brand are plotted in proximity to the brand at the centre (see Figure 12.4). By placing the brand at the centre, it is easy for the consumers to place perceptions, connotations and imagery in relation to the strength of the association with that brand.

Perceptions that are closely associated with the brand are placed near the centre and more distant connections placed further out on the map. The use of two axes can also help to differentiate the perceptions in a meaningful manner. The value of this type of benchmarking is that perceptions from different business categories and thoughts can be related, as they are in the mind of the consumer. This gives the brand manager a holistic picture of how the consumer thinks about a brand personality, in his or her own language. It also reveals associations and connections that may not have been made by the marketing team, but which are clearly relevant to the consumer.

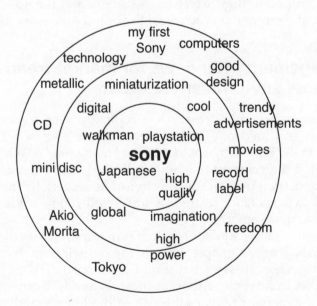

Figure 12.4 Perceptual proximity map, Sony Corporation

Advertising effectiveness (DAGMAR)

Advertising is expensive and it is therefore important to maximize its efficiency in creating awareness and action towards a brand. Defining Advertising Goals for Measured Advertising Results (DAGMAR) is a typical approach to researching advertising effectiveness. It highlights the need to identify a specific objective to be attained through the use of advertising, before commencing a campaign. In this way the results can be measured against this original objective either through direct response or a consumer survey. Direct response research is usually achieved either through retail outlet walk-through figures, or through the use of coded coupons, or response cards. These indicate which publication the advertisement appeared in and can be analysed to develop a profile of the most and least successful ones at attracting the target audience.

Consumer surveys can be used to test advertisement brand awareness and the perceptions of the brand message. In a crowded media world it is vital that unprompted brand name recall is high and that the correct brand message has been received. Often brilliant advertisements obtain high recall for the advert, but low scores on the actual brand name and brand message. In large organizations, it is also worth testing internal staff reactions to an advertising campaign; they are also consumers and the advertisement will affect their own perception of the brand they work for.

Management interviews for market trends and business environment research

Business environment research is typically used for exploratory research and medium- to long-term future research, because it draws on the knowledge of key experts in the field. Usually, a semi-structured interview of one hour will uncover the key issues for a brand or market from the perspective of the expert. By interviewing • several experts from related or unrelated fields, a vision of the future begins to emerge.

The value of this kind of research is that it draws on the accumulated knowledge of people who are top of their field. It enables the brand manager to see what might be coming next in consumer behaviour, building, transport or lifestyle trends. By interviewing a range of experts it reduces the risk of the unexpected, and maximizes the opportunities available to the brand manager. Its weakness is that it is rarely brand-specific and deals more in the realm of categories and trends. By targeting specifics like kitchen trends in the next three years, the brand manager can expect to have a good idea of what consumers will be wanting or how their attitudes to an issue will be changing. It gives enough time to reposition the brand to take advantage of these shifts in attitude before they happen, again synchronizing the brand with the mood of the consumer.

Literature and Internet searching

Literature and Internet searching covers secondary data collection and is generally used as part of an exploratory research programme to grasp the basic ideas and attitudes towards a problem. As Churchill (1988) has suggested, these can fall into either conceptual problems – what is the latest thinking on ecological marketing? – or trade problems – which are the key competitors in the mobile phones category in Germany? These two ideas express how closely they are related to a specific market, brand or consumer group problem.

There are a large number of sources of secondary information that can be divided by how they relate directly or indirectly to the problem:

Direct sources:

* internal company reports;
* internal market test results;
* internal customer feedback;
* TGI indices;
* statistics, Mintel, GFK, A C Nielsen data;
* trade associations and literature;
* government and institutional statistics;
* annual report.

Indirect sources:

* psychological and behavioural journals;
* socio-cultural journals;
* newspapers and magazines;
* case studies of similar businesses;
* management journals;
* business school case studies;
* trend reports;
* art, design and fashion trends;

* technology trends;
* library sources.

The Internet has revolutionized the power and speed of literature surveys: much of the work can now be carried out in the comfort of your office chair. The search engines used to source information are ideal for using keyword or Boolean search techniques. Access to the world's databases has never been more convenient, whether it is dialling into the latest thinking at a leading US business school, or tapping into the Dutch consumer association guide, or surfing through an online version of the *Financial Times* newspaper. Many of the database research businesses such as the Henley Centre for Forecasting or the Future Foundation offer a subscription service for access, while many are also free.

The weakness of the Internet as a research tool is that, as with all research, there is simply too much information available. The skill is in selecting sources that closely match the problem definition and defining a fixed time for the search. Otherwise the search can become a lifelong exercise, as there is always one more link to check.

Another weakness of the Internet, again like real-world research, is that the validity and veracity of the data are difficult to check. There have been cases where deliberately misleading business information has been posted on the Net, and a high-profile investment bank was taken in by the source, losing it millions of dollars. Of course, reputable business sites will want to defend their integrity and brand equity in the virtual world as much in the real world, but with the anonymity of the Net it is always worth checking the source of data.

International research

Conducting international research is particularly important when researching transnationally, since the need for comparability of the results may reduce the explicitness of the questioning in any one country. This has been identified by academics as the Self-Reference Criterion (SRC) that is used by researchers when they research in a country other than their own (Aaker *et al*, 1999). Often the assumptions about the problem and possible areas for investigation reflect the experience of the researcher more than they do the general population of the researched country. This can lead to brand research that asks the wrong questions, of the wrong people, using the wrong variables. To avoid this the researcher should ensure that the cultural relevance of the questions remains equable, rather than concentrating on the exact wording of the questions. For example, when testing a new print campaign for cooking products in Asia Pacific and in Europe, it must be remembered that the strong cultural differences will affect responses. These can range from attitudes to eating out or inviting friends back to the home for dinner, to different expectations of the spiciness of foods and different notions of what represents avant-garde or modern or conservative styles of packaging design. To overcome these, pilot studies and comparable rather than identical questions can be used.

Summary

* The research process typically follows this pattern: problem definition, research structure design, data collection method selection, data collection design, pilot data collection, full-size data collection, results analysis and interpretation, and finally research report presentation.
* Exploratory research aims to provide a wide view of the total field under investigation; descriptive research should describe the specific nature of the problem; causal research should highlight the causes and relationships between parts of the problem.
* Primary research is an investigation that is undertaken specifically for the problem in mind; secondary research is desk research of findings already generated by previous studies.
* Quantitative research covers all forms of statistical data and analysis of how many events occurred, while qualitative provides an analysis of the underlying reasons why those events might have occurred.
* The range of research methods includes: target indexes, hall testing, questionnaires, observation, focus groups, conjoint analysis, databases, loyalty cards, benchmarking, advertising effectiveness, management interviews, literature searches and international research.

CORPORATE BRAND MANAGEMENT

The CEO as brand manager and how to inspire every employee to take responsibility for the brand

This chapter examines the use of brand management as an internal resource for corporate structuring and employee motivation. This starts with a strong brand mission, led by the CEO as the ultimate brand manager. This is developed into the internal brand culture of the business that is shaped by the people and processes that work there.

The importance of understanding employees as internal customers helps to shift the focus of attitude towards an effective dialogue relationship. The use of personal development techniques like NLP (Neuro-Linguistic Programming) has proved popular in shaping internal brand cultures.

The role of the human resources department is key to recruiting and maintaining this resource. The development of the intellectual and emotional capital of internal customers has proved to have a great effect on the coherency of any internal branding programme. This kind of programme can be structured along the four levels of listening, priming, branding and post-message time. Finally, we look at the different tonal variations of language used in internal brand programmes.

Objectives

* Describe the importance of internal brand management.
* Illustrate the shaping of an internal brand culture.
* Analyse the use of emotional capital in employee motivation.
* Describe the four-step internal communication programme.

The CEO as brand manager

As Peter York, founder of SRU Ltd, suggests, 'The CEO is the brand manager, and it's something we have been advocating for the last 20 years.' The true guardian of the brand should be the CEO (Chief Executive Officer) or COO (Chief Operating Officer). It is they who are ultimately responsible to all the stakeholders, internal and external, for the performance of the business. It is only they who can give strategic direction to the brand through their vision of the future of the company, and it is only they who can motivate internal customers to embrace the necessary change and innovation needed in today's competitive markets. Gregory (1997) argues that there is a new role that should be defined at board level, that of a Chief Communications Officer (CCO), whose task would be to concentrate solely on implementing and monitoring the CEO's vision for the brand. He or she would be the brand champion, responsible for the brand's reputation. The aim of the CEO (or CCO) is to build a team with skills, and also to motivate them to be a driving force for the brand, to create acolytes and ambassadors for the brand.

Brand mission

Every brand has a guiding mission statement that summarizes its intent to internal and external customers. The brand name symbolizes these shared values in a single word. Consistency of message is crucial in large corporations as they do not react quickly; any message from the top takes a while to become practice at the front of the business. If that message is constantly changing, then the internal and external customers can easily become confused and almost certainly demotivated. There is a strong reluctance internally to commit to a brand mission if there is an expectation that it will change soon anyway.

Typical brand missions are:

⁕ Hewlett Packard (HP): concerns, trust and respect.
⁕ IBM: customer service.
⁕ Disney: family entertainment.
⁕ Starbucks: quality and service.

There are several proven methods and media for delivering corporate missions to all employees. These range from the direct top-down approach of a video of the CEO, which is shown to all employees as part of their ongoing training. This often takes the form of an annual address to review the previous year's results and share with everyone the new targets and direction for the future. When strong change is required, corporate days are organized around a programme of internal change criteria. In its troubled years, Philips of the Netherlands undertook a 'customer day' in January each year, one day when almost all employees worldwide would pause together to examine best practices, and hear from the CEO, Jan Timmer, about the new tasks for the year, focusing on customer benefits. Smaller versions of these can be held at a regional or local level; they also bring together and consolidate the brand culture of an organization.

Internal brand culture

This brand mission is expressed and developed through the internal culture of the business: the behaviour and practices of internal customers generates an approach to business and a specific viewpoint on the world. These are the shared values of a brand and they have a strong impact on the performance of the brand in the external world. The culture of a business can be explained through its constituent components, shown in Figure 13.1.

The choice of language – directive, requesting or inspirational – and tone of voice of a business culture are an important illustration of the way that a culture behaves. Michael Abrahams suggests that 'You have to balance all your various audiences.' The language both • reflects the cultural status, and shapes and structures the thinking and behaviour of those in the culture.

Beliefs and attitudes are the underlying assumptions that an organization has about the world. It is a collective consciousness that shapes decision making and internal relationships between departments and internal customers.

Rituals and conventions are the symbolic expression of the culture through events and iconic protocols; they are mostly intan-

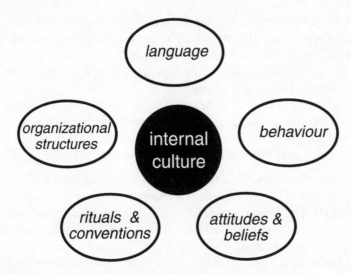

Figure 13.1 Internal brand culture values

gible structuring processes. These can be as simple as buying a cake on a birthday or the deference shown to experienced internal customers.

Organizational structures are the tangible structuring processes of an organization that have been formalized. These might include the management hierarchy, the method of rewards and benefits, the quality systems and associated internal structures such as development processes or TQM (Total Quality Management). These are the basic rules that define the business and its separate elements; they locate the internal customer within that structure.

Behaviour is the action taken by internal customers that reflects the beliefs of the brand and are expressed through their activity within the organizational structures.

Peters and Waterman, in *In Search of Excellence* (1985), have crystallized these issues into a matrix that has become known as the 'McKinsey seven-S framework' (see Figure 13.2). This highlights the seven facets of a business that create a collective value system:

1. Strategy – market/brand maturity, differentiation, mass or niche approaches.
2. Structure – a marketing led organization, tactical approaches and portfolio management issues.
3. Systems – customer database management, customer intelligence networks; investment and market effectiveness measurement tools.

4. Style – competitive stance, brand management style, multiple brand personalities or a single personality around the globe including the tone of voice of the brand.
5. Skills – adding value to brand proposition, training to develop the internal language of the brand.
6. Staff – motivated and brand aware internal customers. The combination of these creates an organization with:
7. Shared values – a branded culture, which drives business performance and innovation, bringing the brand to life.

Each of the elements has a separate role to play in the building of a corporate brand culture and each must be assessed independently and collectively when corporate change is needed. Their collective impact on an organization is vital if significant and sustainable change is to be achieved.

De Chernatony (1999) has divided brand cultures into two distinct types: integrative and differentiated. The essence of an integrative brand culture is that the organization has the brand culture, while the differentiated brand culture is something that the organization is rather than has. The former accents the sense of explicit owning of a set of processes, skills and tools, while the latter accents a business that has an implicit gestalt-like collective sense of its brand. He suggests that an integrative brand culture is structured on three pillars:

1. visible artefacts: like corporate architecture, staff uniforms, office design (open/hot-desking or hierarchical);

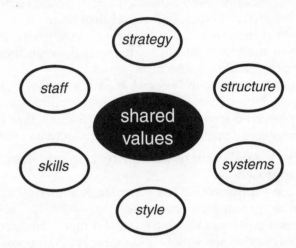

Figure 13.2 Seven-S framework (Source: Peters and Waterman, 1985)

2. employees' values: the explicit articulation of collective beliefs and attitudes;
3. unconscious values: the implicit assumptions and ideology of the collective internal customers.

The value of this type of model is that it emphasizes the mainly tangible elements of an organization and can theoretically be changed via tangible changes in buildings, communication programmes, etc.

The differentiated model of brand culture relies on the complete sense of shared values that are intangible but no less powerful. These are more difficult to audit, and therefore it is tricky assessing the gaps between the current and the desired positioning in the marketplace. However, the strong differentiated culture adds tremendous value to a brand and makes it extremely difficult to compete against. Brands that behave in this way are the cultural brands like Manchester United Football Club and Virgin Airlines.

The value of the internal culture of brand to a business must be clearly understood as a strategic tool and equity; it requires long term-management techniques and not short-term tactics. I cannot emphasize this enough: the aura or promise that a brand represents to consumers can be updated over time, but it is its consistency of core benefit that consumers will buy into and remain loyal to. The evidence of brands that tried to change too quickly or failed to build sufficient trust with the consumer is everywhere. In this age of merger and acquisition (M&A), it will be hard to maintain customer loyalty through consistency of message. The recent spate of bank mergers in the United Kingdom has exposed their weakness, and allowed other, non-traditional banks to take market share. The Midland Bank became the Hongkong and Shanghai Banking Corporation (HSBC), Lloyds and TSB merged to become Lloyds TSB; new entrants include egg from the Prudential, the Sainsbury's bank, banking services from Marks & Spencer and the Virgin One account. For the old banks, the mergers have brought together two distinct corporate cultures, two brand cultures with different heritages and values. The challenge, as with any merger, is to integrate successfully the best of both brand cultures, while eliminating the worst of the previous brand cultures.

Internal customers as brand advocates

The business model of the new millennium is one of people power. When products and services are easily replicable, it is the delivery by people that can create a competitive edge. The power of a well-motivated and knowledgeable group of employees can be harnessed to creating business wealth. The force that can help align these is the brand, as a symbol of what the company is striving for, as a communication channel towards the consumer and other stakeholders. Peter York suggests, 'Rallying people internally and externally around the brand should be one and the same. Businesses that work well are the ones that understand this.' It is no longer possible simply to regard brand management as the domain of the marketing department; every employee must understand the goals and values of the business and exude these in their daily work. Peter Drucker would add that managing and marketing the brand is the responsibility of everyone in an organization.

The human resources department

More than ever, the value of people is being recognized as the differentiator for businesses, especially when technologies can be so easily and quickly replicated by competitors. If the staff is one of the key tools to developing and delivering the brand to all stakeholders, then the HR department must be on the critical path for this. The HR director needs to understand totally the brand and its communication goals. He or she must take these goals into account when searching for new employees; the style of advertisement used should include the key brand values. It is better to recruit people who are implicitly and naturally on-brand, than spend further time and energy realigning them with the brand goals. The employees at Amazon.com have been recruited because they are all enthusiastic● book people and have an inherent service dimension to their personalities. They are people who thrive in the open architecture of the business, developing the product offer as the company develops. This is not the place for employees who are looking for a comfort-blanket approach to employment.

The building blocks of a brand business are its people; this means *everyone* in the organization. A brand business needs everyone pulling in the same direction, using the same language and expressing the same values, consistently and constantly. If a business has 10,000 employees, and each of these has an extended family of 10, a core group of 10 friends and 5 neighbours, then the one-to-one marketing of those employees impacts on at least 5 million people. This is invaluable, as one-to-one marketing is one of the most persuasive forms of communication we can use. The reach of those employees and the sincerity of the message are massive, without spending any advertising or marketing money. The best thing is that those 5 million people are an extra group, outside the daily work of the employees. Now imagine that all your employees are motivated and expressing your brand inside their daily work, every time they answer the telephone, or take an order, or give advice or change to a customer. The power of those brand ambassadors becomes a competitive tool and not just a 'nice to have' benefit.

This kind of employee motivation can provide outstanding performance results when nurtured, and there are several proven techniques for achieving this. They reflect the change in focus towards people, both as the greatest assets a company has, and as recognition that markets are not faceless but real customers with lives and feelings as well. The age of relationship marketing is still greatly misunderstood, as is internal, emotional motivation for employees.

There are many consultants who are trying to motivate and change internal employees' attitudes; most of the successful ones have shifted away from business development towards personal development skills. They help employees to develop themselves, to learn how to define their own comfort zone and how to find interest and challenge in their work. One of the methods currently being used successfully is developed from the work of Mihaly Csikszentmihalyi. He is a psychologist who has created a model about 'flow', his term to describe the optimal balance between the size of challenge we can master and our capability to achieve the goal. A good example is an athlete who races and wins with a feeling of euphoria – a combination of adrenaline and mental satisfaction that the whole mind and body has harmonized to achieve the result.

When a challenge is too great for our skill level, we become anxious, which is expressed as stress. When the scale of the challenge is too low for our skill base, we become bored, which is expressed as apathy. The optimal balance is when our skills are being sufficiently tested that we are not bored, but not tested so hard that we become anxious. This period of flow is constantly dynamic: we must find new challenges as our skill level increases, or find new skills as our challenges increase. For any work task that we must complete, we should have sufficient skill to accomplish it. When the task is new we may be anxious, but as it becomes familiar and we learn how to complete it easily we start to become bored. We require a new challenge to increase our sense of flow.

Creating a sense of flow around the brand is all about encouraging employees to improve themselves and live their lives as well as they can. This in turn results in a greater motivation on their part, with a passion for life and the brand. The total result for the corporation is a highly motivated workforce who are eager to change and meet new challenges with delight; they are also more satisfied with their lives and work situation. The hard part for a brand manager or CEO is to track and manage individual expectations and desires for new challenges, and provide the necessary training to ensure that skill levels continue to rise. The rewards are well worth the effort.

One of the most underestimated but emerging benefits of having all employees as brand ambassadors is the increase in their decision-making ability. When a group of employees implicitly knows how the brand would feel about an issue, or react towards an external problem, the choices they have to make in their daily work are made easier. They already know what the brand would do, and can react more effectively and in a way that continually reinforces the brand message. Any decision-making process, whether for a marketing director on a global brand issue or a receptionist on a telephone call, needs to reflect what the brand would do in the same situation. Businesses like Virgin are renowned as places to work, because what you see is what you get. The Virgin brand is fun-loving and open, because the staff and their way of doing business are like that. The brand attracts people who want to be like that and they in turn build and reinforce the brand values of Virgin.

Crisis management

Crisis management, an implicit kind of brand action, can be particularly important when a crisis hits a business, or it has to react instantly to a competitive threat. When the oil giant Shell wanted to dump one of its old drilling platforms in a deep trench in the Atlantic (in itself a very off-brand thing to do), it was surprised by the speed and depth of consumer reaction. Many petrol stations were boycotted across Europe, as consumers showed their disgust at the large corporation's actions. It is during a crisis like this that all the staff should implicitly understand and react the way the brand would, without having to wait for top-down direction.

Similarly, when a competitor launches a comparative advertising offensive against your brand, you need to consider how and whether the brand would react, rather than entering an advertisement war. If your brand values are based on generosity and freedom, then acknowledge this; do not switch to aggressive power just to win a small point. The strategic management of brands is about winning the war, not just a single battle. The long-term presence of the brand should be carefully refined and guarded; don't be tempted into a short skirmish that is out of character.

Capturing the heart and mind of the employee are the two key dimensions for developing employee buy-in towards the brand values and increasing its competitiveness. The emotional commitment of employees to a brand becomes a driving force that can realize substantial results. It is the difference between people who simply do their job and ones who go beyond the boundaries to make things happen. The intellectual capital that a business has is the store of its knowledge and experience; if the staff leave then often much of that knowledge is lost, even with embedded processes. Thomson (1999) has worked for many years successfully developing these elements as resources for branded businesses. As he describes it, emotional capital (passion) drives intellectual capital (knowledge) delivering business capital (profit).

Information and intellectual brand capital

In today's climate of high technology there is one big problem: too much information. It is the way it is analysed that makes it useful to a brand manager. Translating that information into intellectual capital or knowledge requires a set of filters to help with decision making. These filters are usually based on the range of factors that impact the business. Typical filters might be:

- consumer filter, eg using a youth panel to help lifestyle brands to choose product ranges;
- financial filter, fixing targets and margins like 22% ROI (return on investment) help to filter choices on a profit basis;
- time filter; for example, for service industries and supermarkets it may be necessary to change the offer throughout the day and the seasons;

- spatial filter; for example, brands need to clarify which geographical or micro-regional boundaries they wish to include and exclude;
- technology filter; for example, which new media channel the brand will use as a communication channel;
- people filter; for example, brands can only be built with the right mix of people skills.

All these filters help to reduce the amount of information that needs to be analysed and understood by the brand manager. The remaining information and data form a rich source of intellectual capital that can be used to leverage the brand. The ability to discard information that while interesting is of little saliency to the brand is a crucial skill in these information-rich times. This skill is especially relevant in large corporations, where information floods in from all departments. It cannot be emphasized enough that the initial reduction of the volume of data will allow significantly more time to be spent on the relevant data, rather than spreading the time over all data as though it were equally valuable.

Emotional brand capital

Thomson (1999) describes what emotional capital is and how it can be organized and channelled to create successful businesses. It relies on a large number of the emotional dimensions described in Chapter 8 to motivate driving a branding programme forward. Emotional capital lives in a symbiotic relationship with the brand, as the brand is also the best source to lead the definition of the tone of the emotional capital used internally within the business. For example, the Virgin brand represents a free-thinking and fun brand to consumers in the marketplace; internally, the company has similar values for its relationship between employees. The brand values become the emotional capital of the company, and the emotional capital of the employees drives the brand and its values.

Typical examples of emotional capital are inspiration, pride, success, respect, rejection or angst. Emotional capital can be positive or negative depending on the morale of the employees. When a brand is not performing, a turnaround project may identify that it is largely because the internal customers are not motivated or have a negative emotional capital.

Thomson (1999) has identified the 10 dynamic emotions in business as:

1. obsession: persistent idea that constantly forces its way into consciousness;
2. challenge: desire to rise up, fight and win, especially against the odds;
3. passion;
4. strong affection or enthusiasm for a product, service, personality, concept or idea;
5. commitment: the dedication or involvement with a particular action or cause;
6. determination: unwavering mind, firmness or purpose;
7. delight: the act of receiving pleasure, like fun, laughter, amusement;
8. love: great affection or attachment, to want to give;
9. pride: feeling of honour and self-respect, a sense of personal worth and organizational worth;
10. trust: confidence in the integrity, value or reliability of a person or entity, such as a team or organization.

He identifies the 10 deadly emotions as:

1. fear: feeling of distress, apprehension or alarm caused by a sense of impending danger;
2. anger: feeling of great annoyance or antagonism as the result of some real or supposed grievance;
3. apathy: lack of motivation (give me anger any day – anger can be turned around; apathy is much worse!);
4. stress: mental, physical or emotional strain or tension;
5. anxiety: state of uneasiness or tension caused by apprehension of a possible misfortune;
6. hostility: antagonistic and / or oppositional behaviour;
7. envy: discontent, a begrudging feeling or resentful admiration aroused by the possessions, achievements or qualities of another;
8. greed: excessive desire for wealth and power;
9. selfishness: lack of consideration of others actuated by self-interest;
10. hatred: feeling of intense dislike.

In order to develop internal customers into motivated on-brand advocates it is first necessary to audit the current status of their morale. The above lists are a useful guide to defining the parameters along which they are both successful and unsuccessful, although there will be others as well, depending on the brand category.

An excellent way to check the motivation of the internal customers in a corporate brand is to use the core brand values as the dimensions of the audit. This will tell you if there is a gap between the expectations of the brand and the internal customers' perceptions of their role within the brand delivery systems. For portfolio businesses like Procter & Gamble, it is not necessarily an advantage to match brand values with internal customer values. In this case it is more useful to use the above generic list of emotional capital to encourage and motivate greater performance and satisfaction.

This type of internal brand auditing process is the first step towards developing a strong internal communication network. This should include the internal awareness of the brand, the perception of the brand and the strength of harmony or dissonance with the brand values and personality. The next step is to develop a programme to focus and refine the communication with internal customers. This involves building a dialogue rather than simply a top-down direction for communication. In the same way that external customer needs are mapped and listened to, internal customers must be given the opportunity to express their needs and receive communication materials tailored to them. Like an advertising campaign, the internal customer must be communicated with in a sophisticated manner. Figure 13.3 explains a proven four-step approach to internal communications.

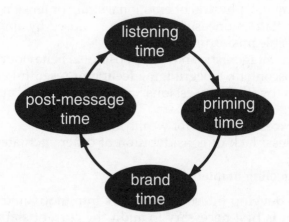

Figure 13.3 Four-step internal communications programme

Four-step internal communications programme

Listening time

Listen very closely to what internal customers are saying and not saying about the brand and the business. Be open to what you are hearing and make sure that part of the conditions of the listening programme are discretion and anonymity. Learn how they perceive the current communication programmes, what their strengths and weaknesses are. Learn how they would like to be communicated with – is there a preference for visual, auditory or kinaesthetic materials? Listen to their assessment of the past, present and future direction of the brand, as this will help to shape the scale of further changes.

Prime time

Once the listening programme is finished, the new internal brand communication must be shaped and developed like any external programme, taking into account the preferences of the internal customers. The first steps in this communication are to prime the audience to receive the message. If this is not done, many of the internal customers will not gain maximum benefit from the campaign because they are not open or ready for the message. Part of that priming is to explain why the message is being communicated and why it is important that they listen and understand it. The context of the new message must also be explained – how this message fits in with the other brand messages they see and hear internally. The best way to achieve this is to map out all the internal communications they receive from all departments and their frequency across the year or month. This will help to highlight the relative hierarchy of the messages and the flow of messages that build up across the year. It may be simple, but it is incredibly effective to visually explain what everyone will hear and in what order, rather than the audience simply receiving a stream of discrete messages that they must build into a structure themselves. It is far better to prime them with that structure beforehand.

The second element of priming is to create a positive platform for the up-coming brand message. This may be achieved with a teaser campaign, or by highlighting the current inadequacies of the brand as it stands, or expressing the future context of socio-cultural trends, technology or business competition that requires the business to progress. The primer should also encourage the internal customer to be open to the brand message by highlighting the specific benefits to each group of employees.

Brand time

Brand time is when the internal brand message is delivered to the internal customers. If the message is complex, it needs to be delivered in a layered approach that can be easily absorbed and understood by breaking it down into a time-phased series of smaller messages. If it is a succinct message, as ideal messages should be, then this should be communicated using multiple techniques and media. The audience has a mixed ability for receiving auditory, visual and kinaesthetic messages, so make sure that each of these is well catered for in any presentation. The audience also probably has a wide range of left- and right-brain abilities across all functions from manual workers, engineers and product managers to salespeople and service managers.

The expense of delivering an internal campaign may seem high, but the brand relies on these internal customers for its delivery at all levels, so it is vital that everyone is well motivated and aligned to the brand. The reward of having a well-informed and energized staff is invaluable, as it drives performance and creates a unique business. This uniqueness also helps to differentiate the brand in the marketplace, thus providing greater profit and further barriers of entry to the competition.

Post-message time

Once the message has been delivered, two things need to happen in the audience: they need to understand the message, and it should motivate them to action. Both these things should be monitored carefully to ensure and measure the effectiveness of the campaign. This means checking what the internal customers understood by the message, how close they are to the original intention and what is the breadth and depth of their understanding. Then indications of action taken by the internal audience as a result of the message should be checked. Without action, the message has been of little value, although it may take time and repeated messaging to generate the desired action. Experience suggests that follow-up messages are crucial to the success of any campaign, otherwise the audience will very quickly fall back into the old routine. Clearly, a campaign that includes a series of messages is to be preferred because of its ability to continue and sustain its programme of change over time.

This four-step process for managing internal communications has proved very successful in realigning internal customers with the desired brand message. For most brands it is better to shape the internal customer base with a new brand message before external-izing it, so that when the external campaign begins, the business and the people who drive it are already tuned in and building the success of the new message from the start. It can also be useful as a test ground of a new direction, since the internal customers repre-sent a small section of consumers for most brands. They should highlight any obvious dissonance in the message before it goes external.

The language of corporate branding

The language we use in any communication is vital to the perceived value of the message to our audience. Michael Abrahams explains this level of detail: 'For Wentworth Club, I felt it was important to define how people spoke to each other.' There are three basic modes of language: directive, requesting and inspirational.

The use of *directive language* usually creates or enforces barriers with internal customers. It seeks to achieve results by demanding action from the audience from a position of strong authority. This type of language should be rarely used, as it will quickly become impotent with frequent use. Internal customers generally react neg-atively to this form of language, which is aggressive and suggests a lack of understanding and interest in the viewpoint of the listener. However, there are certain situations when directive language is unavoidable.

Requesting language is the most commonly used form of commu-nication because it allows the listener to feel included in a dia-logue. While most requests are in fact directives, the language of requesting participation is subtle and encourages greater buy-in from the listener. The implicit power dynamic between the sender and receiver dictates the level of request within the message. The power of motivation within requested language is usually good, as internal customers feel included in the decision making of the business.

Inspirational language is the most powerful type of communication that will fully motivate internal customers because it creates an emotional will to achieve results. It may be in the form of a challenge to reach new levels of service, or the sense of being part of a winning team. Brand managers who can inspire through their use of language can rely on an extraordinary degree of commitment. Great political, sporting or business leaders have shown that inspirational language can squeeze fantastic performance out of even the smallest or least equipped teams.

The choice of language style is therefore crucial to the success of any internal brand communication programme. One of the best ways to develop effective language is to shape a phrase or sound-bite around each message. This crystallizes the message and the tone of that message in a memorable way for the listener; it may use the language of the listener or a colloquial phrase. The power of the phrase is that while much of a presentation may make sense and build the story, the content may also dilute it. The sound-bite is usually the part that most listeners will remember, long after the charts, diagrams and other content have been forgotten. The use of rhythm, pauses, alliteration, allegory and other linguistic tools can help to construct memorable phrases. They should be like the lead line to a hit song: something you cannot get out of your head, something catchy that summarizes a feeling as much as the content. It is always worth spending time to create a separate phrase for each presentation, then using it several times, in a subtle way, throughout the presentation will ensure that the audience retains that specific phrase.

Summary

* Internal brand management can help to realign the whole organization towards the goals of the business. The brand is ideally suited to be this type of catalyst within an organization.
* Internal brand culture is composed of the internal language used, the beliefs and attitudes of the staff, the rituals and conventions, the organizational structures that manage the staff and processes and the behaviours that form the key working practices.
* Emotional capital is the core resource of all employees to an organization. Properly motivated people can achieve higher gains and enjoy their work more than those who are not.
* The four-step internal communication programme is: listening time, priming time, brand time and post-message time.

THE FUTURE

New rules for the new economy

This chapter reviews the most recent trends in business and marketing to demonstrate their impact on the practice of brand management.

Globalization is the most fundamental change that the world is currently coping with, and this will impact on all four of the other trend areas. This ranges from the use of global brands and language, to the need to retain and respect local flavours and desires.

Key business trends include the current western concern for business category consolidation through merger and acquisition (M&A) activities. There is also a strong shift of the future basis for the economy; this represents the continuing journey from the commodity age, to the product economy of the Industrial Revolution, through to the service economy of the late 20th century. In the new millennium, the economy shifts again towards the 'experience economy' or, as the Nomura Economic Research Institute describes it, 'the age of creativity'.

Brands need to match the shifts expressed by the economic model and develop experiential customer interfaces. These will fall into the 5 I's brand dimensions of identify, inform, imagine, immerse and intrigue. Businesses need to define a balanced strategy for the bricks-to-clicks paradigm, as well as the new economy of clicks-to-bricks. They need to create synergy across the traditional and the new media rather than remain purely with one.

Objects

Objectives

* Define the key effects of globalization on brand management.
* Illustrate new business models that affect brand management.
* Describe the latest brand management tools that reflect contemporary consumer needs.

Globalization

The business world is changing rapidly and the meta-shift that faces brands every day is the need to have a global presence. There are several key branding issues that accompany this change:

* the consolidation of regional and national brands into global ones;
* M&A approaches and portfolio management;
* consolidation of regional and national brands into global ones.

The core business approach of many large businesses is to consolidate their brand portfolio into fewer, stronger, global brands. Unilever, the Anglo-Dutch FMCG group, has recently announced that it will be cutting its brand portfolio by 35 per cent in order to concentrate on developing 10 global brands. These cover the fields of soaps, food and drinks and require a strong vision and CEO to push through changes across many markets. Unilever believes that in five years' time the market will be dominated by a few key global brands per category, which take the lion's share of the market. As usual, this will be the profitable part of the market, leaving the unprofitable and lower part of the market to smaller global or regional brands. Kellogg's is a great example of how to successfully dominate a market category: its Cornflakes, Coco Pops and Special K cereals are the market leaders in many countries. It can derive huge savings from economies of scale in production, and brand awareness and communication programmes.

Ries and Trout (1981) have always suggested that if you are not number one in the mind of the consumer then growth will be much more difficult and expensive. They cite the fact that no one remembers who was the second person to stand on the moon, or who was the vice-president to Ronald Reagan. While it is not exactly the same for brands, since most of us can remember two or three brands for any given category, it is true that those at the top of the perceptual list have an innate advantage over the others.

In the global arena, this means consolidating different brands for the same product line to achieve that high position on the perceptual list. Of course, the cost of consolidation will be high – not just the actual change management process, but especially the cost in terms of goodwill. Many local brands have a strong heritage and goodwill associated with them, along with high customer awareness levels. It needs a strong CEO to recognize that in a few years' time, that goodwill may be overtaken by competitors' global brands. The decision is to do it before the competition does; again Ries and Trout cite being first as critical to success in brand positioning.

This kind of activity is particularly relevant in the global raiding atmosphere of international commerce. A quick look at the owners of large utilities reveals that an English water company is owned by a French business, a US business owns a couple of English electricity brands and telecommunications brands are in a constant state of M&A.

Merger and acquisition

Brands like the United Kingdom's Vodafone, Mannesmann of Germany and AirTouch of the United States have realized very quickly that the successful brands will be the ones that have a part of the big picture. The new brand Vodafone AirTouch has recently been formed and has already merged with Mannesmann.

One of the key reasons for this is the need for short-term profit and the generally risk-averse society that we now live in. Board directors who have been successful in shaping a new business realize that it is easier and more efficient to merge with or acquire an ailing competitor and turn it around than to go for organic growth. This is symptomatic of saturated western markets and the lack of real innovation in the marketplace. The core of this issue is that what these companies are buying is not necessarily the technology or product, but the goodwill of another large group of consumers towards that brand. Often the offer price for the business is made up from a majority percentage for the goodwill or brand, and a minority for the capital goods and assets.

Business trends

Clicks-to-bricks business model

The apparently conflicting business models of retail and e-tail have shaken customers' expectations, often hinting at the demise of the high street. But this disregards the social reasons why many of us go shopping on the high street. We often spend our time as well as our money treating the trip as a leisure activity. This reinforces the notion of the retail outlet as theme park and expresses our increasing desire to be entertained. It is also evidence of the fragmentation of our shopping habits across the Net, the high street, out-of-town sites and even cross-border trips. This may be price driven, convenience driven or enjoyment driven.

We select different options depending on our need state, perhaps buying a book from an online seller during the week when we are busy, or browsing over a coffee at the weekend when we have more time. E-commerce brands must decide whether they can fulfil all the customers needs online or whether they should have an offline presence as well.

Less than half of the UK population has current access to the Internet (source: the Internet marketing hit list). This means that the remainder do not have the chance to engage in e-commerce on any brand dimension. Potential customers may not even be aware that certain e-commerce brands exist, and certainly do not know what their key differentiators are. To disregard such a large part of the population is unacceptable to any business and e-commerce brands need to redress this quickly and effectively.

Trust

Any new brand needs to gain the trust of the customer, but especially e-commerce brands. Offline brands achieve this with a high street presence, where customers can view the tangible and legitimate nature of the brand. Online brands need to work harder to achieve this same level of trust. This can partially come from the use of encryption software and explicit privacy protocols. But there is no substitute for seeing a real store and giving your credit card details to a real cashier to convince a customer.

Established offline brands like Tesco have managed to success-fully leverage their real-world brand into the online world through a virtual sub-brand. But it is much more difficult for a new brand to raise awareness with new customers in the online world. Brands like amazon.com and lastminute.com have been successful in doing this by using all the media channels in the offline world as well as online media, but they have been unable to communicate the total brand experience, because of the limitations of those media channels.

Smaller e-commerce brands find it difficult to raise customer awareness levels without any type of offline marketing. Even the larger brands regularly use offline campaigns on TV or in print to generate traffic volume to their online sites.

Brand names as optimal Net-navigators

One of the biggest problems with searching on the Net is that there is too much information on it. Often a search engine will produce thousands of hits, many of which are irrelevant to our needs and this is extremely frustrating. They usually take too long to view and refinements are needed to get close to the chosen subject. This is because the methodology that search engines use does not accu-rately reflect the mental models that people use. The fastest and easiest way to find a site is to use the brand name and go immedi-ately to the chosen site. Our mental model of brands is much more direct than the generic words we might use to describe the subject. To search using the words 'jeans and blue' will retrieve too many hits; to search using 'levi.com' will retrieve only one hit, but it is the one the customer wants. The need for a strong brand and high levels of awareness has become even greater with the proliferation of virtual media.

Delivering total brand experiences

After using the brand name to find a site, the customer now engages with the service, and this should reinforce the experience we have had in the offline world. It should communicate the same brand values in the same brand tone as the customer has experi-enced offline.

Most e-commerce-only businesses do not have these offline channels in place; they rely entirely on the Net for their brand impression. Because of the current technology levels this is often low resolution, slow and lacking multisensorial emotions. The breadth of difference between competitors is also lower than the potential offline distinctions. The most sophisticated ones have animation, downloads and limited sound capabilities, while the simplest are static pages of a brochure. But they all lack the high-impact experience of an offline site and therefore do not truly engage the customer on a high level.

Successful retail brands convey a series of emotional and rational feelings towards customers, immersing them in a rich, seductive environment. They use theatre and perceptual cues to engage the customer and encourage him or her to purchase their brand. Brands that truly live in the mind of the customer are those that will be profitable and resistant to competition. In the contemporary retail landscape, the emotional differentiators will convince customers to be loyal by rewarding them with an attractive and enjoyable experience for the time they have invested in visiting their stores.

Flagship stores

Many e-commerce businesses may not wish to give up the low overheads that the Net provides to invest in a chain of high street locations. But they would be wise to think carefully before avoiding the high street altogether. Customers are people first and shoppers second; they actually find walking around stores and socializing an enjoyable part of their lives.

One of the best solutions to this dilemma has been for e-commerce businesses to open flagship stores. easyJet.com has opened a series of 'easyeverything' stores to help it market its brand on the high street. It raises awareness of the brand and allows access to its product and service offers. It fulfils all four segments for successful retailing:

1. It becomes the home of the brand in the real world by offering an immersive brand experience that will delight customers. It becomes the focus of the brand values, which add depth and texture to those employed on the Net.
2. It generates brand awareness through PR, footfall and word of mouth because it is an entertaining experience. This builds a strong differentiator against Net competition where the threshold for copying is low.

3. It provides first access to the brand and product sampling for the population who are not yet online, and can include terminals to access the Net offer and introduce new customers to the Net. Capturing customers first is always far easier than trying to get them to switch to their brand later.
4. It generates a strong trust in the brand, convincing customers that they are viable and legitimate, which is carried over into their online business.

Seamless integration

The opportunity for bringing e-commerce brands alive and capturing the hearts of customers lies in them enjoying real world experiences. This can best be done by combining the advantages of buying online with those of the high street, rather than following one or the other route. By developing a limited number of flagship stores in key locations like Regent Street in London, the Ginza in Tokyo or Fifth Avenue in New York, online brands can benefit from the best of both worlds. The offline sites promote the total brand experience, opportunities to try the products, and create financial trust in their service handling. The online sites are convenient for purchasing, locating stores and receiving up-to-date news about events. This integrated brand management approach will ensure the competitiveness and profitability of the new e-commerce brands.

The opportunity for integration of retailing channels has never been better for businesses. As e-commerce brands become established and offline brands open virtual stores, there is a growing consensus that the successful companies will be the ones that have a presence both offline and online. The balance between these will be category dependent, but if businesses want to satisfy their customers, they must deliver their proposition across media types and not reside in one. The business model of the future is not the one from offline or the one from online, but the one that successfully integrates them both. •

Brand experiences

The shift in economic model in the western world has led to a change in emphasis on the needs of consumers, raising the level of expectation (see Figure 14.1). Successful brands are now able to

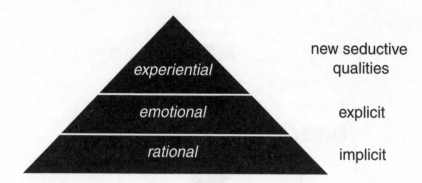

new seductive qualities

explicit

implicit

Figure 14.1 Hierarchy of customer benefits

deliver a higher level of relationship with the customer by offering them a brand experience. The work of Pine and Gilmore (1999) in 'the experience economy' has highlighted the need to reassess our priorities towards customer care.

The product related rational benefits still need to be addressed, as do the emotional benefits, but the biggest opportunity is in developing the experiential nature of the brand. This can be categorized through the 5 I dimensions of a brand experience, the strategies used to express them and the potential tactics to deliver them to the customer. By developing Pine and Gilmore's model we can fully satisfy the consumer across all his or her needs and desires, both latent and articulated. The new 5 I's model (see Figure 14.2) categorizes five key dimensions of consumer experience, representing the five core strategies to total customer satisfaction: identify, inform, imagine, immerse and intrigue.

The dimensions are distinct in themselves, but they also build into a rich experience that covers all levels of consumer need. This approach is strong because it caters to a range of consumer target segments on many different levels and serves many different need states. The second level describes the strategies to deliver those five core benefits.

From these strategies the tactics or tools of execution can be defined, which offer direct opportunities to help build the total brand experience. Like the benefits and strategies, they should be used in combination to achieve the most seductive brand experience, although, it is likely that the brand experience will have one or two major foci and use several other tactics to support the central one. The following is a list of potential tactics for implementing brand experiences:

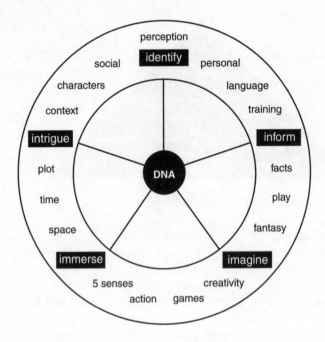

Figure 14.2 The 5 I's brand experience model™

- Identify: perception, social, personal.
- Inform: language, training, facts.
- Imagine: play, fantasy, creativity, games.
- Immerse: five senses, time, space, action.
- Intrigue: plot, context, characters.

Need states

As consumers change their need states throughout their lives, years, days and even hours, it is difficult but extremely important that brands can satisfy them whichever state they are presently in. By taking a layered approach to the brand experience with five dimensions, a brand is able to delight customers whichever need state they may be in at any moment of their lives.

Identify

The expression of self-identity has always been a strong motivator for brand purchases. Consumers wish to balance their need to construct their personality through brands with the need to create visible social identification. These correspond to the inner directed and outer directed psychological types. The mechanism through which these are achieved is the perception of meaning that was discussed in Chapter 7. The brand truly lives in the mind of the consumer. However hard brand managers try to direct the meaning of their brand, the consumer will always define the only important version of the brand identity. The key emotional dimensions discussed in Chapter 8 contribute to the field of self-identity development.

Inform

There is an increasing need for customers to be rewarded for their loyalty to a brand. One way of achieving this is through informing the customer and developing his or her own knowledge base, which creates a sense of achievement and progression.

This may be in the form of training, for example a restaurant showing a customer the best way to eat sushi, or a tailor showing a client the best way to wear a suit, or a car salesperson explaining the best way to check a car's engine. All these types of education help the customer to feel that he or she is gaining a unique and personalized experience from the brand. They also encourage the customer to interact with the brand in a two-way relationship where the customer is helping to define the kind of brand experience he or she wishes to have.

The brand may give customers certain facts that help them grow their mind and bodies. These facts may be expressed through a wine waiter selecting a wine to go with the food the customer has ordered, or customers may receive advice in a health food shop about the best combination of vitamins to take. A supermarket may provide free recipes for the produce that is currently in season and on the shelves.

The education received by the customer may be in the form of learning a new language for drinks, for example a wine waiter describing a fine Taylor's port as fruity, almondy with a hint of nutmeg. It may also be the language to describe an order, like ordering a Starbucks skinny latte (skimmed milk café au lait) from the Barristo (waiter/waitress). The enrichment of the brand experience through language encourages customers to feel closer to the brand, and differentiates it from other brands of coffeehouse.

Imagine

Many brands promise escape as their key value, whether it is a perfume brand like Chanel No 5 promising sexual attractiveness, or a cosmetics brand like Clinique promising eternal youth. The use of fantasy is a cornerstone of most brand campaigns because it stimulates the imagination of the customer, allowing them to escape from their daily lives, even for just a moment. The Sony Playstation TV advertisements 'Double world' draw on the fantasy of a young boy who has 'commanded armies'. It offers customers the chance to fantasize about their role in the world, beyond their physical or age capabilities. The Nike brand encourages us all to 'Just do it', to go beyond our conformity and live for the moment.

This escape may be in the form of creativity, where a brand allows the customer to be creative together with the brand. The Dulux paint brand uses this approach to express its role as a catalyst to unlocking the homeowner's own creativity together with Dulux. Other brands offering creativity as an escape from daily life include Sony, whose latest Minidisc TV advertisements encourage us to find the place we like to hear music, by showing a series of people listening to a minidisc player in unusual but highly personal places. The Gap clothing company, whose TV advertisements encourage us to wear khaki pants any way we like, and do what we like in them, connects its brand with enabling our own ability to be creative with our lives. The Swiss watch brand Swatch encourages customers to escape by wearing a different watch each day or for the mood they are in.

Brand experiences that offer us escape can also be in the format of play and games, like the Häagen-Dazs icecream brand that encourages us to play with food and our partners as an escape from daily life. Car brands like Ford and Land-Rover encourage us to play for the day, instead of going to work, enjoying the escapism of the open road.

Immerse

Brand experiences that immerse the customer in an environmental brand experience will make the most memorable impression about their brand. Every opportunity to deliver a multisensorial brand experience should be used to leverage the brand personality towards the customer. This should include the use of sound (the Direct Line insurance signature tune); visuals (the BMW photography), fragrances (the smell of a new Honda car); the taste and texture of Ben & Jerry's icecream; and the weight and feel of a Rolex watch. Each of the five senses should be defined in terms of the brand's DNA and expressed through its products, services and retail environments. The retail site is a critical expression of the brand in the offline world, because it is able to express the brand in a multisensorial manner. The Ralph Lauren brand has a flagship store on Bond Street in London and at the Rhinelander Mansion in Manhattan to deliver these kind of immersive brand experiences.

Time, space and action are often used to engage and immerse the customer in a total brand experience. The Nike brand uses these elements at its store, Nike Town, where the environment has been designed to create a unique Nike branded atmosphere. The movement of people and staff throughout the store creates the Nike brand, live in front of customers, and engages them to become part of that action.

Service brands are especially good at developing movement to engage the customer. E-commerce brands like amazon.com and lastminute.com continue to send personal e-mails and updates even after the purchase moment. They create action even in the online world. In the offline world the service brands like Iceland supermarket's home delivery service engage the customer in a branded event. Destination shopping malls like Bluewater in Kent have created a walkway to travel along as you move through the mall, immersing you in the unique branded journey.

Intrigue

A key benefit from most brand experiences should be to entertain the customer through intrigue. This means to deliver the brand message in the format of a narrative or story. Research has shown that people like to listen to messages that have a plot and unfold depicting part of a story. Following a plot or story line is an enjoyable and entertaining way for customers to hear the brand narrative. Customers also find it easier to remember messages when they are part of a clear narrative; this is because all stories have fixed elements to them that can be recognized. There are only a few significantly different plot lines and any film watcher or book reader will recognize most of them:

* the drama plot;
* the thriller plot;
* the romance plot;
* the intrigue plot;
* the humorous plot;
* the rise to fame;
* the revenge.

Most of the plots of brand experiences fall into one of these categories and so are already familiar to an audience. The Nescafé coffee advertisements use the continuing romance between two neighbours to deliver the brand experience, with the hero and heroine clearly marked for the audience.

One of the recognizable elements to a narrative is that it contains characters that deliver the story or brand message. Again, many of these characters are familiar to audiences, and so they can easily recognize and remember them as part of the brand message. They include:

* the hero;
* the villain;
* the vamp;
* the heroine;
* the expert;
* the storyteller.

Many cleaning product brands use the product as hero in the narrative. The Flash brand of floor cleaner saves the day by helping a father to clean up safely after the children have muddied the floor. The car recovery brands AA and RAC both use the service as hero, to save the car occupants from a long wait and difficulties. Not all character types are necessary to deliver a brand experience, but using these analogies will help to shape the roles of the brand delivery staff.

The narrative takes place within a context and this will have a significant effect on the perception of the brand experience. If the brand experience is contextualized in a social environment then this will affect the customers' understanding of the brand as a social brand. The context may be historical, continental or ironic, suggesting to the consumer that the brand is the same. The car company Fiat has shot its advertisements for the Punto car in Spain and used the tag line 'Spirito di Punto'. This context encourages the customer to feel that the car is inherently continental and seductive, reminiscent of holidays in warm places.

The branded customer journey

One of the best ways to develop the brand experience is through defining the 'branded customer journey' as a series of elements that build up the brand's message over time (see Figure 14.3). This can work as well for a television commercial as it does for a retail site, an Internet site or even as a customer flips through a brochure or print

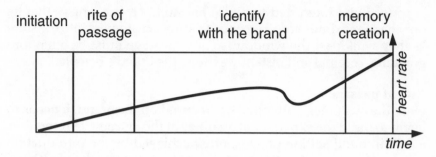

Figure 14.3 Branded customer journey™

campaign. It is powerful because of its ability to lead the customer through a layered story, including elements of the 5 Is that build total brand experiences. It gives the brand manager more control over the delivery of the brand experience and therefore increases the likelihood of its success. There are two layers to a successful journey: the progression through the experiential elements described earlier in this chapter, and the emotional, cinematic journey that customers should feel as they flow through that journey. Both of these layers should be carefully chosen and continually managed to maximize success.

The first layer of the journey
The supermarket brand needs to express itself clearly to all its target groups and across all their reasons for visiting the supermarket. These reasons can be categorized into several core 'shopping missions', like family shopping, lunch buying, emergency supplies, etc. The visits may be of different length and frequency but the desired brand experience should be felt on each occasion. One way to achieve this is to define the entry and exit of the store as portal zones that every customer experiences. Further into the store, different branded customer journeys can be mapped out for different missions, offering different facets of the store's brand.

Initiation
Like the cover on a brochure, first impressions help to align the expectations of the customer, whether it is their first or hundredth time of experiencing the brand. This is the first point of differentiation that builds a brand's positioning and effectively communicates it with the customer. The fashion designer Paul Smith changes his store window on a weekly basis to ensure that customers are always

surprised and interested to notice his store. He recognizes that he only has a maximum of 30 seconds to attract customers into the store as they walk past the window, so any message must be attention-grabbing, original and instantly express the brand's benefits.

Rite of passage

Once the customer's attention has focused on the brand, it needs to begin to build the experiential qualities of the journey. This requires a certain mind-setting process, often achieved by the introduction in a brochure or advertisement. It needs to change the emotional state and define the new points of reference of the brand towards the customer to ensure full engagement with the brand. This is most successfully achieved by a stimulating multisensorial experience. It ensures that all of the customer's attention is tuned to the experience and emphasizes the distinct nature of that brand over competitors.

Identify with the brand

This phase of the journey should deliver the main feature of the brand in a seductive and experiential presentation. It should draw on all the 5 I dimensions and the surrounding tactical tools to create a vivid and enjoyable experience. Depending on the mission, this may be short or long but should not miss out any elements; it can simply reduce the time for each. One of the criteria is the separation of the functional needs of the customer from start to finish. For a supermarket like Asda or Wal-Mart, there may be a series of customer missions that need to be fulfilled by the store. Customer research has segmented needs into five broad categories that are linked to the major shopping trips and target audiences:

1. lunch time food and snacks;
2. emergency supplies and last-minute items;
3. family or household major weekly shopping;
4. family or household minor weekly shopping;
5. newspaper and cigarettes/sweets.

Each of these would need a different brand accent, so the lunchtime food mission requires freshly made delicatessen-style branding, while the family major mission would require more detailed advice or a wider range of possibilities. The identifying with the brand phase of the customer journey in this case would have several different sub-journeys that customers would follow. This needs to be started with a choice-making phase or point of departure, and a final joining phase at the end so that customers return to the meta-journey, and end this with the memory-creation phase.

Memory creation

The final phase should create a positive residual memory of the brand; an imprint of the experience or, as Woodhuysen calls it, 'the memory muscle'. This is the mental closure that customers like to have when they are changing states of mind; it allows them to consolidate one experience and move on to another without losing the first. It is crucial to get this right because it turns first-time buyers into regular customers, or a transaction into a customer relationship. It is the brand's calling card for a return visit and should confirm the distinctive experience that the brand offers over the competition.

Flexibility and adaptability

The above description is the core-branded customer journey and there are many alternative routes and phases in between, depending on the nature of the category, the customer base and the media channel required. It may be necessary to have a choice and selection phase for instance for a Warner Brothers 18-screen cinema multiplex brand, or the large British Telecom Internet brandsite. Or it may need to shorten or lengthen the phases depending on the nature of the brand's message or location. The Nike Town flagship store or the trainline.com Internet site devotes more time to rites of passage than the Matalan warehouse store. The luxury chocolate brand Godiva has a long rite-of-passage opening ceremony to its packaging, while the Colgate toothpaste brand's pack is minimal. The lounge for Cathay Pacific's first-class airline passengers has a different rite-of-passage brand message from that given to its economy passengers, who remain in the airport lounge. The important issue is the flexibility and adaptability of the brand journey to specific target customers, segments, regions and needs. It needs to
• be tailored to meet their requirements; monitored and updated to remain successful.

Layer 2: Emotional state journey

The second layer of the brand journey should plot the change in the emotional state that customers should experience in order to fully engage in the brand experience. Some of the most successful of these are based on the award-winning cinematic journeys of cult films like James Bond, *ET*, *Raiders of the Lost Ark*, *Room with a View* and *Hellraiser*. Cooper's (1997) work on film screenplays is an excellent reference for developing the value and dimensions of a branded customer journey. The cinematic experience provides a strong analogy with the kinds of brand experiences that customers will enjoy as they open a piece of packaging, receive a travel service, or browse a site.

This emotional state journey has several advantages:

* It helps customers to follow the brand message because it follows the expected rules of performance.
* It ensures a vibrant 'live' performance feel for the customer every time.
* It reduces the reliance of the performance on the staff, and increases overall quality across the business.
* It can be changed depending on the season or time of day to create further uniqueness in the market.
* It provides a meta-story that audiences remember first, then fills in the details.
* Most importantly, it delivers the sense of build-up of tension then relief and relaxation that customers enjoy and need in their lives.

There are a few core, recognizable silhouettes of the emotional state journey to choose from that should match with the needs of the brand message. But within these, the lines can be adjusted to suit local needs and preferences, and hybrids and variations can be created. The core silhouettes according to Cooper (1997) are:

1. mountain: a simple and steady rise to the climax of the story;
2. alpine: a continuous rise with several distinctive sub-peaks of action and brand messages;
3. dinosaur: a steady rise to a peak, which turns out to be a false ending, a dip to take time out then a sharp rise to the climax;
4. tick: an explosive start, followed by a relaxed period that rises steadily to the climax.

As Figure 14.4 suggests, each one has its own structure and development and is therefore suitable for different brand situations and message delivery. Using these analogies we can also start to see how competitors' brands approach brand communication in different ways, reflecting their brand's personality.

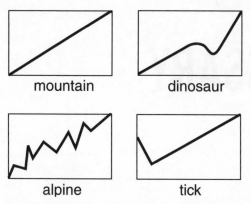

mountain   dinosaur

alpine   tick

Figure 14.4 Emotional state journey (Source: Cooper, 1997)

Summary

- The future of brand creation, development and management should reflect the emerging business models of the key markets of an organization. This will ensure that it can maximize its potential gains and minimize the risks of business growth. This means embracing new technologies as well as new cultural and social needs to optimize customer satisfaction and loyalty.

- The opportunity for greater breadth of communication across markets and target groups has never been higher. But there is also an opportunity for greater depth through direct contact with individual customers to ensure that they are totally satisfied, every time. It is important to define the target goals of these activities and put in place structures that can tactically deliver them.

- One of the key effects of globalization is the increase in product availability and choice for the consumer. This is combined with the increase in communication pollution developed by those businesses. The brand becomes increasingly important as the easiest navigator in this frenetic world.

- The key new business models that will impact on brand management arise from the new economy models of e-commerce and transformational change.

- The latest brand management tools create multisensorial brand experiences based on the 5 I's model of identify, inform, imagine, immerse and intrigue customers.

GLOSSARY

above the line   A group of media including the press, radio, television, cinema and outdoor and transport media.

act of passing off   A legal definition of when a competitor tries to sell a product with a visual identity, brand mark or trade dress that is too similar to another business's.

aesthetic codes   The symbolic or visual meaning of an image or text, eg the colour gold represents wealth and luxury.

AIDA (Attention, Interest, Desire and Action)   Strong's (1929) model of an effective advertising process.

below the line   A group of media including point of purchase (POP), public relations, direct mail, in-store promotions and all other media.

benchmarking   An analysis of best practices in the market or category.

brand   A set of characteristics that give added value to a product or service beyond its tangible benefit. The product or service can be visualized as a hard, white golf ball, while the brand is a large, translucent, multi-coloured balloon of gas surrounding that golf ball. The balloon's membrane is the flexible personality that can be squeezed and changed to different accents or personalities, while the central golf ball remains. The consumer's decision to buy is mostly based on the character of the balloon, while the underlying use is often based on the character of the golf ball.

brand breadth   A measure of the stretchability of the brand across the widest possible range of consumer groups.

brand custodian blueprint   A sequential process for new brand creation that starts by defining the brand DNA in a media-neutral frame of reference.

brand definition   A process to determine the most appropriate set of characteristics that a brand should communicate.

brand displeasure   A dimension expressing a customer's deep dissatisfaction with a brand.

brand DNA   A term used to describe the core essence of a brand's characteristics. It should be evident in every part of a business, from its internal culture to its product or service and their communication.

brand equity   A term used to describe the financial value of a brand.

brand experience   A totally immersive happening that engages the customer with all the five senses in a live event.

brand extension   A term describing the technique of adding new products to the range using the same lead brand name and adding a sub-name to it.

brand force field mapping   A method of understanding a customer's needs and a brand's ability to fulfil them.

brand identity   A visual or design style that expresses the core brand values.

brand leader   The number one or two positioned brands that customers expect a store to have.

brand length   A measure of the stretchability of the brand across product or business categories.

brand logo/brand mark   The visual design or stylistic identity of the brand name that can be trade marked or registered.

brand mapping   A visual technique of representing the core positioning of a brand; often used to compare competitors' footprints on the same axis.

brand media   All media types that can communicate the brand: advertising, PR, packaging, product, store, staff, including above the line and below the line media.

brand name   A name that represents the brand and often the structure of the business or product range or service level.

brand narrative   A biography of a brand that develops over time, matching a developing relationship with the consumer.

brand perception   The customer's received comprehension of the brand's meaning.

brand personality   A chosen character that best communicates the brand's positioning; it may be represented by any media or style such as using a cartoon, a watercolour, using humour or aggression, etc.

brand planning   A strategic role in a business, responsible for the holistic development of the brand. Also a method of brand creation and development.

brand pleasure   A dimension expressing the customer's deep satisfaction with a brand.

brand portfolio   A term for the collection of brands and sub-brands in a business that need to be managed simultaneously.

brand power   A measure of a brand's ability to influence customers, often related to customer loyalty.

brand proposition   A succinct description of the benefits that the brand delivers to consumers.

brand spread   The spread of a brand across categories, rather like brand breadth.

brand theme   A conceptual framework that connects all elements of the brand message, eg pagan-Scottishness for a whisky brand.

brand weight   A measure of the dominance of a brand in a market, often related to its market share.

branded customer journey   A chart that describes the optimal emotional feeling that customers should receive from a brand experience.

branded identity company   A business that uses individual brand names for each of its products.

brandsite   A virtual or new media site that communicates the brand.

broadcast codes   A media term for defining symbolic images and meanings that will attract a wide target audience.

business culture   The internal attitudes, behaviour and practices of a business.

buying process   A recognized four-step process of anchor, search, choose and check that customers go through when purchasing.

cash cow brand   A brand that delivers healthy revenues for a minimum investment.

causal research   A research methodology that illustrates the existence of any cause-and-effect relationships between market phenomena.

cognitive brand dimension   A brand value perceived by the customer through logical reasoning.

conjoint analysis   A research methodology that compares different combinations of variables of a brand.

consumer culture   The attitudes, behaviour and practices of the westernized world, whose economy is based on the consumption of material goods and intangible services. It also refers to the increasingly *consumer-centric* nature of society, business and the economy.

copyright Legal protection against copying a distinctive and unique intellectual property.

corporate identity A visual identity communicating the name and typically the structure of a business.

cultural brand pleasure A brand dimension that is based on fulfilling consumers' cultural beliefs like aesthetics, spiritualism and icons.

DAGMAR (Defining Advertising Goals for Measured Advertising Results) One of the testing methods for advertising effectiveness.

descriptive research A research methodology that leads to a detailed portrait of a consumer segment, brand proposition or brand management issue.

design patent Legal protection of a visual design or intellectual property that is protected because of its originality.

diffusion brand (Identical to sub-brand.) A term describing a product that forms part of a range or line of goods and uses the core brand name of the original brand.

digital television A television signal based on digital technology rather than analogue; its main benefits are increased quality and the potential for two-way interactivity.

dilution A legal definition of the reduction in value of one brand by another because of its similarities, often specified as an infringement in legal cases.

DMU (Decision Making Unit) In the context of this book, a group of people who will collectively choose a brand, typically in business-to-business marketing. It may contain the finance manager, technical experts and line manager.

e-commerce A business model that relies on digital or virtual sales.

• **emotional benefit** A definition of a brand's benefit perceived through intuition and inspiration.

emotional capital A term used by Thomson (1999) to describe the value of an employee's emotional commitment to a brand.

entry brand A brand that encourages customers to trial a brand for the first time.

essentials A must-have brand that a store needs to attract customers.

exploratory research An initial research methodology that defines what the question or scope of the question should be.

extranet   A computer network that allows suppliers to access a company's internal database.

flanking brand   A brand that supports a core brand and acts as a barrier to competitors.

FMCG (fast-moving consumer goods)   A type of cheap consumable product like toothpaste, washing powder, newspapers, chocolate bars, shampoo, canned drinks, etc.

focus group   A research method involving a small group of typical consumers or non-consumers of a product who discuss their attitudes with a trained facilitator.

gestalt   A psychological term for a collective or group's understanding of a brand's meaning, the sum of all the parts; the brand experience is the sum of the name, the identity, the packaging, the services, etc.

goodwill   The associated loyalty and tolerance that a brand commands from the customer, often used to create and specify the financial value of a brand.

grey imports   (Identical to parallel imports.) A type of good bought legally in another, cheaper country and then imported and sold at a price lower than the manufacturer's specified price.

high-end brand   A brand that occupies a premium position.

ideological brand pleasure   A brand dimension that is based on fulfilling consumers' highest level beliefs, like nationalism or the environment.

interactive television   A process and technology that allows consumers to react and request services and products via television programmes.

Internet   A computer network that allows a computer to access databases all over the world via the telephone line. Significantly, the total information is not stored in one specific computer's memory.

intranet   An internal computer network that allows all internal employees access to the same database at the same time.

KVI (known-value item)   A daily product like bread, milk or cheese, whose price and value are typically known to customers.

left-brain thinking   The left part of the brain is responsible for the inspirational and intuitive, irrational ideas and thoughts.

line brand   A brand name that is used across a range of products, often similar.

Maslow's hierarchy of needs   A consumer behaviour model that can be used to distinguish the levels and the order of potential brand benefits.

merger and acquisition (M&A)   A business term for the activity of buying businesses to achieve growth rather than through organic growth.

MUD (multiple-user dungeon)   A controlled virtual environment that allows social games and fantasy to be experienced.

narrowcast codes   A media term for defining symbolic images and meanings that will only attract a narrow, specified target audience.

niche brand   A brand that provides a specific but narrow proposition to a smaller target audience.

NVR (nominal value ranking)   A system of scoring a list of brand attributes to easily prioritize them.

own-label   A brand name on a range of products belonging to the store that sells them.

parallel imports   (Identical to grey imports.) A type of good bought legally in another, cheaper country and then imported and sold at a price lower than the manufacturer's specified price.

passing off   Trying to sell a product with a visual identity, brand mark or trade dress that is too similar to another business's.

perceptual grouping   A psychological concept of the customer's perceived grouping of a number of brands that offer similar benefits.

perceptual proximity mapping   A methodology to illustrate the received meaning that a consumer associates with a brand; the closer the association, the nearer the middle of the map.

positioning statement   A description of the key distinguishing attributes of a brand.

power retailing   A business model of the increasing strength of retailers' brands over manufacturers' brands.

primary research   A research methodology that requires the collecting of original data specific to the problem.

product brand   A brand that represents a single product, eg a Snickers bar.

• **profit brand**   A brand that generates high margins and profit.

psychological brand pleasure   A brand dimension that is based on fulfilling consumers' personal beliefs like achievement, success or the five senses.

QFD (Quality Function Deployment)   A Japanese management system that analyses a brand's values against the customer's needs.

qualitative research   A research methodology that tries to define the reasons why market and consumer phenomena occur.

quantitative research A research methodology that tries to describe the facts and figures concerning consumer and market phenomena.

range brand A brand name that is used across a range of products, often dissimilar.

rational benefit A definition of a brand's benefit perceived through logical reasoning.

registered mark A legal definition of a distinctive and unique visual sign, text or intellectual property that represents a business, often the brand name. It indicates that this has been registered and is protected.

retail branding A business model that uses own-label goods to generate and communicate brand identity.

right-brain thinking The right part of the brain is responsible for the rational and logical thought processes and ideas.

secondary research A research methodology that uses already collected sources of data; it usually comes before primary research.

self-image A sociological term for an individual's sense of his or her own individual identity.

semiotics A study of signs that is a popular method of understanding how consumers comprehend the meaning of a brand.

SMART (specific, measurable, achievable, realistic and time-based) A model for effective target setting, often used in ISO 9000 quality management processes.

social image A sociological term for an individual's sense of his or her group belonging and identity.

sociological brand pleasure A brand dimension that is based on fulfilling consumers' social or group beliefs like status and group membership.

sole identity company A business that uses a single brand name across all its products or services.

SSAP-22 – accounting for goodwill A UK accountancy rule to determine the value of a brand.

sub-brand (Identical to diffusion brand.) A term describing a product that forms part of a range or line of goods and uses the core brand name of the original brand.

SWOT (strengths, weaknesses, opportunities and threats) A business process of internal and competitor analysis.

trade dress The defining tangible and intangible characteristics of all the elements of a brand.

trade mark   A legal definition of a distinctive and unique visual sign, text or intellectual property that represents a business, often the brand name. It indicates that this has been protected but is unregistered.

validated identity company   A business that uses a business name across all its products as well as a sub-brand name.

weak brand   A brand that should be divested or recombined.

BIBLIOGRAPHY

Aaker, D A (1991) *Managing Brand Equity*, Free Press, London
Aaker, D A (1994) *Building Stronger Brands*, Jossey-Bass Wiley, New
    York
Aaker, D A (2001) *Strategic Marketing Management*, Wiley, New York
Aaker, D A and Joachimsthaler, E (2002) *Brand Leadership*, Free Press,
    New York
Aaker, D A, Kumar, V and Day, G S (1999) *Marketing Research*, Wiley,
    New York
Adcock, D, Bradfield, R, Halborg, A and Ross, C (1995) *Marketing
    Principles and Practice*, Pitman, London
Allen, D (1988) *Creating Value: The financial management of brands*,
    Chartered Institute of Management Accountants, University of
    Loughborough
Amber, T and Barwise, P (1998) The trouble with brand evaluation,
    The Journal of Brand Management, **5** (5), pp 367–77
Anderson, A H and Barker, D (1994) *Effective Business Policy*,
    Blackwell, Oxford
Angehrn, A A, *et al* (1998) Mastering marketing series: marketing and
    new media, *Financial Times*
Angell, I (1998) Who needs the Internet?, *Computing*, November,
    p 26
Barnard, M (1996) *Fashion as Communication*, Routledge, London
Barthes, R (1993) *Mythologies*, Palladian, London
Baudrillard, J (1998) *The Consumer Society: Myths and structures*, Sage,
    London
Bernstein, D (1991) *Company Image and Reality: A critique of corporate
    communications*, Cassell, London
Best, S and Kellner, D (1991) *Postmodern Theory: Critical investigations*,
    Guilford Press

Blythe, J (1998) *Essentials of Marketing*, FT Pitman Publishing, London

Bocock, R (1993) *Consumption: Key ideas*, Routledge, London

Bray, P (1998) We're mostly cowards on the techno diving board, *Daily Telegraph*, November 25, p 36

Brearly, R A and Myers, S C (1991) *Principles of Corporate Finance*, McGraw-Hill, Maidenhead

BRMB (1998) *Internet User Growth: Research findings*, BRMB, London

Butcher, M (ed) (1998) *New Media Age*, 15 October, p 15

Calvino, I (1996) *Six Memos for the Next Millennium*, Random House, London

Caminiti, S (1996) Ralph Lauren, the emperor has new clothes, *Fortune*, 11 November

Campbell, C (1998) *The Myth of Social Action*, Cambridge University Press, Cambridge

Carratu, P (1996) *Carratu International* [online] www.carratu.com

Chowdhury, S (1999) *Management 21C: Someday we'll all manage this way*, Financial Times/Prentice Hall, London

Churchill, G A Jr (1988) *Basic Marketing Research*, Dryden Press, London

Connolly, A and Davenport-Firth, D (1999) Visual planning – the power of thinking visually, *The Journal of Brand Management*, **6** (3), pp 161–231

Cooper, D (1997) *Great Screenplays for Film and TV*, Macmillan, New York

Cotton, R and Oliver, R (1993) *Understanding Hypermedia: From multimedia to virtual reality*, Phaidon, London

Csikszentmihalyi, M and Rochberg-Halton, E (1995) *The Meaning of Things: Domestic symbols and the self*, Cambridge University Press, Cambridge

Davidson, M (1992) *The Consumerist Manifesto: Advertising in postmodern times*, Routledge, London

Davis, M P and Zerdin, D (1996) *The Effective Use of Advertising Media: A practical handbook*, Random House, London

• Davis, S (2000) *Brand Asset Management*, Jossey-Bass Wiley, New York

Dearlove, D and Crainer, S (1999) *The Ultimate Book of Business Brands*, Capstone, Oxford

de Chernatony, L (1999) *Journal of Marketing Management*, **15**, pp 157–79

de Chernatony, L and Dall'Olmo Riley, F (1998) Defining a 'brand': beyond the literature with experts' interpretations, *Journal of Marketing Management*, **14**, pp 417–43

de Chernatony, L and McDonald, M (1992) *Creating Powerful Brands*, Butterworth Heinemann, Oxford de Chernatony, L and McDonald, M (1998) *Creating Powerful Brands in Consumer, Service and Industrial Markets*, 2nd edn, Butterworth Heinemann, Oxford

de Saussure, F (1996) *Course in General Linguistics*, McGraw-Hill, New York

Drucker, P (1989) *Managing for Results: Economic tasks and risk-taking decisions*, Heinemann, London

East, R (1997) *Consumer Behaviour: Advances and applications in marketing*, Prentice Hall, Hemel Hempstead

Eliot, R (1994) Exploring the symbolic meaning of brands, *British Journal of Management*, **5** Special issue S13–S19 (June 1994)

Ellsworth, J and Ellsworth, M (1995) *Marketing on the Internet: Multimedia strategies for the World Wide Web*, John Wiley, New York

Ellwood, I (1998) The future of retail sites, a paradigmatic shift from the retailing of commodities to the commodification and consumption of brand experiences, The International Annual Design History Society Conference, Proceedings papers

Ellwood, I (1999) *Borders Research*, RCA, London

Ellwood, I (2000a) *Clicks to bricks*, Supermarketing

Ellwood, I (2000b) Be brave, e-commerce, e-business conference proceeding papers, Access, London

Ellwood, I (2000c) Why e-commerce businesses need a flagship store, *New Media Age*

Ellwood, I (2000d) Store experience is the main attraction, *Retail Week*

Ellwood, I (2001a) Seeing purple, *The Economist*

Ellwood, I (2001b) How psychology can help create a brand culture, *Marketing*

Ellwood, I (2001c) Intel must get beyond its 'chipmaker' image, *Marketing*

Ellwood, I (2001d) Making an impact in the B2B market, *Marketing*

Ellwood, I (2001e) The leisure principle, branding experiences, *Financial Times*

Ellwood, I (2001f) Fine teas and poor management, *The Economist*

Falk, P and Campbell, C (eds) (1997) *The Shopping Experience*, Sage, London

Featherstone, M (1996) *Consumer Culture and Postmodernism*, Sage, London

Gilmore, F (ed) (1997) *Brand Warriors: Corporate leaders share their winning strategies*, HarperCollins Business, London

Gregory, J R (1997) *Leveraging the Corporate Brand*, NTC Business Books, Chicago

Guiltinan, J B and Paul, G W (1994) *Marketing Management Strategies and Programmes*, McGraw-Hill, Maidenhead

Hamilton, D and Kirby, K (1999) A new brand for a new category: paint it orange, *Design Management Journal*, Winter, pp 41–45

Hankinson, G and Cowking, P (1996) *The Reality of Global Brands: Case studies and strategies for the successful management of international brands*, McGraw-Hill, Maidenhead

Hart, S and Murphy, J (eds) (1998) *Brands: The new wealth creators*, Interbrand, Macmillan, London

Hemsley, S (1998) Net navigators, *Marketing Week*, 26 November, p 45

Hodge, R and Kress, G (1995) *Social Semiotics*, Polity, Cambridge

Hutchinson, J (1998) The new disc standard: a case of DVD and Goliath, *Daily Telegraph*, 25 November, p 37

Ind, N (1990) *The Corporate Image: Strategies for effective identity programmes*, Kogan Page, London

Ind, N (1998) An integrated approach to corporate branding, *The Journal of Brand Management*, **5** (5), pp 323–29

Jefkins, F (1994) *Advertising Frameworks*, FT Pitman, London

Jeremiah, J R (1996) *Merchandising Intellectual Property Rights*, Wiley, Chichester

Joachimsthaler, E and Aaker, D (1997) Building brands without mass media, *Harvard Business Review*, **75** (1), pp 39–50

Johnson, I (1998) The death of the adbreak, *Campaign*, 6 November, p 38

Joliffe, R (1999) *Financial Times*, 8 June

Jolley, B (1988) Brand extensions, in L Leuthesser (ed), *Defining, Measuring, and Managing Brand Equity*, Marketing Science Institute, Cambridge, Mass

Jordan, P (1996) *Designing Pleasurable Products*, Taylor & Francis, London

Journal of Marketing Management, 1991, No 7, pp 3–13, Academic Press, London

Kapferer, J N (1998) *Strategic Brand Management: Creating and sustaining brand equity long term*, Kogan Page, London

Kassin, S (1995) *Psychology*, Houghton Mifflin, Boston, Mass

Kavanagh, M (1998) UK retailers must embrace e-commerce, *Marketing Week*, 5 November, p 40

Keller, K (1999) Designing and implementing branding strategies, *The Journal of Brand Management*, **6** (5), pp 315–32

King, S (1991) Brand-building in the 1990s, *Journal of Marketing Management*, **7**, pp 3–13

Kochan, N (ed) (1996) *The World's Greatest Brands*, Interbrand, Macmillan, London

Kohli, C and Thakor, M (1997) Branding consumer goods: insights from theory and practice, *Journal of Consumer Marketing*, **14** (3), pp 206–19

Kozinets, R V (1999) E-tribalized marketing? The strategic implications of virtual communities of consumption, *European Management Journal*, **17** (3), pp 252–64

Lash, S and Urry, J (1996) *Economies of Signs and Space*, Sage, London

Lauren, R (1998) Ralph Lauren biography, Press Release, Ralph Lauren Corporation, London

Law, A (1998) *Open Minds: 21st century business lessons and innovations from St Luke's*, Orion, London

Leonard, M (1997) *Britain TM: Renewing our identity*, Demos, London

Leonhardt, D (1998) Bringing hit products abroad back home, *Business Week*, 7 September

Leuthesser, L (1988) *Defining, Measuring, and Managing Brand Equity*, Marketing Science Institute conference summary no 88-104, Cambridge, Mass

Lowes, B, Pass, C and Sanderson, S (1994) *Companies and Markets: Understanding business strategy and market environment*, Blackwell, Oxford

Lury, C (1993) *Cultural Rights, Technology, Legality and Personality*, Routledge, London

Lury, C (1996) *Consumer Culture*, Polity, Cambridge

Lury, G (1998) *Brand Watching: Lifting the lid on the phenomenon of branding*, Blackhall, Dublin

McCarthy, E J (1987) *Basic Marketing: A managerial approach*, 9th edn, Irwin, Homewood, Ill

McLuhan, M (1968) *The Medium is the Massage*, Bantam, New York

Mahony, K (1998) Interview, Mahony Associates, London

Maio, E (1999) The next wave: soul branding, *Design Management Journal*, Winter, pp 10–16

Maltz, E (1991) Managing brand equity, Marketing Science Institute, conference summary, Cambridge

Marling, S (1993) *American Affair: The Americanisation of Britain*, Boxtree, London

Maslow, A H (1954) *Motivation and Personality*, Harper & Row, London

Millichamp, A H (1997) *Finance for Non-financial Managers*, Letts, London

Mort, F (1996) *Cultures of Consumption: Masculinities and social space in late twentieth-century Britain*, Routledge, London

Mullins, L J (1999) *Management and Organisational Behaviour*, FT Pitman, London

Murphy, J (ed) (1991) *Brand Valuation*, Business Books, London

Nava, M B, MacRury, I and Richards, B (eds) (1997) *Buy this Book: Studies in advertising and consumption*, Routledge, London

Negroponte, N (1995) *Being Digital*, Hodder & Stoughton, London

Neuborne, E with Hof, R D (1998) Building brands on the Net, *Business Week*, 16 November, pp 1001–08

O'Connor, J and McDermott, I (1996) *Thorson's Principles of NLP*, HarperCollins, London

Olins, W (1989) *Corporate Identity: Making business strategy visible through design*, Thames & Hudson, London

Packard, V (1991) *The Hidden Persuaders*, Penguin, Harmondsworth

Peacock, R (1997) Rebuilding the value of the Xerox brand: brand development and positioning for the document company, *The Journal of Brand Management*, **5** (1), pp 23–27

Penrose, R (1998) in J-N Kapferer (ed) *Strategic Brand Management*, Kogan Page, London

Perry, N (1998) *Hyperreality and Global Culture*, Routledge, London

Peters, T J and Waterman, R H (1985) *In Search of Excellence*, HarperCollins, London

Pickering, C D G (1998) *Trademarks in Theory and Practice*, Hart, Oxford

Pilditch, J (1961) *The Silent Salesman: How to develop packaging that sells*, Harper & Row, London

Pine, B J II and Gilmore, J H (1999) *The Experience Economy: Work is theatre and every business a stage*, Harvard Business School Press, Boston, Mass

Porter, M E (1986) *Competition in Global Industries*, Harvard Business School Press, Boston, Mass

Randall, G (1997) *Branding*, Kogan Page, London

Rice, C (1997) *Understanding Customers*, Butterworth-Heinemann, Oxford

Ries, A and Trout, J (1981) *Positioning: The battle for your mind*, McGraw-Hill, Maidenhead

Rijkens, R (1992) *European Advertising Strategies*, Cassell, London

Robertson, K (1989) Strategically desirable brand name characteristics, *Journal of Consumer Marketing*, **6** (4), pp 61–71

Samways, A and Whittome, K (1994) UK brand strategies, facing the competitive challenge, *Financial Times* management report, pp 8–10

Savage, M, *et al* (1992) *Property, Bureaucracy and Culture: Middle class formation in contemporary Britain*, Routledge, London

Schmitt, B and Simonson, A (1999) *Marketing Aesthetics: The strategic management of brands, identity and image*, The Free Press, London

Senge, P M (ed) (1994) *The Fifth Discipline Fieldbook: Strategies and tools for building a learning organization*, Nicholas Brearley, London

Shannon, J (1998) E-commerce is risky business, *Marketing Week*, 5 November, p 39

Shields, R (ed) (1992) *Lifestyle Shopping: The subject of consumption*, Routledge, London

Slater, D (1996) *Consumer Culture and Modernity*, Polity, Cambridge

Sloane, A (1996) *Multimedia Communication*, McGraw-Hill, Maidenhead

Smith, G V (1997) *Trademark Valuation*, Wiley, New York

Smith, P (1998) Objects and observations, Design and Art Directors Association, president's lecture, Royal Geographical Society, London

Smith, P (2000) How to create a distinctive online brand, *Jaring Internet Magazine*, February

Smith, P R (1998) *Marketing Communications: An integrated approach*, Kogan Page, London

Southgate, P (1995) *Total Branding by Design: How to make your brand's packaging more effective*, Kogan Page, London

Sterne, J (1999) *Worldwide Web Marketing*, Wiley, Chichester

Stewart, B (1996) *Packaging as an Effective Marketing Tool*, Kogan Page and PIRA, London

Strong, E K (1929) *The Psychology of Selling and Advertising*, Ladd-Franklin, New York

Tauber, E M (1990) Brand leverage: strategy for growth in a cost control world, *Journal of Advertising Research*, August/September, pp 26–30

Thompson, B (1998) Safe shopping, *Internet Magazine*, December, p 123

Thomson, K (1999) *Emotional Capital*, Capstone, Oxford

Thwaites, T D and Lloyd Mules, W (1994) *Tools for Cultural Studies: An introduction*, Macmillan, Sydney

Tiger, L (1987) *The Pursuit of Pleasure*, Transaction Publishers, London

Tomkins, R (2000) *Financial Times*, 1 February

Trout, J with Rivkin, S (1996) *The New Positioning: The latest on the world's #1 business strategy*, McGraw-Hill, Maidenhead

Turkle, S (1997) *Life on the Screen: Identity in the age of the Internet*, Phoenix, London

Uhlig, R (1998) Families switch off television to surf the Net, *Daily Telegraph*, 18 November, p 48

Vishwanath, V and Mark, J (1997) What really drives profit? In consumer goods, market share alone is not the answer. Your brand's best strategy, *Harvard Business Review*, **75** (3), pp 123–29

Warren, L (1998) Update time, *Computer Weekly*, 3 December, pp 32–33 •

Webb, G (1998) Digital TV won't sound the death knell of PC – yet, *Marketing Week*, 26 November, p 16

Webb, I R (1994) The world according to Ralph, *The Times*, 5 September, p 13

Williamson, J (1978) *Decoding Advertisements: Ideology and meaning in advertising*, Marion Boyars, London

Yusuf, N (1994) Past perfect, *The Times*, 15 May, pp 9/32

INDEX